All the Queen's Men
Elizabeth I and Her Courtiers

OPPOSITE The Barbor
Jewel, made in about 1580.
Tradition has it that
Richard Barbor, who died
in 1586, ordered this
jewel to be made to
commemorate his delivery
from the stake during the
Catholic persecution.
He had been saved from
death by Mary's own death
in November 1558.

OVERLEAF Queen
Elizabeth I, by Nicholas
Hilliard, c. 1580.

NEVILLE WILLIAMS

All the Queen's Men

Elizabeth I and Her Courtiers

THE MACMILLAN COMPANY
New York, New York 10022

For Lucy

The Macmillan Company
866 Third Avenue, New York, N.Y. 10022
Collier-Macmillan Canada Ltd., Toronto, Ontario

All the Queen's Men was first published in 1972 by
Weidenfeld and Nicolson, London

Designed by Karen Bowen
Library of Congress Catalog Card number: 72-84882

First American Edition 1972
Printed in Italy by Librex, Milano
Photoset by BAS Printers Limited, Wallop, Hampshire.

942.055
W(,?

Contents

Acknowledgments

Photographs and illustrations were supplied by, or are reproduced by kind permission of the following. The pictures on pages 87, 99 and *156 (above)* are reproduced by gracious permission of H.M. the Queen; on pages 53 (right), 107, *192 (above)* and *255 (below)* from the Woburn Abbey Collection by kind permission of His Grace the Duke of Bedford: on page 58 by courtesy of the Archbishop of Canterbury (copyright reserved by the Courtauld Institute of Art and the Church Commissioners): on pages *46 and 47* by permission of Viscount de L'Isle VC, KG from his collection at Penshurst Place, Kent: on page 50 by permission of the Earl of Pembroke from the painting at Wilton House: on pages *17*, 44, *237* and 245 by courtesy of the Marquess of Salisbury, KG: on pages 56, 88 and 135 by permission of Mrs P.A. Tritton from the collection at Parham Park, Sussex: on page *48* by permission of the Trustees of the Wallace Collection (Crown Copyright). Armourers and Brasiers of the City of London: 157; Ashmolean Museum, Oxford: 25; Hon. Gavin Astor, Hever Castle: 140, 145; Sir Edmund Bacon: *81*; Marquess of Bath, Longleat: *153*; Batsford Limited: 184; Bibliothèque Nationale: 68, 69; Bodleian Library, Oxford: 34, 133; Denis Bower, Chiddingstone Castle: *112*; British Museum: 13, 15, *18*, 20/1, 23/1, 64, 100–1, 108, 116/2, 121, 127, 130, 151, 152/1, 152/2, 165, 178, 179, 182, 193, 194, 197, 203, 205/2, 207, *228*, 229/2, 258/1, 258/2, 261; Duke of Buccleuch and Queensberry: 38, 113, 205/1, 214, *238*, *255/1*; George Bushell: 250; Marquess of Bute: 254; Sir John G. Carew-Pole: 213; Earl of Carlisle: 53/1; College of Arms, London: 12, 14, 14–15, 222/2; Country Life: 80; Courtauld Institute of Art: 30, 58, 73; Mrs Dent-Brocklehurst, Sudeley Castle: 103; Department of the Environment (Crown Copyright): 63, 90, *111/2*; Mary Evans Picture Library: 79, 259; Mr Fitzroy-Newdegate, Arbury: 251; Syndics of the Fitzwilliam Museum, Cambridge: *226–7*, Giraudon: 68, 69, 139; Glasgow Art Gallery and Museum (Burrell Collection): *45*, 159; Jack B. Gold Esq: 41/2; Trustees of Goodwood Collection: *84*, 105; Captain Loel Guinness: 233; Hampshire Field Club: 184–5; Lord Hampton: 20/2; Hawkley Studio Associates: 123/1, 123/2; Earl of Jersey: 212; Kunsthistorisches Museum, Vienna: 229/1; Kunstsammlungen, Kassel: 170; Lambeth Palace: 58; London Museum: 21, 26–7, 28, *154–5*, 208; Magdalene College, Cambridge: 206; Manchester City Art Gallery: 53/1; Mansell Collection: 164; Lord Methuen, Corsham Court: *256*; Mrs More-Molyneux, Loseley Park: 123/1, 123/2; National Galleries of Scotland: 240; National Maritime Museum: 120, 223/2, 231; National Monuments Record: 29, 162/2, 184, 184–5, 185; National Museum, Stockholm (SPA): 65; National Portrait Gallery: 23/2, 41/1, 49, 91, *94*, 147, *156/2*, 162/1, 183, *192/2*, 222/1, 242; National Trust, Hardwick Hall: 167/1, 167/2; Northampton Art Gallery: 149, 150; Duke of Northumberland, Alnwick: 80, 248; City Art Gallery, Plymouth: 177; Duke of Portland, Welbeck Abbey: *93*, 136; Private

Collections: *4*, 61, *111/1*; Public Record Office: 124, *155*, 209, 235; Radio Times Hulton Picture Library: 100–1; Rothersfield Greys Church, Oxon: 250; Royal Academy of Arts: 61, 213, 251; St Faith's Church, Gaywood, King's Lynn: *190*, *191*; Scala: *189*, 217; Brigadier Schreiber: *225*; Sidney Sussex College, Cambridge: 186; Sir John Soane's Museum: 30, 73; Nigel Stopford-Sackville, Esq: 37; Tate Gallery, London: 223; Uffizi Gallery, Florence: 139; Earl of Verulam, Gorhambury: 43, 74, 75, 221; Victoria and Albert Museum: *3*, 92, 116/1, *156/3*, 210, 223/1, 244, 260; M. Ward-Thomas, Esq, Horham Hall: 143; Simon Wingfield Digby, Esq, Sherborne Castle: *82–3*; Worshipful Society of Apothecaries of London: *190–1*.

Foreword

This book is primarily about political power, to some an end, to others the means of grace and favour, at the court of Queen Elizabeth I. In those days men came to court for much the same reasons that their descendants would enter Parliament in the eighteenth century, for the Tudor court was the hub of the kingdom's affairs, the fountain of patronage and profit. The Queen could not help but act as a powerful magnet attracting men to her service and, indeed, she counted on the attendance of many men and some women to people the stage that she contrived to dominate throughout her reign. The courtiers were in fact 'all the Queen's men' of different degrees and capacities – her ministers of state, senior officials of her household, peers of the realm and other members of the grand cousinage of royal relatives, and favourites who sought to convince her of their undying devotion. Then there were men of humbler creation who looked first to a patron as the essential intermediary for craving their sovereign's blessing on their suits, and so around the leading courtiers formed factions, the distant ancestors of political parties. We shall follow the shifting pattern of alliances as major issues on the succession, the Queen's marriage and religion became debated, and also take stock of the changes in personnel in the most significant offices, as sons succeeded fathers in their peerage titles or as other new faces appeared at court. Though our principal concern is with the Queen's men, our eyes – like their's – cannot be averted from their sovereign lady, who was the centre of their universe.

It is not usually very easy for an author writing a foreword some weeks before book proofs are in his hands to make due acknowledgement to his publishers; yet in my case the encouragement I have received from the staffs of both George Weidenfeld and Nicolson in London and The Macmillan Company in New York has been fundamental. I am particularly indebted to Christopher Falkus for stimulating discussion of so many points, from early synopsis to final text, and to Margaret Willes for her lively appreciation both of the Elizabethan scene and of the historian's problems in interpreting it. I am most grateful to Jane Dorner for her detailed work in identifying and selecting the illustrations and to Dulcie Ashdown for drawing up the family trees. Peggy Hill once more typed the greater part of my manuscript with her customary skill. Finally, as always, my wife and family have been my greatest allies. N.W.

The gent pencionars on foote withe pollaxes in their handes barehed

The Quieres and footemen nexte about her highnes litter barehed

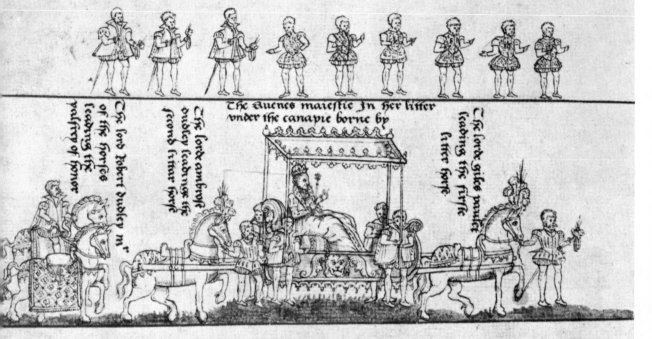

The Quenes maiestie In her litter vnder the canapie borne by

The lord Robert dudley m[r] of the horsse leading the palfrey of honor

The lord ambruse dudley leading the second litter horse

The lord giles pawlet leading the firste litter horse

The Quieres and footemen nexte aboute her highnes litter barehed

The gent pencionars on foote withe pollaxes In their handes barehed

1 The Magnet of Ambition

The later sixteenth century was above all an age of queens, but it was Elizabeth of England who gave her name to the epoch. 'It is more to have seen Elizabeth than to have seen England,' wrote one visitor who had come under her spell for the first time, for she dazzled like a Sun Queen, making her court the most resplendent in Christendom. Many of her subjects sought 'to have the twinkling of one beam of the splendiferous planet,' others, drawn irresistibly to her service, felt in the shadows when they were away from her side. The court, appropriately in a personal monarchy, was the setting in which the sovereign lived out her public and private lives so that attendance on her became the social obligation of the aristocracy and the goal of lesser mortals. Everybody who was anybody came to court for at least part of the year. This was the centre of affairs – political, social and cultural – the fount of patronage and power, the avenue to profit and promotion, and it exercised a magnetic attraction that few could resist.

Elizabeth I held sway in three capacities which were so inter-related that it is not easy for us, any more than for her subjects, to distinguish them clearly. First, as her father's daughter, she had inherited what was a firmly-based throne. She was the lawful sovereign and had at last come into her own on an unprecedented wave of popularity; from the first she was 'much attached to the people' and in her long reign was to nurture them into a nation. The crowning in the Abbey, the throne in the Presence Chamber and the distinctive sign manual all symbolised undisputed power, and the ceremonial guard and the traditional pageantry of everyday life at court emphasised the Queen's unique position.

Her second capacity was as a sovereign, anointed as well as crowned, so that she was 'God's Creature', ordained to rule by divine right; though a woman, Parliament had made her Supreme Governor of the Church. 'She is our God in earth,' Lord North was to remind the Bishop of Ely, and 'if there be perfection in flesh and blood, undoubtedly it is in Her Majesty.' The sacrament of her coronation had endowed her with a quality that no subject, not even an archbishop, possessed and she was thus hedged about by a mysterious divinity. She touched for the Queen's Evil at Whitehall and on progress, following the hallowed rite (though with the prayers revised and set in English), feeling it her bounden duty to extend a healing hand to scrofulous persons. Each Maundy Thursday she distributed alms, food and

13

clothing to the same number of poor women as she had years, after she had washed their feet, even as Christ had washed his disciples' feet before the Last Supper. At every service in every church prayers were required to be said for her, and when bishops, deans and chaplains recited the familiar versicle, 'O Lord Save the Queen,' they knew that royal supremacy in the Church was not an empty phrase but a self-evident fact.

Finally there was the significance of her sex, and where many queens found this a matter of weakness Elizabeth made it a source of strength. Living in an essentially masculine society she succeeded in evoking a remarkable emotional response from courtiers in general, not merely from the few she highly favoured, who felt moved to pay her a special kind of homage simply because she was a woman. This secular devotion owed most to the old ideal of chivalry, which had kindled a deep respect for spotless maidenhood, and it had little in common with the religious homage paid her as anointed Queen and Defender of the Faith. This 'courtesy' was evident from her first days as Queen but with the passing of the years and her persistent refusal to marry, it developed through her own encouragement into a strong personal cult, so that she charmed courtiers into participating in the sophisticated idyll of the Virgin Queen. Poets and composers lauded Elizabeth as Fair Oriana, Cynthia the moon goddess, or as the immortal shepherdess of a pastorale, and these allegorical fantasies reached a peak when she was sixty – a mystical romance lived out on a public stage. At her accession day tournament each November courtiers would break a lance for the honour of their sovereign lady and the champion would treasure the prize he received at the end of the day from her beautiful hands.

The court over which she presided resembled a large family, with its members closely knit by ties of kin and the obligations of allegiance. As a family it had its feuds, where personalities clashed, its favourite sons with their nicknames, and its ill-favoured daughters. Factions – the ancestors of political parties – developed round leading courtiers, and Elizabeth sought to maintain a nice balance to keep the peace. As a matriarch she expected these her 'relations' to be about her, justifying aristocratic privilege by personal service.

This was, on the face of it, a compact society comprising privy councillors, peers and senior officials both of the royal Household proper and of the departments of state that had technically broken away from it, and the wives of some of the great men held posts as ladies of the Bed Chamber or Privy Chamber, or found a niche for a daughter or a niece as a maid of honour. Though servants of the Crown were entitled to board and lodging at court, their wives could not expect to share this privilege as of right and whatever exceptions the Queen made, the rule itself remained. Below the ushers, grooms and pages were the armies of servants in the 'below stairs' departments, from the pantry to the woodyard – not courtiers, indeed, any more than were the servants of the stables or the kennels, but each performing tasks that were vital for the smooth running of the court. The great brought their own retainers and attracted their hangers-on seeking patronage, and these in turn brought their own servants.

This compact, intimate society was very far from being static since (unlike the peerage) the ranks of courtiers were constantly being extended by new arrivals, especially by the young men of the next generation. The luckiest

newcomers had a father or uncle to introduce them, or the pull of a name with a pedigree of service to the Crown. Consider the Throckmortons, for example: in the middle of the Queen's reign Thomas Throckmorton wrote a family history in verse in which his uncle, Sir Nicholas the ambassador, is made to tell of his rise to service in King Henry's court through old Sir George Throckmorton's connexions.

> Lo! then my brethren, Clement, George and I
>   Did seek, as youth do still, in Court to be:
> Each state as base we did defy,
>   Compared with Court, the nurse of dignity.
> 'Tis truly said, No fishing to the sea's,
> No serving to a King's – if you can please.

In due course, despite Sir Nicholas's early death, his son Arthur made his début and was given a place. After a kindly word from the Queen with remembrances for his mother, he successfully angled for his sister Bess to serve in the Chamber. Such was the power of a name. Others needed to start from scratch and find a patron prepared to take them up on his own terms. In practice anyone who could boast the status of gentleman had access to the court but, as William Cecil put it, a man without a friend there was like 'a hop without a pole'. Much use was made of mutual acquaintance to gain the first rung of the precarious ladder, and so in an age of large families men exploited the intricate web of cousinage, used the ties of neighbourhood and gave lip service to the loyalties of college and inn of court.

To approach Her Majesty and gain her ear could involve making a series of gifts from a coin in the palm of a minor official to a piece of plate for the Vice-Chamberlain. Then, at the appropriate time, the humble suitor for royal favour would need to send in a gift to the Queen herself – a jewelled fan, perhaps, or a handsomely-bound book – and wait on tenter-hooks to see if the offering was accepted or rejected. Happy the youth whose figure, standing out among the crowd, earned interest or recognition as the Queen passed by. The seventeen-year-old Welsh squire who was to become Lord Herbert of Cherbury came to court in 1600 more from curiosity than ambition and years afterwards related his fortunate début:

> As it was the manner of those times for all men to kneel down before the great Queen Elizabeth, I was likewise upon my knees in the Presence-Chamber when she passed by to the Chapel at Whitehall. As soon as she saw me she stopped and, swearing her usual oath, demanded 'Who is this?' Everybody there present looked upon me, until Sir James Croft, a pensioner, finding the Queen stayed, returned back and told who I was, and that I had married Sir William Herbert of St Julian's daughter.

When Charles Blount arrived in Whitehall in 1583 with his looks and his wit as his sole assets, he made an immediate impression on the Queen who advised him, 'Fail you not to come to court and I will bethink myself for to do you good.' When Essex came on the scene a little later both he and his sovereign took the giving and receiving of such advice for granted.

The young gentleman eager to impress would run up bills with tailors, hatters and bootmakers to clad himself in extravagant clothes of gorgeous hues and stylish cut with gold buttons and buckles and the other accessories in vogue, wearing an estate upon his back, as it was said, simply to shine

The Genealogy of Elizabeth I at Hatfield House. With the succession to the Crown unsettled, politicians drew up royal descents, often illuminated or pictorial. These were a counterpart to the genealogical trees made by the newly-ennobled like Sir William Cecil, Lord Burghley, with the help of the College of Arms to establish the antiquity of their families, even if their origins were humble. But a royal genealogy, unlike a subject's, could have no spurious entries.

HONI SOIT QVI MAL Y PENSE

CASSIS TVTISSIMA VIRTVS

TVTIS SIMA

QVÆ NATVRA POTEST HATTONO CONTVLIT VNI;
ET FORT VNA DEDIT, QVÆDARE, CVNCTA, POTEST;
CERTATIM VIRTVS CVMVLVM SVPERADDIDIT ISTIS;
ANGLICA DIVA TAMEN PLVS TRIBVS VNA DEDIT.
ECQVID HABENT TANTAM SATVRNIA SECVLA DIVAM?
ECQVID HABENT TALEM TEMPORA NOSTRA VIRVM?

above rivals on this highly competitive stage. To be noticed was very heaven, the initial dividend from a heavy investment. In vying for attention novelty was all, with the twists of high fashion defying prediction: 'today there is none to the Spanish guise, to-morrow the French toys are most fine and delectable,' whether it was boots or beards, gloves or gaskins, choice of fabric or style. The prentice courtier no less than the seasoned campaigner was a chameleon, preening himself in composite fineries, for England was 'the ape of all nations' superfluities, the continual masque of outlandish habiliments', as Thomas Nashe put it rather devastatingly in 1593. The rules about what one could or could not get away with in dress had become utterly confused, though in spite of the triumph of dandyism the Queen always expected a man to look like a man. Nevertheless, away from the court, effeminate attire could run riot at times, so that William Harrison could write of some individuals he saw 'it hath passed my skill to discern in London whether they were men or women' – striking a note that we can appreciate. It was not about any young buck that Gabriel Harvey wrote his satirical lines on the Italianate Englishman, but about the seventeenth Earl of Oxford:

> A little apish hat, couched fast to the pate, like an oyster;
> Fresh cambric ruffs, deep with a witness, starched to the purpose;
> Delicate in speech; quaint in array; conceited in all points;
> In courtly guiles, a passing singular odd man.

Waiting at court for the right moment to embark in earnest on a suit for favour involved a great deal of hanging around, yet there was danger in dawdling and indecision, for sooner or later Queen and court would move on to another residence. Yet there was plenty to enliven the tedium of waiting, and the man who became bored with the court was generally tired of life itself. There was the excitement of being on the periphery of events, identifying who was who among the great in the land, observing their gait and even overhearing their casual remarks. Gossip about personalities was the staple of conversation. For the initiated there was much to be gleaned about the pecking-order of precedence and the rivalries of men in different liveries, while for the novice there was much to be learnt about the ordered ritual of court affairs where splendid ceremony elevated so many ordinary, daily events in the sovereign's life into quasi-religious observances. The table in the Withdrawing Room, on which dishes were placed before being carried to the Queen's own table in the Privy Chamber, had to be laid in a particular way, taking thirty officials at least half an hour:

A gentleman entered the room bearing a rod and along with him another who had a table cloth which, after they had both knelt three times with the utmost veneration, he spread upon the table and, after kneeling again, they both retired. Then came two others, one with the rod again, the other with a salt-cellar, a plate and bread. When they had knelt as the others had done and placed what was brought upon the table, they too retired, with the same ceremonies performed by the first.

A little later a lady-in-waiting and a maid of honour arrived and, after graceful genuflexions, 'rubbed the plates with bread and salt with as much awe as if the Queen had been present'. The yeomen of the guard in full pomp brought in from the kitchens twenty-four gilt dishes which had to be placed in a strict order on the table. Trumpeters and drummers 'made the Hall ring

for half-an-hour together' to summon Queen and courtiers to their respective dinner-tables. As a precaution against Her Majesty being poisoned, a lady-in-waiting with a tasting-knife gave each yeoman of the guard a mouthful of the dish he had carried in, and other maids of honour brought the dishes to the Privy Chamber for Elizabeth to make her choice of courses. Something of the ornate ritual that had been expelled from divine service had been annexed by the palace.

There was much music-making in the palace, in Chapel, Hall and Presence Chamber, a fine display of tapestries, paintings and *objets d'art*, the masques staged by the Master of the Revels and the performances of the dramatic companies supported by the various peers, which taken together gave the court the character of a great academy. Then there were the side-shows of the cockpit, the butts, the tennis court and the tiltyard, and some would find irresistible the invitations to throw dice or join in games of primero and ruff, until their purses were empty. On ordinary days, when the Queen dined by herself in the Privy Chamber, plain victuals were plentiful in Hall – 'the good piece of court beef and mustard, a cowsheel and a piece of ling and sodden oysters' that Sir Thomas Smith missed when he was ambassador in Paris – and on red-letter days there were state banquets with a profusion of dishes, when the uninvited could jostle for a place in an upper gallery to feast their eyes on the assembled guests. Amidst all the bustle and noise the young spectator would surely stand entranced and a little bewildered, more than ever determined to play an active role himself in this great gathering.

One further attraction of court for the young man of birth was that, being away from the eyes of strict parents, he could associate openly with young ladies from much the same background as himself. It was a great place for

ABOVE LEFT 'The Effeminate Courtier', a woodcut from *Ship of Fools*.
ABOVE RIGHT Sir John Pakington (1549-1625), handsome, athletic and spendthrift, whom the Queen nicknamed 'Lusty Pakington'.

RIGHT A salt-cellar of silver gilt, 1560.

20

love matches, though the peril lay in striving too high. Winning the heart of a maid of honour was a vain conquest unless the Queen thoroughly approved of the intended marriage, and those who presumed on her indulgence by failing to seek her permission were invariably in trouble. Well-wishers suggested to Lady Bridget Manners that she feign an attack of measles to gain her a month's 'quarantine' away from court and then, at the end of the month when Elizabeth would almost have forgotten her, she should write in humble strain seeking her leave to marry. The ruse might have succeeded, but instead of employing it Lady Bridget improvidently played truant, married her beau without any petition and in consequence saw him sent to prison. When Sir Henry Shirley secretly married Frances Vavasour, a lady-in-waiting, the Queen, as predicted, was furious and defended her fury: 'She hath always furthered any honest and honourable purposes of marriage or preferment to any of hers when, without scandal and infamy, they have been orderly broke to her.' She would never relinquish her proprietary rights over 'any of hers'.

We shall notice other cases where Elizabeth blighted the honeymoon days of runaway lovers, and if marriage was being entered because the lady was pregnant the Queen's temper knew no bounds. Marriage of one of her ladies or maids meant breaking up the intimate family circle and, especially in later years, she became extremely jealous of those near her who found happiness in matrimony. Right at the end of her reign it was not really so remarkable, considering the warped feelings of an old maid, that she banished Leicester's natural son from court for daring to kiss Mistress Cavendish. At that time, said Harington, 'she did oft ask the ladies around her Chamber if they loved to think of marriage. And the wise ones did conceal well their liking thereto, as knowing the Queen's judgment.' Court, as she intended it, was the place where subjects paid court to *her*, not the place where the young indulged in easy courtships.

To prepare oneself for court required rather more than a fashionable wardrobe. The Queen valued intelligence in a man no less than she appreciated the courtly graces of music and poetry or the energetic performances in the tiltyard. Gentle compliments from a man of wit were on quite a different plane from the empty flattery of a dullard. Ideally she expected those about her to be well-read, though firm avoiders of pedantry, discriminating in their conversation, men of taste who escaped the shortcomings of the affected dilettante. As a woman who never set foot outside her native land she was intrigued by the tales of much-travelled men, though she held no great store by their experiences and was firmly convinced that the inestimable benefit of proficiency in foreign tongues could be acquired, as her own had been, without protracted tours abroad. Elizabeth might have defined a courtier as one whose manners and conversation she found pleasing. Those who broke rules of etiquette on formal occasions were left in no doubt of their effrontery; a young buck 'being more bold than well-mannered' at a palace reception in 1582 'did stand upon the carpet of the cloth of estate and did almost lean upon the cushions' where the Queen was sitting, and as it was beneath her dignity to reprove him herself she reprimanded her Chamberlain for allowing such behaviour. Yet any man who had the intuition to abandon formality when she was in an unbuttoned mood, and regard her as a woman, stood a strong chance of gaining her favour as a Queen, and if he could convey by gestures, or a song to the lute, that he was a little in love with her and play the masquerade in the way she wanted, he would feel he was treading on air.

Theorists and men of affairs in England, as elsewhere, discussed the best means of training youth for the public service, for they recognised that the two distinct branches of education of medieval times – that for the clerk in school and university, and that for the knight at arms in chivalric courtesy and the art of war – needed bringing together. The courtier of the later sixteenth century, whatever his country, was expected to be something of a clerk and something of a knight – a rounded Renaissance man, as versatile in his parts as the prince he served.

A majority of the privy councillors at Elizabeth's accession had in fact been to Oxford or Cambridge and a number had, in addition to or instead of a university training, been to an inn of court. It became quite usual for peers to send their sons to university, even if they did not proceed to a degree, or to study at one of the inns. The first Earl of Pembroke's illiteracy was a remarkable exception to the standards of learning which his fellow councillors had achieved; he retained the military qualities of a medieval knight but was a stranger to 'courtesy'. Some felt the universities with their strict classical curricula were a poor training-ground for employment at court, and indeed their morale was low at the beginning of the reign, when religious changes had created an unprecedented upheaval. Sir Humphrey Gilbert in 1564 proposed an imaginative scheme for founding 'Queen Elizabeth's Academy' in London, 'for education of Her Majesty's wards and others, the youth of nobility and gentlemen.' Here boys from the age of twelve were to study 'matters of action meet for present practice, both of peace and war'. After a grounding in Latin, Greek and logic they were to learn modern languages, political science, mathematics, civil and common law, divinity and the rudiments of medicine, and practise horsemanship, fencing, dancing and music. Gilbert's plans for the training of courtiers were, alas, stillborn.

Three years before Gilbert's blueprint for an Academy, Sir Thomas Hoby's translation of Castiglione's *Il Cortegiano* had appeared. The Italian had published this manual on the education of a gentleman in 1528, drawing on his own experiences at the ducal court of Urbino, and the ideals he set down were to have a profound effect throughout Europe. Hoby had been steeped in the humanism of St John's, Cambridge, in its zenith and as a Marian exile had heard Johann Sturm lecture in his gymnasium at Strasbourg (where the curriculum was not dissimilar to that later proposed by Gilbert) before visiting Italy. Since he was brother-in-law to Cecil and Bacon, we may expect Hoby's translation to have caused no little stir in Whitehall on its publication, and for years to come a copy of it would be found on the shelf of many a country gentleman with few pretensions to learning, alongside Tusser's *Five Hundred Points of Good Husbandry*, Foxe's *Book of Martyrs* and the Bible.

Although Castiglione has nothing much to say about the education of women as such, what must have struck the Queen as she read it was the picture of the court in Urbino, in which women shared with men a common culture, sitting in a circle alternately with men in the ducal salon to engage in polite conversation; the Italian was concerned 'to exalt the gentlewoman of the palace so much that she may be equal with the courtier'.

The courtier in Castiglione's ideal served his prince as a companion in his Privy Chamber in off-duty hours as well as in tendering advice in affairs of

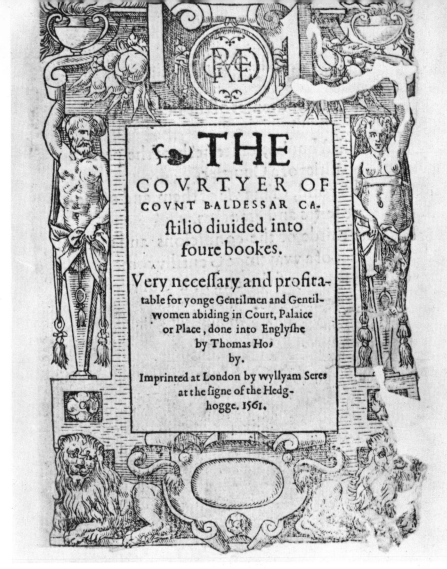

The COVRTYER OF COVNT B·ALDESSAR CA-stilio diuided into foure bookes.

Very neceſſary and profita-table for yonge Gentilmen and Gentil-vvomen abiding in Court, Palaice or Place, done into Englyſhe by Thomas Hoƀ by.

Imprinted at London by wyllyam Seres at the ſigne of the Hedg-hogge. 1561.

ABOVE Title page of Sir Thomas Hoby's translation of Castiglione's *Il Cortegiano*, published in 1561.

BELOW Sir Edward Hoby (1560-1617), painted by an unknown artist in 1583. This son of Sir Thomas married Hunsdon's daughter.

state; he was not just a grave councillor framing high policy or a skilled soldier ready for action in the field, but a man of wit and fashion as well, able to discourse knowledgeably with his sovereign on art and poetry, to play an instrument when called upon and sing a part in tune, to be an accomplished dancer, horseman and tennis-player and to be unfailingly dressed for the occasion 'in moderate preciseness', since clothing always revealed 'the fancy of him that weareth it'. To achieve such all-round excellence was, no doubt, expecting too much of mere mortals, for Castiglione was setting before his readers a portrait of the ideal, yet not a few of Elizabeth's courtiers would have achieved high marks in several branches of the Italian's essential accomplishments and Leicester, Sidney, Hatton, Raleigh and Essex would each have been reckoned a virtuoso of versatility.

The vogue for Italian manners ushered in by Hoby's translation led numbers of young Englishmen to undertake a grand tour of the Italian states to gain first-hand experience of a society that would be a passport to the court on their return. But as the Elizabethan religious settlement hardened, it seemed a dangerous course for young men to sojourn in the states of the Counter Reformation. 'Suffer not thy sons to pass the Alps,' warned Burghley, and those who did journey to Rome, like Lawrence Hyde, Lord Clarendon's grandfather, were thought to be imperilling their lives as well as their souls, for the city was reckoned 'very dangerous to all the English nation who did not profess themselves Roman Catholics'. In fact the grand tour remained popular, though with the coming of the war, service afloat, or with the forces in the Netherlands or France, became a more exciting way of completing one's education for court. 'Virtue once made that country [Italy] mistress over all the world,' wrote Ascham in *The Schoolmaster*. 'Vice now maketh that country slave to them that before were glad to serve it.' Ascham related how the Queen's kinsman, Sir Richard Sackville, had asked him once, when discussing education in the Privy Chamber at Windsor, what he thought about so many young men's fancy to travel to Italy, and the Queen's Secretary for the Latin Tongue did not mince his words. Italy was 'Circe's Court' and any who stayed there was transformed into an 'Italianate Englishman, who is the devil incarnate'. Ascham commended Hoby's book, but in a homespun way: 'advisedly read and diligently followed but one year at home in England would do a young gentleman more good, I wis, than three years travel abroad spent in Italy.'

For all his scholarship, blunt Yorkshire Ascham lacked the courtier's graces; perhaps he felt they were unattainable, for he believed that a courtier's place was a matter of birthright, even if blue blood itself was not enough. 'Nobility without virtue and wisdom is blood indeed, but blood truly, without bones and sinews . . . . But nobility governed by learning and wisdom, is indeed much like a fair ship, having wind and tide at will.' The children of great and noble families could deserve to inherit their fathers' places at court only by following the Platonic path of virtue and worthiness.

Practice accorded ill with theory. Roger Ascham knew that the loyal service his mistress attracted would not go unrewarded and that upstart families could beget brilliant men. He would have been amazed had an astrologer correctly predicted for him that from a yeoman farmer of West Hatch near Salisbury, named Lawrence Hyde, recently allowed by the heralds to assume the status of an esquire, would spring two great-great-

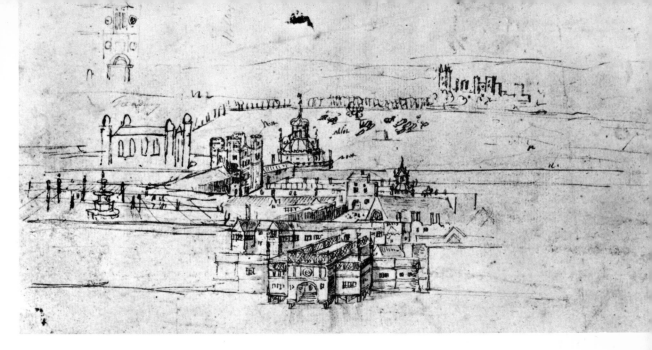

Whitehall Stairs, with
other buildings of the
palace in the background;
a drawing by Anthony van
Wyngaerde, *c.* 1555.

grand-daughters, Mary and Anne, who would in turn be queens regnant of
England, Ireland and Scotland. Despite Queen Elizabeth's reluctance to
create new peers, her reign was to develop as an era of great social mobility,
and the surest way of climbing the ladder of 'gentility' was in fact through
the royal court.

Whitehall, though not Elizabeth's favourite palace, was her principal residence. Coming to the Crown on Wolsey's fall, it had been rebuilt and
extended by her father to become the largest palace in Christendom. Apart
from its size, its importance lay in its being sited right in the capital city so
that the court was integrated with the life of London, instead of being withdrawn from it; indeed, there were rights of way for the public through the
Holbein and King Street Gates, while Old Palace Stairs on the river
remained a public landing-place. When the court was in residence the popu-
lation of the cities of London and Westminster combined topped a quarter
of a million in 1558, greater than that of all the other cities and corporate
boroughs put together, yet this metropolis was still compact, distinctly rural
away from the chief roads and on quite a different scale from the Great Wen
of a later age. Courtiers' houses were concentrated in no more than four
main districts and it would have been possible for a messenger to go the
rounds on horseback in term-time with letters to the houses of the fifty most
important subjects of the Queen in the course of two hours. The metropolis
was a microcosm of the realm when the great landowning magnates of provincial England were in residence: the Earl of Shrewsbury from Yorkshire
and the Midlands, Derby from Lancashire and Cheshire, the Earls of
Northumberland, Cumberland and Westmorland from the far north, Pembroke and Worcester from South Wales, Bedford from the West Country,
Southampton and Winchester from Hampshire, Arundel from Sussex, and
Norfolk, the greatest of them all, from East Anglia.

Fewer courtiers were living within the city's square mile in 1558 than a
generation earlier and most of them were neighbours in Aldgate Ward. Here

stood Bevis Markes, a mansion noted for its fine courtyards and spacious rooms, which had passed at the Dissolution from the abbot of Bury St Edmunds to the Heneage family; next door to it was The Papey, formerly an almshouse for old priests, which Francis Walsingham took as his first lodgings; and a stone's throw away, in St Mary Street, was the house built by the diplomat Sir William Pickering, who fancied his chances of winning Elizabeth's hand. Lord Lumley, a staunch Catholic, lived at the Crutched Friars in Aldgate in the residence built by Sir Thomas Wyatt, the poet, and near Aldgate Pump was Northumberland House, for four generations the London home of the Percies, but soon to be converted, for the sake of the rent-roll, into gambling dens and the pleasant gardens into bowling alleys. Through his second marriage with Margaret Audley, the Duke of Norfolk had acquired the mansion built by Lord Chancellor Audley out of the ruins of Holy Trinity Priory, and this Cree Church Place became the Duke's London home until 1564, when he bought the Charterhouse from Lord North. Though pageantry was commonplace in Tudor London, the Duke's arrivals at Cree Church Place from the country always attracted much attention, with his retinue of one hundred horse, the riders in velvet livery. Almost next door to the Duke's was Sir Nicholas Throckmorton's house, which had formerly belonged to the abbots of Evesham, and not far away was the house in Seething Lane belonging to Lord Robert Dudley. Aldgate was, indeed, the Park Lane of early Elizabethan England.

Lord Treasurer Winchester had established himself in the Austin Friars in King Henry's day, building a superb mansion over the remains of the

refectory, dormitory and cloisters, though he left the church standing – the west end of it a place of worship for the Dutch Community, the rest as storehouses; Winchester's gardens were the largest in the city, extending down to London Wall. Near the river, by Dyers' Hall, was Cold Harbour, belonging to the Earl of Shrewsbury. Unlike most peers, the Earls of Oxford kept to the city when they changed houses, instead of moving west. Old Oxford House by London Wall had come by a marriage to the Wingfield family from Suffolk, powerful at court under Queen Mary, and at the end of the century would be sold to Sir Edward Coke. At the dissolution the Earl of Oxford had acquired a large house at London Stone in Walbrook that had belonged to a Sussex priory; backing on to it were the houses where Empson had lived next door to Dudley under the first of the Tudors. Here the sixteenth Earl of Oxford would come with his retinue of eighty gentlemen with gold chains round their necks as outriders and one hundred tall yeomen riding behind him, all in his livery of Reading tawney with the blue boar embroidered on the left shoulder. His son was to exchange the house at London Stone for 'a beautiful house, with gardens of pleasure, bowling alleys and such like' at Bishopsgate, built by a goldsmith.

In the west of the city near Puddle Dock was Baynards Castle, which Henry VII had rebuilt, not as a stronghold but as a mansion 'far more beautiful and commodious, for the entertainment of any prince,' and here now lived the Earl of Pembroke. His neighbour was Lord Hunsdon, whom Elizabeth had installed at Blackfriars. The south bank of the river was out of favour, except with certain bishops, and the only temporal peer living

Wallis's map of the cities of London and Westminster, 1563.

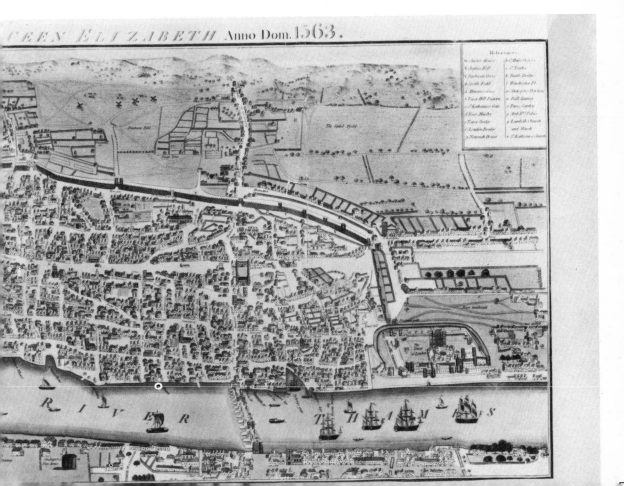

there was Lord Montague, at St Mary Overy, Southwark. The remaining courtiers were establishing themselves along the Strand and Fleet Street, replacing 'with fair buildings' the inns in which medieval bishops and abbots had resided when they had come down for Parliament and Convocation. The surface of the Strand had been improved when Protector Somerset began building his great residence, but the road was still secondary to the river. The convenience of the properties along the south side of the Strand owed most to the Thames, still London's chief thoroughfare, and the busiest entrances to the great houses were the water-gates. By the middle of Elizabeth's reign this had eclipsed Aldgate to become the most fashionable quarter of the capital. Besides Somerset House the Queen had at her disposal Durham House, which Bishop Tunstal had effectively surrendered to her father.

It is worth looking at the topography from St Bride's to Charing Cross in detail. Salisbury Court by St Bride's Church, formerly the residence of the bishops of Salisbury, was now owned by Sir Richard Sackville, while on the site of the White Friars were 'many fair houses built, lodgings for noblemen and others', on short leases. In term-time, noted the Lord Mayor, 'all the houses in Fleet Street and the streets and lanes adjoining . . . do use lodgings, victualling, or letting out chambers'. Near Temple Bar, to the west of Middle

ABOVE Part of an Elizabethan map of the City of London: this shows the great houses with their gardens, and brings out the rural character of the city with Finsbury Fields, Moorfields and Spitalfields. Sir Francis Walsingham's house of The Papey, just off Bishopsgate, is marked at the bottom right-hand corner of the map.

Temple Lane was the great house which the first Lord Paget had bought from the Bishop of Exeter and enlarged; his son was to let it to the Spanish ambassador, until 1569 when the Earl of Leicester acquired the lease and transformed it into 'the stately place' that so amazed Edmund Spenser. Dudley occupied it as his London house until his death, when his stepson Essex took over the lease and the mansion was renamed Essex House. Beyond the tenements on the other side of Milford Lane lay Arundel House. This had belonged to the bishops of Bath and Wells until it had been acquired by Lord Thomas Seymour, the Admiral, and on his fall it had been bought by Henry FitzAlan for the bargain price of £40. Here Arundel kept his collections of marble statues, busts and other treasures from Greece and Rome in spacious galleries and maintained a rich library. Next came Somerset House, built for the Protector between 1547 and 1552 with stone taken from the dissolved monastic properties of St Paul's Cathedral and Westminster Abbey. This house was unquestionably one of the most interesting buildings of the day. The front onto the Strand was composed entirely in the Classical style, with a central gatehouse of three superimposed orders echoed in the two projecting window bays, and a flat balustraded roof. Old Somerset House must indeed have provided a startling contrast to the traditional houses around it. For beyond lay John of Gaunt's medieval palace of the Savoy, restored as a hospital by Queen Mary but still partly used by her successor in her earliest months. Moving west we reach the Earl of Worcester's house, not so long ago owned by the Bishop of Carlisle, and beyond it, near Ivy Bridge Lane, lived the Earl of Rutland, where late in the reign Sir Robert Cecil would build his brick and timber mansion.

Durham House, to the east of Ivy Bridge Lane, was perhaps the most extensive site on the Strand, with its gate-house approximately opposite today's Adelphi Theatre. Beyond the inner courtyard, towards the river lay the house itself, 'high and stately with marble pillars', boasting two great turrets on either side of the water-gate whose steps led straight into the

BELOW The Strand waterfront, showing Durham, Salisbury and Worcester Houses, from a drawing by Hollar, c. 1630.

The Strand façade of Old Somerset House, the great Classical mansion built by Protector Somerset. Drawing by John Thorpe.

mansion. There had been many changes since Catherine of Aragon's unhappy residence here as a spurned princess in the years following Prince Arthur's death. It had been Elizabeth's own London house in her brother's reign, though she had little chance of occupying it. Queen Mary had assigned it to the Spanish ambassador, Count de Feria, who was still in residence in 1558 with his English bride, Lady Jane Dormer; De Feria's successor, Bishop de Quadra, retained the use of Durham House, and mass in his private chapel was secretly attended by English Catholics from the court. On the Bishop's disgrace the Queen regained possession, and the house became a 'grace and favour' residence for courtiers and distinguished foreigners. Sir Ambrose Cave, Chancellor of the Duchy of Lancaster, was allowed to hold his daughter's wedding festivities here when she married a son of the militantly Protestant Sir Francis Knollys; for a time Leicester had a suite in Durham House before he moved to Lord Paget's; the first Earl of Essex, who had no London house of his own, also resided here, and Leicester may first have become enamoured of Lettice Knollys at Durham House. When Princess Cecilia of Sweden came to England, the first member of another royal House to pay Elizabeth an official visit, she was lodged here. In 1583 the Queen was to lease the house to Sir Walter Raleigh.

The last notable building before Charing Cross was Norwich or York House which enjoyed a frontage on the road roughly the same as Peter Robinson's store today, but extended down to the river, with gardens and a landing-place; its changes of occupation are themselves a commentary on Tudor politics. The last pre-Reformation bishop of Norwich had exchanged this 'inn' with the Crown for property in Norfolk and Henry granted the house to his sister's husband, Charles Brandon, Duke of Suffolk. Archbishop Nicholas Heath, Queen Mary's Lord Chancellor, had cause to regret that with Wolsey's fall the archbishops of York had lost their centrally-placed residence, and he soon exchanged his house in Southwark for 'Suffolk House by Charing Cross'. When he declined to serve Elizabeth as Chancellor he had no need of 'York House' and leased it to his successor, Lord Keeper

Bacon; at the end of the reign the house was leased to Lord Keeper Egerton, and later on to Lord Chancellor Bacon, who had been born there. (Even though the site was to be granted by Charles I to his favourite Buckingham, the water-gate was still known as York Stairs.)

On the north side of the Strand were 'divers fair buildings, hostelries and houses for gentlemen and men of honour'. The chief was Sir William Cecil's house on the site of the rectory of St Clement's Dane, where Sir Thomas Palmer had erected 'a magnificent house of brick and timber' during Protector Somerset's rule. On Palmer's attainder the property passed to the Crown, and Elizabeth granted it to her Principal Secretary, who extended it into 'a noble pile', adorning it with four square turrets. The only other house of note in this area before the middle of the reign was Russell House, the Earl of Bedford's London home. A landmark on the north side of the Strand was the Chequers Tavern (later known as The Queen's Head) standing opposite Durham House. This hostelry was much frequented by the 'men-at-arms, court-danglers and serving men' passing to and fro from Whitehall and was an ideal place for acquiring the latest gossip.

To the west of Whitehall Palace were the houses belonging to Lord Grey of Wilton and Lord Dacre in Tothill Street, giving on to St James's Park. In Canon Row, beyond the King Street Gate, where the canons of St Stephen's had resided before the Dissolution, were the town houses of a number of peers, including Admiral Clinton and Protector Somerset's widow, who earned Elizabeth's displeasure first by marrying beneath herself, choosing as her second husband her steward Francis Newdigate, and then by the dynastic marriage of her son to Lady Catherine Grey. It was in Canon Row that Sir William Cecil lived, in a house bought from Lord Paget before he moved to St Clement's Dane. The Earl of Southampton lived in an almost rural retreat in Holborn, by Lincoln's Inn Fields, a few minutes' walk from the Bishop of Ely's palace with its rose gardens (that would one day belong to Sir Christopher Hatton) and not so much further from Lord North's Charterhouse, Lord Rich's house at St Bartholomew's, Smithfield, and the neighbouring house that Sir Walter Mildmay, Chancellor of the Exchequer, had bought from Rich when residence at Hackney seemed too far from the hub of affairs.

Court and capital were two arms of the same magnet, exerting an unprecedented attraction. John Norden, who by his maps did more than any other Elizabethan to make known provincial England, categorised London as 'that adamant which draweth into it all the other parts of the land and above the rest is most usually frequented with Her Majesty's most royal presence'. Another called it 'the garden of England', since the produce of all the counties could be picked there; and more, it was the great emporium for foreign wares. Stow, the Londoner, praising the range of commodities for sale, could not but regret the decline of provincial trading centres, for 'the daintiness of men cannot be restrained, which will needs seek these things at London, yet other places also might be relieved'. It was no wonder, he wrote at the end of the reign, that people abandoned country towns, since the court 'which is now-a-days much greater and more gallant than in former times ... is for the most part either abiding at London,' or close to it, and in consequence gentlemen flocked thither, 'the younger sort of them to see and show vanity, and the elder to save the cost and charge of hospitality and housekeeping' in the provinces. For all who had tasted the delights of the metropolis, provincial life seemed tedious and uneventful, but for the courtier proper it was banishment. Those whose positions at court did not warrant official accommodation, or whose income was insufficient to purchase or lease a London residence, rented accommodation by the term. Wives, eager to enjoy the amenities that London offered, joined their husbands when they could, and Sir Robert Sidney, not wanting to leave his wife shut up in Penshurst without company while he was in the capital in 1594, hired a town house for the winter. Only two factors reduced the numbers staying in London; one was the plague, whose outbreaks invariably provoked a general exodus of all who could leave, the other was the Queen's summer progress, for Elizabeth's was still an itinerant court in the old tradition.

Progresses were unpopular with senior courtiers and many begged to be excused from attendance. The summer was their chief opportunity of returning to their own homes and they did not want to be obliged to be on duty, on the move between one stately home and another – but whether or not they could take a holiday rested with the Queen herself and it was risky to play truant. Elizabeth expected to be well served by courtiers and officials as she toured the less far-flung parts of her realm showing herself to her people, with an entourage of some five hundred persons bringing colour to the countryside as they noisily progressed at three miles an hour. The 'prodigy houses' like Burghley's Theobalds and Hatton's Holdenby were specifically designed for entertaining Her Majesty, however much their owners dreaded the bills incurred by playing host, and every nobleman's seat was a palace in miniature, with its principal suites of rooms modelled on the domestic arrangements at Hampton Court or Greenwich, so that the Queen should be as little inconvenienced as possible. Yet the assignment of lodgings was always a ticklish business, and tempers were easily frayed by makeshift arrangements in cramped quarters. On a visit to the Archbishop's palace at Croydon, for instance, there was an awkward scene when the Lord Chamberlain allowed Raleigh to occupy the rooms ear-marked for Hatton. Lower down the hierarchy the emphasis on the rights of rank was no less insistent, and old Sir Henry Lee refused to sleep under canvas when the Queen visited Hampshire, seeking permission to leave the progress because his servant could not find a fit lodging for him.

Queen and court taking the road during most summers complemented the arrangements in the royal calendar whereby Elizabeth held court in her palaces in Greater London for the rest of the year. Even if law term was over and Parliament in recess, the fact that the Queen was in residence at Whitehall still drew great numbers to the capital.

Some still regarded a journey to London as a great adventure and, because of the perils of travel and of the vicissitudes expected on arrival, made their wills before setting out, as did the gentry from the Isle of Wight who thought of it as 'an East India voyage'. Others in the country, less attracted to gadding about or more careful of their purses, made a virtue of their homespun inclinations, perhaps rather proud to be so determinedly against the fashion. This was especially so with women who disliked the hours spent in the side-saddle in the days before the coach became general and less an expensive luxury. Attendance at court meant that many men in the middling rank of royal servants were parted from wives and families for much of the year – men like John Gamage of Kingsey in Oxfordshire, who was tied to his office in Westminster throughout term, while his wife for her part was tied to their children and the farm she managed. She found time to bake duck pies and tench pies, to stew eels and roast joints which the carrier brought to stock John's London larder. She would also send pippins and artichokes from their garden, convinced that the fruit and vegetables sold in London were unwholesome, and for a Shrove Tuesday party she loaded a hamper with plovers, teals and partridges. Mrs Gamage was far too busy to contemplate visiting London herself, but merely counted the days until John would be home from court. Men much more eminent about the Queen than John Gamage relied on bulky food parcels from their country estates – sides of venison, barrels of bacon and even oats for their horses.

Clarendon's grandmother never left Wiltshire, though her husband had travelled in Italy and came to Westminster as an MP, because gentlemen only came to London 'upon important business and their wives never'. Mrs Hyde never saw for herself the wonders that the shops in Cheapside held or went sightseeing in the Strand, and by the time the fashionable clothes her husband had talked about had reached Salisbury they had generally been replaced in London, for 'new fashions came first to the court and then (by the time they have been copied by the common people and stage-players) the courtiers have taken up something else'.

For men for whom a place at court was unattainable, a seat in the Commons was a consolation prize, since during the hectic weeks of a Parliamentary sessions they were on the fringe of the court. 'I am one that loves to see fashions, and desires to know wonders, therefore, if I be elected, I will not refuse it,' wrote the Recorder of Beaumaris. His stock in Anglesey rose by his sojourn in London.

Life at court was not unalloyed joy and not every man had a suitable temperament. The successful courtier needed to be fortified by an inner toughness to survive disappointments, disfavour and disharmony, and to be able to keep his balance when he was the victim of malicious tongues. Reputation was so often fragile, power illusionary, the future plagued by uncertainty. The Queen not only dazzled; she could burn like the sun with a fiery intensity and it was remarked that successive lords of Berkeley prospered because they had experienced 'the warmth of the court in a moderate distance, not in too near an aspect'. 'When she smiled,' wrote her godson Harington, who perhaps understood the Queen as well as any man in her last years, 'it was pure sunshine that everyone did choose to bask in if they could,' but the fine spell could not last indefinitely and when a storm arose without warning 'the thunder fell in monstrous measure on all alike'.

Despite the rich pickings from patronage, the costs of maintaining oneself at court, keeping up appearances and retaining royal favour could be crippling. No one made a fortune at the final balance, many suffered losses and some were heavily in debt; apart from sums due to others the favourites Leicester and Hatton died owing the Queen £34,000 and £42,000 respectively, and in each case their private debts were not much smaller. One who achieved an impartial assessment of the court scene, weighing carefully its merits against its hardships, wrote 'It is a world to be here, to see the humours of the time. Blessed are they that can be away and live contented.'

2 Sovereign's Choice

In the weeks during which her sister was slowly dying, Elizabeth had ample time to select potential councillors and other holders of the chief offices. She weighed their capabilities and experience, pondered their known political and religious affiliations in the light of their past and, perhaps above all, looked carefully at their family trees. 'I mean to direct all my actions by good advice and counsel,' she said in a speech at Hatfield in the first days of her accession, when she classified potential advisers into three groups. The first were 'the ancient nobility, having your beginnings and estates of my progenitors, Kings of the realm,' who should have a natural care in maintaining the commonwealth; then there were those 'of long experience in governance' under her father, brother and sister; finally there were men who had not previously held high office but seemed eminently suitable to serve her. She asked those councillors, peers and commoners who were not to be reappointed to realise that they were not being dropped 'for any disability in them', but because she wanted a smaller council, and she urged them to serve her in their counties as good and faithful subjects. Her appointments certainly resulted in a more compact body than had served Mary, with a full council of twenty instead of her predecessor's thirty, although in recent months absentees had outnumbered those meeting in the council chamber; and yet Elizabeth was being less than frank in announcing that her dismissals would not be on grounds of personal disability, for the nineteen she did not retain were all staunch Catholics.

Among the peers left off the council were Lords Montague and Hastings, who had been elevated to the peerage by Mary. Both were ardent papists. Like his father before him, Lord Montague, as Sir Anthony Browne, had held the post of Master of the Horse, and led an embassy to the Pope before taking the field at St Quentin, though he was to remain loyal to Elizabeth who sent him as ambassador to Madrid. Lord Hastings of Loughborough was younger brother of the second Earl of Huntingdon and it was incongruous that while his nephew, who succeeded as third Earl in 1561, was an ardent Protestant, Hastings voted against Elizabeth's Act of Uniformity and remained a fierce opponent of her settlement. Richard Lord Rich, an ambitious careerist, had been through Cromwell's service, perjuring himself at Thomas More's trial to secure his downfall and execution. He later became Edward's Lord Chancellor, but under Mary he played only a minor role in affairs, and with the

Sir William Cecil, Lord Burghley (1520-98), riding a mule in his garden.

new Queen his political career ended and he now devoted himself to his estates and to founding Felstead School in Essex.

Lord Paget, by contrast, had been the mainstay of Marian policy after Gardiner's death, and his dismissal by Elizabeth, as we shall notice, was the one major change in personnel. Among Mary's councillors were the group of East Anglian knights who had rallied to her cause at Framlingham while Lady Jane Grey was being proclaimed Queen in London, and who had been rewarded with posts at court – men such as Elizabeth's jailer at Woodstock, Sir Henry Bedingfield, Sir Thomas Cornwallis, Sir Richard Southwell and the lawyer Sir Edward Waldegrave. These, with other commoners undistinguished except for their loyalty to Catholicism, including Sir John Bourne, John Boxall, Sir William Dormer, Sir Francis Englefield and Sir Thomas Wharton, all found that their appointments had lapsed and that their wives had lost their places in the royal household. Sir John Baker, the Chancellor of the Exchequer, died in the first weeks of the new reign.

Henry Carey, 1st Baron Hunsdon (1524-96), first cousin to the Queen.

Elizabeth reappointed no more than eleven councillors – seven peers and four commoners – of the thirty who had served Mary, and nearly all of these had been at the hub of affairs under her father and brother. Of the peers all except the Earls of Derby and Pembroke held a major office; these were Howard of Effingham as Lord Chamberlain, Arundel as Lord Steward, Clinton as Lord Admiral, Winchester as Lord Treasurer and Shrewsbury as Lord President of the Council in the North. The commoners retained were Sir Thomas Cheyney, Treasurer of the Household, who had not long to live; Sir William Petre, a Secretary of State from the end of Henry's reign until his resignation in 1557, who was in outlook a civil servant, as loyal to the new sovereign as he had been to her predecessors, but already an old man, anxious to spend what remained of his life at Ingatestone Hall, his charming house in Essex; and two professional diplomats, who had each begun their careers in holy orders, Sir John Mason, Treasurer of the Chamber and Chancellor of Oxford University, and Sir Nicholas Wotton, by far the most experienced of Elizabeth's ambassadors, who contrived to cling to the deaneries of both Canterbury and York.

Of the nine new members, two had served on the council before Mary's accession – Sir William Parr, now restored to the marquisate of Northampton, and Sir William Cecil, the Principal Secretary. Four more had previous experience of the court and administration – Sir Nicholas Bacon, the Lord Keeper, Sir Richard Sackville, the Under-Treasurer, Sir Edward Rogers, a Somerset squire who had served in Edward's Privy Chamber and became first Vice-Chamberlain and then Comptroller of the Household, and Sir Francis Knollys, his successor as Vice-Chamberlain, who had been prominent at Edward's court. A seventh, old Sir Thomas Parry, had been steward of the young Princess Elizabeth's household; his incautious answers to his interrogators long ago about Admiral Seymour's plans to marry Elizabeth had never weakened her confidence in him and he became Master of the Wards and, on Cheyney's death, Treasurer of the Household. The final two councillors were indeed new men; they were Sir Ambrose Cave, the Chancellor of the Duchy of Lancaster, in place of Sir Edward Waldegrave, and Francis, second Earl of Bedford, like Knollys an outspoken Protestant, who had not long succeeded to his title.

For us to appreciate the significance of ancestry and the legacy of the past in influencing Elizabeth's choice of these men, we need to explore the labyrinth of cousinage and be almost as aware as the Queen herself about who was related to whom. Like her, we also need to be sure not merely about the stance an individual had taken in Mary's reign, but also how his father had served her father and why his father-in-law had fallen out with Protector Somerset or failed to come to terms with Northumberland.

There was a new generation of Boleyn kin at court, now that Anne's daughter was Queen, headed by Henry Carey. Mary Boleyn, the elder daughter of Sir Thomas, had been Henry VIII's mistress for some years before he met Anne. She had married William Carey, an esquire of the Body, and their son Henry, born in 1526, was in consequence first cousin of Elizabeth and possibly her half-brother as well, for King Henry had certainly continued his liaison with Mary after her marriage. When William Carey died of the plague in the hot, distressing summer of 1528 she had married a

Stafford. Though Henry Carey sat in the Commons during Edward's and Mary's reigns he was inconspicuous, keeping clear of conspiracy and biding his time for Elizabeth's accession. When she created him a peer at the time of her coronation – where he cut a splendid figure in the ceremonial jousts – she chose as his title Baron Hunsdon, after the Hertfordshire manor where she had spent so much of her childhood away from court. The Queen placed great trust in cousin Harry's judgment and capacity, and kept him busy from the beginning with diplomatic, military and administrative tasks, though it was not until 1561 that she appointed him to her council and bestowed on him a post at court as captain of the Gentlemen Pensioners.

Catherine Carey, a year or so older than her brother (itself suggesting she had a stronger claim to royal parentage than he), had married Sir Francis Knollys, the eldest son of an usher to the Chamber under the first two Tudors. He had attended on Anne of Cleves when she landed in England and later identified himself with militant Protestantism; after Henry's death he was frequently at court, where his zeal for religion impressed both King Edward and Princess Elizabeth. When with the Marian reaction he decided to leave England, Elizabeth wrote Lady Catherine a characteristic letter looking forward to their safe return. Francis corresponded with Calvin, was a close friend of both Peter Martyr and John Jewel, and enrolled as a student at Basle University. Among those who had taken refuge abroad while Protestant reformers were burned at Smithfield, he was the only layman to be placed in a key post on Elizabeth's accession, for he became a Privy Councillor and was appointed both Vice-Chamberlain of her household and captain of the Halberdiers, while Lady Catherine and her younger sister both became gentlewomen of the Privy Chamber. In view of Elizabeth's mistrust of the *revenants* from Zurich and Geneva, who regarded her as Deborah, 'judge and

A miniature by Hilliard, reputed to be of Catherine Carey, wife of Lord Hunsdon.

restorer of the house of Israel' and expected her to bring about a root and branch reform of the Church, it is clear that it was only Knollys's marriage to a Carey that had secured his sovereign's favour, though this fact was far from clear to him.

Another Boleyn connexion was Sir Richard Sackville, whose mother was a sister of Sir Thomas Boleyn. Though Anne Boleyn was thus a first cousin he succeeded in laying the foundations of a career at court after her fall, becoming Chancellor and Under-Treasurer of the Exchequer. Under Edward VI he also held the lucrative post of Chancellor of the Court of Augmentations, supervising the sales and leases of former monastic and chantry lands. Sackville had remained in office rather as a permanent civil servant with a flair for finance throughout Mary's reign and it was natural, too, for Elizabeth to confirm him in his appointments; she also appointed him a councillor and gave him responsibility for making many of the arrangements for her coronation. After his death in 1566 his widow was to marry Lord Treasurer Winchester, whose moderate political outlook he had largely shared. Elizabeth was to show no little favour to Sackville's son Thomas, whom she created Lord Buckhurst and granted the reversion of Knole.

Two more distant members of the Boleyn family to be found places at court are worth noticing less for the posts they occupied than for their relationship with other courtiers. One, John Fortescue, who became master of the Wardrobe, was stepson of Sir Thomas Parry, Treasurer of the Household. The other, John Ashley (or Astley), whose mother was a niece of Anne Boleyn's mother, had understandably come to court on Anne's marriage in 1533, but somewhat surprisingly had clung to his minor preferment after her fall. The friend of Cheke, Ascham and the Cambridge humanists, he was to find a post in Princess Elizabeth's household, perhaps as confidential secretary, and he endeared himself to Elizabeth by marrying Kate Champernowne, once her governess, now her mistress of the maids. Kate's elder sister Joan had also married a Cambridge scholar, Sir Anthony Denny, the courtier closest to Henry VIII in his last months. While Kate remained with the Princess at Woodstock, Hunsdon and Hatfield when she was under suspicion in Mary's reign, John Ashley had left for the Continent to study at Padua. Husband and wife were well entrenched in the royal household from the accession, with John becoming Master of the Jewel House.

The Howard cousins of the Boleyns still dominated the peerage in 1558 in numbers, wealth and honours, and it was Elizabeth's connexions through her mother's family with the prolific Howards that gave her so numerous a cousinage. The House of Howard had survived the falls of Anne Boleyn and Catherine Howard, the attainder of Surrey and the regimes of Somerset and Northumberland, to regain political power under Mary. At the head of the family was the poet Surrey's eldest son, the fourth Duke of Norfolk, now twenty, cousin of the Queen, England's sole duke and hereditary Earl Marshal. His father had gone to the block as a victim of Hertford's schemings in King Henry's last days, and his mother, a Vere, had married again to a Suffolk squire. While his grandfather, Lord Treasurer Norfolk, had languished in the Tower throughout Edward's reign, Howard had been tutored by John Foxe, the martyrologist. Later he was weaned from Protestant dogma by Bishop White, and was thought by some to have inherited the third Duke's sympathies for the old religion, as well as his disdain for such ewly ennobled families as the Dudleys. A youthful marriage to Mary FitzAlan, the Earl of Arundel's daughter, had made Thomas Howard a father and a widower in swift succession. In the first days of Elizabeth's reign he married again, choosing as his bride a young widow, Margaret Lady Dudley, by birth an Audley, whose husband, Lord Henry Dudley, elder brother of Lord Robert, had been killed at the battle of St Quentin. To Norfolk fell the task of arranging the secular ceremonial of the coronation and the banquet which followed, but his youth and inexperience left him outside the circle of his royal cousin's advisers. Of the Duke's three sisters Catherine, an expert falconer, was married to Henry Lord Berkeley; her younger sisters were both to marry northerners – the Earl of Westmorland and Lord Scrope.

Two Howards of earlier generations were prominent; William Lord Howard of Effingham, a son of the second Duke of Norfolk by his second wife, and another Thomas, Surrey's younger brother. Howard of Effingham, born in 1510, had behind him a distinguished career as soldier, sailor and diplomat. He had earned his barony from Mary for his defence of London against Sir Thomas Wyatt the Younger, but he had the courage to speak up for Elizabeth when she was under suspicion in the Tower. This threw doubts on his own loyalty to Mary and he even contemplated leaving public life, but in her last year Mary appointed him Lord Chamberlain. Elizabeth continued her great-uncle in his posts at court and council. Thomas Howard, another royal cousin, was advanced to the peerage at the coronation as Viscount Bindon. Two of Howard of Effingham's sisters, both dead by now, had married into the peerage; one had been the mother of Thomas Radcliffe, third Duke of Sussex, who was consequently an uncle of the Queen; the other had been first wife of Edward Stanley, third Earl of Derby and mother of the heir to the title.

Elizabeth also had connexions springing from her father's final marriage with Catherine Parr. Catherine had taken her role of stepmother conscientiously, bringing the young Princess back to court and providing her with a house at Chelsea in the first months of Edward's reign. The Queen Dowager had married Sir Thomas Seymour, who dallied with Elizabeth's affections before and after Catherine's death in childbirth. Catherine's brother, William Parr, in and out of the Tower in Mary's reign, was now restored to the marquisate of Northampton and the Privy Council; he had a tangled matrimonial history but was now married to a daughter of the Lord Cobham who had helped to bring about the fateful match between Lady Jane Grey and Lord Guildford Dudley. The Queen had always been fond of Northampton.

There was one further royal connexion. Lord Clinton, the Admiral, as a royal ward had married Elizabeth Blount, widow of Lord Tailboys, the former mistress of Henry VIII and mother of Henry Fitzroy, Duke of Richmond. Before her early death Bessie had presented Clinton with three daughters – Bridget, who married Robert Dymock of Scrivelsby, the son of Sir Edward, the Champion of England at the coronation banquets in turn of Edward VI, Mary and Elizabeth; Catherine, who became the wife of William Lord Burgh; and Margaret, who married Charles Lord Willoughby of Parham. Bridget Dymock died before her husband hardened into recusant ways, but her sisters survived well into the next century. Clinton's second wife, a Stourton, provided him with sons as well as daughters, but by Elizabeth's

RIGHT Edward Fiennes
de Clinton (1512-85), 1st
Earl of Lincoln and Lord
Admiral: portrait by an
unknown artist.

BELOW Lady Elizabeth
FitzGerald, Countess
of Lincoln, the 'Fair
Geraldine' of
Surrey's sonnets.

accession he had been married for six years to a third wife, like his first one of the most beautiful women of the century. This was Lady Elizabeth FitzGerald, 'the Fair Geraldine' who as a young girl in Princess Mary's household at Hunsdon had inspired Surrey's finest verse. At fifteen she had been married off to an aged widower, Sir Anthony Browne, Henry's Master of the Horse and Lord Montague's father, to live till his death at Battle Abbey, but there were no more than sixteen years between Lady Elizabeth and Admiral Clinton. They had no children. In the summer of 1561 she was on the windy side of the law, being closely questioned about some offence, probably within the jurisdiction of the ecclesiastical courts, and Archbishop Parker was outspoken about her behaviour: 'It were honourable to God she were chastised in Bridewell for example, and if my Lord hath given her frailty any just accusation of forgetting her duty she were well worth to be thoroughly chidden.'

Admiral Clinton himself, who had inherited his peerage at the age of five, was already at forty-seven something of a veteran servant of the Crown. A skilled performer in the tiltyard, he had first gone to sea with John Dudley. In the wars with France and Scotland he had helped to repel French invasion, shared with Somerset the victory at Musselburgh and against all odds held out in Boulogne. He succeeded his master Dudley as Lord Admiral in 1550 but after the failure of Lady Jane Grey's conspiracy he managed to make his peace with Mary, though he lost his office to Howard of Effingham. With Pembroke, Clinton commanded the English forces at St Quentin, which enhanced his reputation. When, in the dark days following the fall of Calais, Mary reappointed him Lord Admiral, his recall put fresh heart into the navy's efforts to defend the Channel and attack Brest. Elizabeth confirmed his commission and regarded him as her expert on military and naval affairs, so he sat in council much as a minister of defence down to his death in 1585. As a man who retained royal favour in four successive reigns Clinton clearly had no strong religious feelings, but henceforward on most issues he stood close to Cecil, whose new mansion at Stamford was not so far from his own Lincolnshire house at Sempringham.

William Cecil, Principal Secretary and *primus inter pares* of councillors, was thirty-eight. His Welsh grandfather had fought for Henry Tudor at Bosworth, come to court as yeoman of the guard and risen to be serjeant-at-arms and to serve as sheriff of his adopted county, Northamptonshire. Richard Cecil, William's father, had been found a place as a page of the Chamber, but his career was undistinguished; during a lifetime spent in Henry VIII's service, he rose no higher than groom of the Wardrobe. William, with the benefit of six years at Cambridge followed by a period at Gray's Inn, entered the royal service later in life and at a very different level. He cemented his friendship with the Cambridge humanists (free from the suspicions of unorthodoxy while Henry lived) who were, in the next reign, to shape Protestant doctrine by marrying a sister of his tutor, Sir John Cheke, and after her early death he married Mildred Cooke, the eldest of the remarkable daughters of Sir Anthony Cooke of Gidea Hall, Essex, who were renowned for their classical scholarship; three of Mildred's sisters were to marry men who distinguished themselves at Elizabeth's court – Sir Nicholas Bacon, Sir Henry Killigrew and Sir Thomas Hoby. Cecil, like Bacon, had embarked on a career

ATIS SVÆ. 51.

1580

Anne Cooke, wife of Lord
Keeper Bacon and sister
of Lady Burghley: portrait
attributed to George
Gower, 1580.

at the bar at a time when, through Queen Catherine Parr's influence, Cheke
and Cooke were tutoring Prince Edward.

On Henry's death, Cecil entered Protector Somerset's service, later becoming his secretary, and his flair for public affairs made him indispensable to
Northumberland, who appointed him Secretary of State. He had lost this
post with Mary's accession, yet while Cheke, Hoby and Killigrew left England
in the face of persecution Cecil remained, trimming his Protestantism to the
times. He stayed aloof from affairs, devoting himself to sheep-farming and
building, though he obeyed Mary's summons to serve on diplomatic missions
and sat in Parliament in 1555. He saw as clearly as Elizabeth that Mary's
regime was but an interlude and with cautious opportunism he waited on
events, steering clear of conspiracies. This aloof conformity was to be of
immense significance, for Elizabeth would never have chosen as her chief
minister a man who had plotted against an anointed Queen, nor one who
had gone into exile to be nurtured in the ways of Zurich and Geneva. In 1550
the Princess had shrewdly appointed Cecil surveyor of her lands and over the

LEFT Mildred Cooke, Lady
Burghley: portrait painted
by the Master of Mildred
Cooke, c. 1565.
RIGHT Sir William Cecil,
Lord Burghley, holding
his staff as Lord
Treasurer: portrait
attributed to Marcus
Gheeraerts the Younger,
after 1585.

years his work had won her trust and his discharging of it her affection.
During 1558 he had maintained discreet communication with Hatfield,
under cover of his duties as surveyor, and received her instructions on how
he was to act on the demise of the Crown. Her choice of him as Secretary
aroused no surprise, for he had held the office with distinction under her
brother and he was the one official with whom she had consistently enjoyed
cordial relations over almost a decade. Because of their past associations, at
times each thought they were closer in outlook during the first years of their
new partnership than they really were.

Somewhat surprisingly, Elizabeth was prepared as an interim measure to
reappoint Nicholas Heath, Archbishop of York, as Lord Chancellor, but he
had declined, wishing to be 'utterly disburdened' of office. An uncompromis-
ing Catholic, he was to be deprived of his archbishopric the following July,
though he survived in the wilderness for another twenty years. In Heath's
place, the Queen chose Cecil's brother-in-law Nicholas Bacon, though his
status was that of Lord Keeper of the Great Seal, not Lord Chancellor. At

OVERLEAF Painting of
a lady, said to be the
Queen, dancing with
Robert Dudley, now
hanging at Penshurst
Place.

COR·VNV·VIA·VNA

William Herbert,
1st Earl of Pembroke
(1501-70), soldier and
politician of renown,
who remained illiterate,
yet built Wilton House
(see p. 162).

in office because his great administrative experience outweighed any dis-advantages of age. Born while Edward IV was on the throne, he was now at least seventy-five, but showed no signs of senility. In the first days of the reign he lost his wife, and when the Queen visited him at Basing House, Hampshire the next summer, thoroughly enjoying the entertainment he provided, she made fun of his grey hairs, for 'if my Lord Treasurer were but a young man I could find it in my heart to have him for a husband before any man in England'. The old man was to marry again, living to see 103 of his own descendants. Truly he spanned a great tract of political life, perhaps the sole link with a more staid world, so that the upheavals of the last two reigns appeared as mere interruptions in England's natural development. He had been sheriff of Hampshire in the year of the Field of Cloth of Gold, sat in all sessions of the Reformation Parliament and become Comptroller of the royal household before Henry VIII had married Anne Boleyn. When, on her fall, Anne accused other councillors of twisting her words she excepted the Comp-troller, who 'was a very gentleman,' and perhaps Elizabeth eventually came to hear of this. His flair for tackling financial problems in the household brought him in succession the posts of Treasurer, Lord Chamberlain and Great Master, as well as the lucrative office of Master of the Wards, and before Henry's death he had become Lord President of the Council. Essen-tially a bureaucrat, Winchester made a virtue of being a trimmer in politics under Edward and Mary. Northumberland had elevated him to a marqui-sate, although he was suspected of papist leanings, and the man who swore he would set upon Philip of Spain when he arrived to marry Mary, found himself rather enjoying entertaining the bridal couple on the morrow of their wedding. Winchester wanted no further changes in religion in 1558, and said so, though having voted against the alteration of church services in the Lords (where he acted as Speaker in 1559) he decided to accept the situation as he had continued to accept political change all his life, being sprung, as he remarked, from the willow not the oak. It was the national budget not the national conscience that remained his concern.

Of the peers whose services Elizabeth retained on her council the Earl of Pembroke was closest to Cecil in these early years. William Herbert had had a colourful past. A promising career in the royal service seemed in jeopardy when this 'mad young fighting fellow' killed a tradesman for lack of respect and fled to France, but Henry VIII, assured of his bravery, welcomed him again at court. Herbert's subsequent marriage with Anne Parr, whose elder sister became Henry's last wife, set the seal on his fortunes; he was granted the extensive estates of Wilton Abbey as well as lands in South Wales, and was promoted to the Privy Chamber and to the Keepership of Baynards Castle, the royal house by the Thames, which he retained until his death. Under Edward VI he put down the Prayer Book Rising in the West with his Welsh retainers and successfully made terms with Northumberland; on the day that John Dudley was created Duke of Northumberland, Herbert became Earl of Pembroke and at the same ceremony Cecil was knighted. His son Henry Herbert had been married at the age of nine to Catherine Grey, Lady Jane's sister, as part of Northumberland's attempted *coup*, though the mar-riage was soon dissolved. The Duke later ascribed the origins of his conspiracy to Pembroke on the grounds that under a Catholic Queen he would lose his monastic properties, yet Pembroke had declared for Mary in the nick of time and, though suspicions about his fidelity remained, he was too useful a servant to be cast aside. Philip of Spain thought highly of him, despite his Protestant views, recommending that he should command the English army in France, where he distinguished himself at St Quentin.

On Mary's death Pembroke had ridden to Hatfield to swear he was a true liegeman of the young Queen, and though he was given no office at court he was a most regular attendant of council meetings until in the summer of 1560 he became seriously ill. He was perhaps the most successful of the men who had profited by the fall of the abbeys, for he survived the turbulence of the next two reigns unscathed, wealthy, established and respected. After Anne Parr's death he had married a daughter of the sixth Earl of Shrewsbury and in 1562 cemented his family's relations with the house of Talbot by arranging a remarkable double wedding: his son Henry, who had been the child bridegroom of Lady Catherine Grey, married the sixth Earl of Shrewsbury's daughter, Catherine (so that she now counted her sister as her step-mother-in-law), while Pembroke's daughter Anne married Lord Francis Talbot, Catherine's brother and the heir to the earldom.

Pembroke's inclinations to Calvinism outstripped Cecil's and in time would lead him to support Robert Dudley and his schemes for alliances with Continental Protestants, but for the present he threw himself heart and soul behind the Secretary. When Cecil had to leave court to negotiate with the Scots in 1560 he regarded Pembroke as the most reliable man left behind in Whitehall, and then when the Earl became ill Cecil lamented that he had not a friend in council. Despite the elegance of his new house at Wilton, his friendship with Protestant theologians and the regard Elizabeth had for his judgment, Pembroke remained a rough diamond – an old soldier, blunt in his expressions. A boisterous career had done nothing to smooth his manners. He was happiest with his dogs or egging on his retainers to brawl with neighbouring landowners and he was the only privy councillor of the reign, if not of the century, who was illiterate, and rather proud of the fact.

Henry FitzAlan, Earl of Arundel, was confirmed in his post of Lord Steward of the Household and in his seat on the council. His high rank and experience of affairs had marked him out for favour and in 1559 (as in 1547 and 1553) he was appointed High Constable of England for the coronation, the highest office a subject could hold. He was from the first the leading conservative on the council, a Catholic in religion, anxious to steer England into a Habsburg alliance. Born in 1512, he had been named Henry after the King, his godfather, and had come to court before he was fifteen. As Lord Maltravers he had been present at Anne Boleyn's trial and on Lisle's fall became deputy at Calais. Succeeding to the earldom, he distinguished himself in Henry's last war with France and was rewarded with the office of Lord Chamberlain. He continued to hold it under Edward VI, though he was outmanœuvred by Northumberland, who kept him in the Tower for a year without trial. Restored to the council he acquiesced in the schemes for Lady Jane Grey's succession in order to betray them to Mary, and it was Arundel who won over the City of London and had Mary proclaimed Queen, for which loyal service she appointed him Lord Steward and a councillor.

In the war with France, Arundel became lieutenant-general of the forces for the defence of the realm. Mary had cared little for her father's folly at

Nonsuch and when she talked of demolishing the palace and selling the estate Arundel persuaded her to grant it to him, and spent considerable sums on completing the outer court and extending the gardens 'for the love of honour he bare to his old master, his godfather'. His affection for King Henry's memory certainly endeared him to Elizabeth, and in the early months of her reign there were rumours that she might marry this well-proportioned widower of forty-seven. He was the 'English spouse' members of Parliament had in mind when they pressed her to marry from among her own subjects, and in the summer of 1559, when he entertained her for a giddy week of festivities at Nonsuch, some were so confident that a betrothal would be announced before the Queen resumed her progress that they laid wagers.

Arundel was soon to be as disappointed in political power as he was in courting his Queen. The man who had been at court for longer than Elizabeth's other councillors and whose seniority in the royal household was unquestioned, found himself no match for Cecil. Whereas he had been a key councillor under Mary, when his opinions were always treated with great deference, he now found himself too often in a minority of one in matters of high policy; he was not even playing second fiddle to Cecil and after Robert Dudley's emergence he faded even further into the background. Though he had found a seat in the Parliament of 1559 for the Queen's cousin Francis Knollys, he was slow to realise the strength of Protestant feeling in men like Knollys, and it was probably on the score of religion that Arundel resigned the chancellorship of Oxford University after a matter of months. Like his son-in-law Norfolk, the Earl felt himself undervalued; he became disillusioned with the new regime and in 1565 was to resign his staff of office in a

53

huff and leave England for a sojourn in Padua, on the pretext of taking a course of baths to cure his gout. Over the years he assembled a magnificent library at Arundel House and though he made light of his own learning, his two daughters, Mary, Norfolk's first Duchess, and Jane Lady Lumley, were both considerable scholars. Arundel was quite militant in his aversion to foreign languages, which made his conversations with the Spanish ambassador somewhat awkward and, indeed, his ingrained habit of speaking English extremely fast sometimes made his remarks in the council chamber unintelligible to his colleagues.

Francis Russell, second Earl of Bedford, had been implicated in Wyatt's plot and fled to the Continent on Mary's accession. In 1557 the Queen pardoned him and he returned to England. Like Clinton, he had a penchant for widows. His first wife was Margaret St John, widow of Sir John Gostwick and, after her death, he would marry the Earl of Rutland's widow. His four sons predeceased him, so that a grandson succeeded him in the earldom in 1585, but his daughters made great marriages – the eldest to Ambrose Dudley, Earl of Warwick, her sisters to the Earls of Bath and Cumberland. Countess Margaret must have found Bedford, the friend of Bullinger, very different from her first husband, Gostwick, who had aroused King Henry's wrath for questioning Archbishop Cranmer's orthodoxy in the Commons. In 1551 as Sir Francis Russell, MP for Buckinghamshire and possibly the first heir to a peerage to sit in the Commons, he had attended private discussions on the nature of the Eucharist with divines and interested laymen, such as Northampton, Knollys and Cecil, and their fervour had helped to shape the second Edwardian Prayer Book.

Bedford's pronounced Protestant sympathies and his involvement in Northumberland's conspiracy led to imprisonment. He gave secret support to Wyatt and may even have carried messages between Elizabeth and the rebel; at any rate on succeeding to the earldom he escaped abroad, first to Geneva, then to Venice, sitting at the feet of Continental reformers. At some risk he returned home in 1557, and his service under Pembroke at St Quentin earned him the appointment of Lord Lieutenant in the western shires. Appointed a councillor from Elizabeth's accession Bedford was, at thirty, regarded as the principal hope of English Protestantism, especially by those returning from exile, and he hoped to persuade Peter Martyr to come to England. Apart from minor diplomatic assignments Bedford was not given a specific office until 1564, when he became Warden of the East Marches and Governor of Berwick. Until her death in 1562 Countess Margaret served at court as a lady-in-waiting.

Francis Talbot, fifth Earl of Shrewsbury, whose father had been Henry VIII's first Lord Steward, spent more of his time on the Scottish border than at court and by Elizabeth's accession he had already given ten years service as President of the Council in the North, to keep the northerners from rising against the government in repetition of the Pilgrimage of Grace. Shrewsbury would periodically come south for occasional meetings of Parliament and council, and as England's premier earl he found himself summoned for special duties, such as sitting in the court of claims for the coronation. He owned considerable estates in the West Riding, Nottingham and Derby, which he ruled from Sheffield Castle, so that next to the Duke of Norfolk he was England's wealthiest peer. With the uncertainties of Scottish politics Shrewsbury's loyalty to the Crown was fundamental to the peaceful establishment of the new regime and though his sympathies were Catholic, like those of many lesser northern landowners, so that he despised the 1559 Prayer Book, he died the next year before his loyalty had been put to the test. His successor, George Talbot, the sixth Earl, was by contrast to inspire Elizabeth's entire confidence.

The other northern peer on the council, Edward Stanley, Earl of Derby, had had a more varied career than Shrewsbury. Born in 1508, he had become a ward of Cardinal Wolsey and served as cup-bearer at Anne Boleyn's coronation. Though the dissolution of the monasteries had extended his properties in Lancashire and Cheshire, he was opposed to religious change and spoke out in the Lords against the Edwardian Prayer Books and Act of Uniformity. He first became sworn a privy councillor under Somerset, on condition that he need attend meetings only when specifically summoned, and this proviso saved him from the intrigues of Edward's reign, even if his eldest son was principal witness at Somerset's trial. Derby happily identified himself with the Marian reaction, coming to council meetings much more frequently and playing an active part in persecuting heretics. Under Elizabeth he received no office at court beyond his seat on the council, which he rarely occupied. Cecil was well informed about his recusancy and the more militant Catholicism of his sons, and although Elizabeth was suspicious about the intentions of this great provincial magnate Derby himself remained loyal to her.

Of the remaining councillors we need only glance at Sir Ambrose Cave, a Leicestershire gentleman, who had been bred to the law and was now Chancellor of the Duchy of Lancaster. From his associations with the Cambridge humanist circle he was reckoned to be 'well affected to the Protestant religion'. Cecil's sister married into his family and in general he was a staunch Cecilian at court, but in local affairs Cave came to a working arrangement with Lord Robert Dudley, with whom he shared the lieutenancy of Warwickshire. It was from Dudley, not from Cecil, that he learnt the manners of a courtier. Once when the Queen's shoe slipped off while she was dancing, Sir Ambrose picked it up and with sundry gallantries offered to restore the trophy, but she playfully declined to receive it, so he tied it then and there to his left arm and said he would wear it in this way until the end of his life.

The two surprising omissions from the list of councillors were Lord Paget and Sir Thomas Smith. Paget, who had served as Secretary to Henry VIII in his last years and to Somerset, survived both the Protector's fall and a flirtation with Lady Jane Grey's cause to become Mary's Lord Privy Seal. He had opposed Bishop Gardiner's proposal to exclude Elizabeth from the succession, but had later won Philip of Spain's confidence and as chief councillor after Gardiner's death people blamed him for England's entry in the war, with the consequent loss of Calais. Paget was, it is true, in poor health at the end of 1558 and would be dead within five years, yet, more than any other factor except Cardinal Pole's death, his removal from the political scene gave the new government a complete break with the past. Smith, now forty-five, had become Vice-Chancellor of Cambridge before he was thirty and had left the university for court in the first weeks of Edward's reign to put into practice the precept he imparted to students who attended his lectures as regius professor of civil law – that the study of civil law offered marvellous opportunities for those intending to enter the royal service. He became Paget's colleague as Secretary, throwing himself into diplomatic and economic affairs, and though he remained a layman was appointed Provost of Eton and Dean of Carlisle before Somerset fell. Unlike Paget, Smith had been out of office under Mary, when so many more outspoken Cambridge friends had been abroad, but with Elizabeth's accession he expected preferment; he counted on Cecil's friendship, for the new Secretary had studied with him at Cambridge and served with him under Somerset.

Although Cecil sought Sir Thomas's help in preparing legislation and found a seat for him as MP for Liverpool, he found himself 'utterly forgotten' and he was not even called in to advise on the recoinage, a topic on which he was the acknowledged expert. Some misunderstanding, nurtured by Smith into a sore grievance, led to a quarrel with Cecil and it was not until 1562 that he was summoned from Essex to undertake an uncongenial embassy to France when what he wanted was a post at the hub of affairs. Perhaps Cecil regarded him as essentially an armchair statesman, penning donnish treatises about government but lacking the personality to translate political decisions into action. Sir Thomas also lacked an essential quality of a courtier – polished manners – without which a great intellect was almost a handicap at Whitehall. Yet though he was sensitive about his 'rude and homely ways' he never made any efforts to acquire social graces and counted it a matter of pride that 'at compliments I am the veriest calf and beast in the world'. 'My fault,' he once correctly diagnosed, 'is plainness and that I cannot dissemble enmity or pleasure'; music, dancing, gallantry and wit bored him, and he said as much, but expected everyone to be fascinated by his own dreams. In his eyes all women were frivolous, feckless and rather stupid, and blunt Sir Thomas took no pains to conceal his opinion that Queen Elizabeth was no exception. As her reign developed he hovered between standing close to Cecil and allying himself with Dudley, and he necessarily found himself caught in the cross-fire.

Among the appointments to lesser offices was that of old Lord Williams of Thame – who had befriended Elizabeth at Rycote on her journey to Woodstock in 1554 – to the Presidency of Wales, though he died within the year. Lord Cobham, who had been a supporter of Wyatt, became Lord Warden of the Cinque Ports while Sir Walter Mildmay, a friend of Cecil much experienced in public finance, now held the office of Chancellor of the Exchequer, an administrative post at this time, with no hint of its later supremacy.

Looking back over the chasm of her sister's reign Elizabeth restored to favour the children of Protector Somerset and of the Duke of Northumberland. At her coronation Edward Seymour regained the earldom of Hertford (but not the dukedom of Somerset), while Lord Ambrose Dudley and his brother Lord Robert, who had both been restored in blood with the rank of duke's sons by Queen Mary for their services in the wars, each had posts at court. Lord Ambrose was Master of the Ordnance, in place of Sir Richard Southwell, and Lord Robert was Master of the Horse, as successor to Lord Montague. One sister, Catherine, had married Henry Hastings, heir to the earldom of Huntingdon, the other, Mary, was the wife of Sir Henry Sidney, whom Elizabeth was soon to recall from Ireland, where he

Sir Henry Sidney, Lord Deputy of Ireland and President of the Council of Wales, (1529-86), the father of Sir Philip Sidney.

was aiding Sussex against Tyrone, to follow Lord Williams as President of the Council of Wales. Unlike Ireland and the Scottish border, the Principality was basically peaceful, so that Sir Henry and his wife were able to leave Ludlow for court for months on end and Lady Mary became one of Elizabeth's most devoted ladies-in-waiting.

Elizabeth aimed at being the very antithesis of her sister, whose rigid Catholicism and Spanish marriage had divided the nation. Not a few misunderstood her goal and fondly supposed that being the opposite of Mary would lead her to pursue a fervently Protestant policy. Such people expected that she would not merely put back the clock to embrace the tenets of the Edwardian reformers but even bring both doctrine and Church organisation into line with the advances made since then in the godly congregations of Zurich and Geneva and, more recently, in the Scotland of John Knox.

For the Queen, however, reversing Mary's policy meant not a violent swing of the pendulum but a delicate adjustment so that it came to rest centrally. Though she was utterly sincere in her own beliefs and was intensely interested in matters of doctrine, Elizabeth was not, as her sister had been, deeply religious. She saw her mission as to heal the divisions rending the nation, making her Church comprehensive, with room in its many mansions for the vast majority of her subjects – all except the extremists of the Catholic and Protestant wings. Instead of partisan exclusiveness she would choose moderation and as a matter of principle would not open windows in men's souls.

Such moderation had no appeal for the Protestant exiles returning from the Continent, who, now that the fires of Smithfield were extinguished, expected Elizabeth as their 'Protestant Bride' to show herself from the beginning as a vigorous supporter of their party programme. 'The wolves be coming out of Geneva,' thundered Bishop White of Winchester, preaching Queen Mary's funeral sermon, yet in not so very different a tone of voice Matthew Parker was soon saying 'God keep us from such a visitation as Knox has attempted in Scotland.' The Presbyterian system of elders as an alternative system of Church government to the rule of bishops was a warning, not an example. Elizabeth insisted that her Church settlement was a domestic affair and that she must preserve continuity in organisation to give the Church the stability which was essential to the State, and so retained the episcopacy. Treading a *via media*, she was accused of fostering a 'leaden mediocrity' by zealots who wanted a thorough reformation, seeing the Anglican Church of her devising as 'a cloaked papistry or a mingle-mangle'.

Unlike her ministers, the Queen recognised that the real challenge to religious unity came not from the right but from the left. Staunch Catholics unlikely to conform had been excluded from the council, yet around the Queen were men only too anxious to see the Church become specifically Protestant. Bedford and Knollys, who had both drunk deeply in the springs of the Continental Reformation, never ceased to work towards a Calvinistic solution of England's problem, while Cecil, despite the restraint under which his oath of office placed him, would hanker for some years after a distinctly Protestant Church and a foreign policy which would make Elizabeth the natural leader of Protestantism in Europe. Northampton was understandably reckoned a great favourer of the reformed faith, though not a 'party' man in the sense of Bedford. Lord Robert Dudley, though outside the council, was even in 1559 building up a following that would make him the spokesman of Protestant truth, and the new Earl of Huntingdon, too near the throne for high office, echoed the views of Bedford.

Such men looked to John Jewel, the *revenant* who became Bishop of Salisbury, as their prophet. Jewel reported to his friend Peter Martyr that 'the Queen openly favours our cause, yet she is afraid of allowing any innovations,' but in time he came to realise how limited her favour was. He was constantly exerting such pressure as he could to abolish requirements about vestments and ritual and to permit extempore prayers, sermons and discussions. 'There is a little too much foolery. That little cross of ill-omened origin still maintains its place in the Queen's chapel,' he lamented, and his friend Sir Francis Knollys could do nothing about it. The reforming party, later to acquire the nickname 'Puritans', never gave up their intention of a wholesale reform of the Church, and highly placed patrons such as Bedford, Huntingdon and Dudley secured Parliamentary seats for men with a religious programme that aimed at undermining the 1559 settlement.

As the Marian bishops, beginning with Bonner of London (who had been forced to lend his richest cope to little Oglethorpe of Carlisle who crowned

Matthew Parker, Archbishop of Canterbury, 1559-75. Biblical scholar and joint architect with the Queen of the Church settlement. To Elizabeth, his former service to her mother made up for his indiscretion in marrying.

the Queen), became deprived of their sees for refusing to take the Oath of Supremacy, the need for consecrating a new Archbishop of Canterbury to succeed Cardinal Pole became acute. Elizabeth had early on singled out Matthew Parker, who had long ago been chaplain to her mother. Unlike most Cambridge reformers of his generation Parker had not been tainted with European Protestantism; he was a scholar in the Erasmian tradition, learned in patristic studies and an undisputed authority on Biblical texts. Like Cranmer before him he had secretly married, and since the new Queen was outspoken on the subject of clerical celibacy he feared her wrath. At first he declined her offer of the archbishopric on grounds of ill health, but when pressed again he pleaded with her that Canterbury was 'above the reach of mine ability'. At length she persuaded him to accept; years afterwards he maintained that if he had not been so bound to the memory of Anne Boleyn he would not so easily have agreed to serve her daughter.

Matthew Parker proved an ideal archbishop for forwarding Elizabeth's grand concept of a comprehensive Church, for he shared the Queen's views about almost every detail of policy except that of clerical marriage. It was as much due to Parker as to his sovereign that the transition from the Roman Mass to the Anglican Eucharist was achieved so smoothly. 'All Christendom admired that it was wrought so easily and without commotion,' wrote the chronicler with admiration, for Queen and Archbishop had captured the middle ground, giving short shrift to neo-Calvinists and parsons who would not wear the regulation vestments. It is worth remembering, however, that despite his high office Parker was not in his early years a member of the select Privy Council.

Intermingled with the religious issues was the problem of the succession to the Crown, for claimants in the Stuart line, stemming from Henry VIII's elder sister Margaret Queen of Scots, were Catholics, while those in the Suffolk line, springing from the second marriage of Henry's younger sister Mary with Charles Brandon, Duke of Suffolk, were Protestants. Elizabeth would recognise none of the claimants since all of them, however reluctant in making their bid, were in her eyes potential traitors. Her own experience in her sister's reign had taught her the lesson that an heir presumptive bred faction, and once she acknowledged the right of a successor she would, she said, be back in the Tower 'within a month'.

The Stuart claim aroused her chief suspicion, since it was the most plausible. Mary Queen of Scots, the only surviving child of James V and Mary of Guise, had married the Dauphin, who in July 1559 became King Francis II of France for seventeen months. On his death Mary would return to her Scottish realm. From the first days of Elizabeth's reign Mary had claimed to be not merely her heir, but the rightful Queen of England in her place. In Scotland, during Mary's absence, the Lords of the Congregation, inspired by John Knox, deposed the regent, Mary of Guise. With difficulty, as we shall see, Cecil persuaded Elizabeth to send an army to expel the French from Scotland in what was characteristically called 'The War of the Insignia', because Mary was using the royal arms of England. The Treaty of Edinburgh, signed in July 1560, protected England from a renewal of the 'Auld Alliance'. In it the Scots recognised Elizabeth's right to her throne and undertook that Mary Stuart should relinquish her claim, but Mary subsequently stated that she would ratify the treaty only if Elizabeth recognised her as her successor.

A second Stuart claimant was Lady Margaret Douglas, Countess of Lennox, the only child of Queen Margaret of Scotland's marriage to the Earl of Angus. Lady Margaret had in turn married Matthew Earl of Lennox, himself a claimant to the Scottish throne, yet it was at Temple Newsam in Yorkshire that the Countess lived with her son Lord Darnley. In the eyes of men such as Arundel, Darnley's English birth made his claim to the English throne more acceptable than Mary's, certainly while Mary remained Queen of France. After attendance at the coronation, Lady Margaret withdrew from court to the north.

In contrast to the Catholic Stuarts there were the claimants in the Protestant 'Suffolk' line. Frances Brandon, the daughter of Mary of Suffolk, had three daughters by Henry Grey – Jane, Catherine and Mary. On Lady Jane Grey's execution in 1554 the Suffolk claim passed to her sisters, whom Elizabeth decided to keep under her supervision at court. Born in 1538, Lady Catherine had been married at fifteen to Henry Herbert, as we have seen, as part of Northumberland's conspiracy, but the union was never consummated and young Herbert divorced her. In 1559 there were tales of a madcap scheme for her to be kidnapped and sent to Spain as a bride for Philip II – or even Don Carlos – 'since she is supposed to be the next heir to the realm'. And then in the last weeks of 1560 she was secretly married to the Protector's son, Edward Seymour, Earl of Hertford, at Hertford House in Canon Row, Westminster; the ceremony, performed rather remarkably by a Catholic priest, was unknown to all but a few until the following August when Catherine was great with child. Elizabeth promptly dispatched her to the Tower and Hertford was also sent there on his return from France, though to different quarters from his wife. Catherine gave birth to a son, Edward, on 24 September. Cecil thought the Queen unnecessarily harsh in her treatment of Lady Catherine; while she saw 'some greater drift' in this match than mere love, he was, he said, unaware of any conspiracy. The following spring a commission headed by the Archbishop of Canterbury investigated the marriage, and as neither priest nor witness could be produced the union was declared invalid. As a result Hertford was fined £15,000 in the Star Chamber for the crime of 'seducing a Virgin of the blood royal'.

But though they were not man and wife in the eyes of the law, the couple continued to meet, thanks to bribes to jailers, and in February 1563 Lady Catherine was delivered of a second son within the Tower, thus dashing any hope she might have had of the Queen's mercy. Later on, Elizabeth was greatly alarmed that there was a conspiracy afoot to legitimise Catherine's marriage. She had been permitted to leave the Tower while the plague was raging in London and continued her captivity in the country, but now she was deemed too dangerous a figure, with her two healthy infant sons, to be allowed this comparative freedom, and left the Tower only for periodic visits to the lieutenant's house at Cockfield Hall. Fuller's 'Lady of Lamentations', Lady Catherine was seldom seen with dry eyes for years together, until in 1568 she died. Elizabeth, much relieved at her passing, paid £76 to give her a stately funeral in Salisbury Cathedral. At one time her boys appear to have been brought up in Cecil's household. Much later their father married Frances Howard, but in 1595, when he sought to have this marriage set

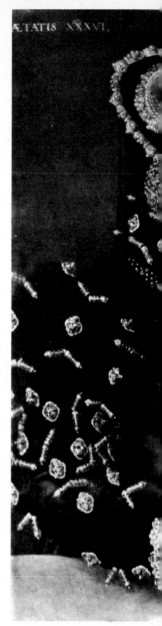

Frances Brandon, Dowager Duchess of Suffolk, with her second husband, Adrian Stokes, her Master of the Horse, and sixteen years her junior. Frances was the elder daughter of Henry VIII's sister Mary by her marriage to Charles Brandon, Duke of Suffolk. She first became the wife of Henry Grey,

M·D·LIX.   ÆTATIS XXI.

Marquess of Dorset, and
gave birth to the Ladies
Jane, Catherine and Mary
Grey. Double portrait
by Hans Eworth, 1559.

aside to clear his sons' claims to the throne, he was arrested. For such matters, so closely touching her regality, Elizabeth had a long memory.

Catherine's younger sister, Lady Mary Grey, fared no better. She had stayed on at court as a maid of honour, despite her sister's disgrace, so that Elizabeth could keep an eye on her. Alas, after six years of life at court, fearing at twenty-five that she was becoming an old maid, Mary turned her attention to Thomas Keys, the Queen's serjeant porter. It was an incongruous match, for Lady Mary was petite and Keys an enormous fellow with a huge girth. One evening in August 1565, after a quiet supper in her rooms in White-hall Palace with Lady Stafford's daughters, she walked over to the Privy

Chamber and thence to the council room, where she found a messenger to take a pre-arranged token to the serjeant porter. At 9 p.m. they were married by candlelight in Keys' chamber near the water-gate by an unidentified priest, 'apparelled in a short gown, being old, fat and of low stature'. But Elizabeth soon heard and was furious. That a maid of honour – let alone a candidate for the succession – should marry without her permission was *lèse-majesté*, but that she should marry so far beneath her, and right under the Queen's nose, was unpardonable. Keys was packed off to the Fleet Prison, where he spent three miserable years, hoping in vain to be given a second chance; he even volunteered to serve in Ireland. At length he was freed, on condition that he lived quietly at Lewisham and did not attempt to see his wife. Even a letter Keys sent with Archbishop Parker's blessing, begging for the Queen's mercy to live with his wife 'according to the laws of God', was flatly refused.

Lady Mary meantime had been placed in the custody of William Hawtrey at Chequers in Buckinghamshire. Then she was allowed to live at Greenwich with Catherine, the Dowager Duchess of Suffolk, a kindly soul, who bemoaned that she had no decent furniture 'for the dressing up of' the girl's room. Out of loyalty to the serjeant porter Mary continued to sign herself 'Mary Keys' and on his death unsuccessfully petitioned Elizabeth to be allowed to wear mourning. The hapless Mary died in 1578.

A weaker claim in the Suffolk line, but still sufficiently strong to perturb the Queen, was that of Margaret Lady Strange, first cousin to the unfortunate Grey sisters, being the only child of their Aunt Eleanor, who had married the Earl of Cumberland. In Queen Mary's time some regarded her claim as far more weighty than her Grey cousins, for her side of the family had stood aloof from Lady Jane's conspiracy; and the Venetian ambassador of the day, dismissing Princess Elizabeth's title under bastardy, wrote of Margaret as 'the nearest of all to the blood royal – and to her the succession belongs'. She had already married Henry Stanley, Lord Strange, later to become Earl of Derby, but theirs was a far from happy union and they were ever squabbling about money. A postscript of a letter to her Derby in-laws was so blotted with tears that it could not be read. For the first dozen years of the reign Lady Margaret attended at court; when, on leave of absence she was reluctant to return to Whitehall, Elizabeth peremptorily required her attendance 'as one very near in blood to us'; she wanted any possible claimants who were not already in the Tower under her eye at court. Unhappy to the end, Margaret tried to find consolation in the company of magicians and wizards.

The final claimant was a man, Henry Hastings, Earl of Huntingdon, who was descended on his father's side from Edward III and on his mother's from George, Duke of Clarence. The 'Puritan Earl', as he was called from his strong Protestant convictions, had married Dudley's sister. He remained a most loyal servant of the Queen who, as he told Dudley, would sometimes give his wife 'a privy nip especially concerning myself' when she came to court – a playful warning not to be ambitious on account of his Plantagenet blood – and he never was.

Henry Hastings, 3rd Earl of Huntingdon (1535-95) – 'the Puritan Earl' who was a claimant to the throne: portrait by an unknown artist.

Een Grave oft Lord
van den Parlemente

Een Lord van
der Ordre, zoo sy
ghecleedt
gaen op St.
Gooris dach.

Eenen ha
rdier aer
Magesteit

3 Dudley's Bid for Power

ABOVE King Eric XIV of Sweden (1533-77). During his suit for Elizabeth's hand, the Queen sent the artist Steven van der Meulen to Stockholm to paint this portrait, in 1561.

LEFT Drawing of two peers of the realm, with a halberdier: executed c.1567.

In 1558, everyone assumed as a matter of course that Elizabeth would marry quite soon and mother an heir to the throne, so the question of the succession was regarded as incidental to the Queen's marriage. Marriage would mean the establishment of a consort's household, with a series of posts from chamberlain down to page largely duplicating the Queen's personal officials, while in the fullness of time people anticipated that the court would be swollen even further with a separate establishment for the children that marriage would bring. Those unlucky in the distribution of places at court at the accession looked forward accordingly to the Queen's early marriage. As a Princess, she had had no shortage of candidates from abroad, ranging from the Archduke Ferdinand at Prague, who was 'high-spirited and lusty' as well as being militantly orthodox, and Emmanuel Philibert of Savoy, the energetic ruler of an enlarged duchy who was a kinsman of Philip of Spain, to the Protestant Crown Prince Eric of Sweden, yet Elizabeth had then made it plain that she had 'no wish to marry'. Now, as Queen, she was free to make her own choice and courtiers did not expect the palace to be long without a consort.

Philip II, as husband of the late Queen, was the first to press his candidature through his ambassador, Count de Feria. Elizabeth, who had no wish to make enemies, responded at first with apparent interest, though she knew perfectly well that the match would be politically unacceptable to many of her subjects, who were urging her to marry an Englishman to show herself the antithesis of Mary. In fact the affair was conducted half-heartedly on both sides, and when eventually Elizabeth declined Philip's proposition (on the grounds that she was a 'heretic', and could never acknowledge the Pope's authority to give Philip the dispensation on which he insisted) he accepted the situation as final and at once opened negotiations with Catherine de' Medici for the hand of her daughter, the beautiful Elizabeth of Valois, who had only three months earlier been betrothed to his own son, Don Carlos. Henceforth de Feria and his successors were to turn their attentions to canvassing the merits of Philip's cousins, the Archdukes Ferdinand and Charles, sons of the Emperor Ferdinand I, and because a Habsburg match received quite considerable support among Elizabeth's courtiers the chances of success seemed to be much greater than with the King of Spain's candidature.

In February 1559 the House of Commons had been bold enough to discuss the question of royal matrimony, a topic Elizabeth was convinced their predecessors would never have dared to debate in her father's reign. Various members had asked for a humble address to be made to Her Majesty to marry an Englishman, though Mr Speaker had tactfully amended this to a request to take a husband without any limitations, and a few days later he was reading to the House her considered reply. She assured her faithful Commons, that had so irritated her by raising this issue, that if she decided to marry she would never sacrifice national and religious interests by her choice of spouse, as her sister had done. Characteristically she left the matter vague; if she remained a spinster provision would be made, by God's help, to settle the succession on a worthy heir. 'And in the end, this shall be for me sufficient, that a marble stone shall declare that a Queen, having reigned such a time, lived and died a virgin.' Very few of those who heard these words believed in their hearts that she would remain single, for an unmarried monarch was unheard of, and before long it seemed that she was being swept off her feet by two Englishmen concurrently, providing a fund of gossip at court. One was Lord Robert Dudley, her Master of the Horse, who by April had established himself as her favourite; their special relationship was destined to endure, despite all the quarrels and misunderstandings, down to his death in 1588. The other was Sir William Pickering, a diplomat, whom she had forgotten after six months.

Pickering, as the son of Henry VII's Knight Marshal, had been nurtured in the ways of the court and been friendly with the poet Surrey and the younger Wyatt before being sent on embassies. Only a severe fever had detained him in Flanders when he had wanted to hasten home to lay himself at Her Majesty's feet. A bachelor of forty-three, he was tall, handsome and proud of his reputation as a ladies' man. On his first visit to court Elizabeth saw him privately – a rare privilege – and the next day they were closeted together for five hours while Lord Robert was away at Windsor. Not a few reckoned that Pickering would succeed in his courtship – 'they are giving 25 to 100 that he will be King' – for he was assigned chambers in Greenwich Palace. He spent a fortune with his tailor and another on entertaining', yet to cultivate an impressive image he 'always dines apart with music playing'. Bishop Jewel of London, who recalled that he had been a pupil of Cheke at Cambridge, reckoned him a man of prudence and even detected 'a royal countenance'.

Sir William trod on a good many toes by taking liberties such as his insistence on the right to worship in the royal pew. Dudley thought he deserved to be put in his place rather smartly, while Bedford spoke out against the newcomer at a banquet and challenged him to a duel. In October Arundel, who had seen his slender chances of winning Elizabeth's affections shattered, stopped Pickering on the threshold of the Privy Chamber and told him with the authority of Lord Steward that the place for men of the degree of knight was the Presence Chamber, not the inner apartments, entrée to which was the privilege of peers alone. He answered that he knew the rule quite as well as he knew that Arundel was 'an impudent, discourteous knave' and went on into the inner sanctum. Elizabeth had no intention of marrying him, but for the present she was amused by his company. Before he faded out of the life of the court he jokingly told the Spanish ambassador, then presenting the suit of the Archduke of Austria, that he was wasting his time, 'for he knew she meant to die a maid'.

Lord Robert's swift ascent was much more disturbing to the court than the nine days' wonder of Pickering who had, indeed, appeared to some as a relief from Dudley, so assured yet so enigmatic. By mid-April he was monopolising Elizabeth's company, there were reports that she visited him frequently, day and night, and tongues wagged to de Feria that 'Dudley's wife has a malady in one of her breasts and the Queen is only waiting for her to die to marry Lord Robert'. The Venetian ambassador endorsed this: the Master of the Horse was 'a very handsome young man, towards whom in various ways the Queen evinces such affection and inclination that many persons believe that if his wife, who has been ailing for some time, were perchance to die, she might easily take him for her husband'. On the first St George's Day of the reign he was installed as a Knight of the Garter in token of his sovereign's regard.

The fifth son of the Duke of Northumberland, Dudley had been born in the year before Elizabeth and at seventeen had married Amy Robsart, from Syderstone in Norfolk, at Richmond Palace. With his father triumphant over Somerset, he was made a gentleman of the Privy Chamber and then Master of the Buckhounds, though he was implicated with the rest of his family in the fatal bid for the Protestant succession. But for Robert's own marriage in 1550 it might well have been he, instead of his younger brother Guildford, who married Lady Jane Grey. Robert had been sentenced to death as a traitor with all his brothers, but after fifteen months in the Tower all except Guildford were pardoned and the war with France gave him the opportunity of redeeming himself, so that Queen Mary restored him to his rank as a duke's son.

It was uncommon under the Tudors for families to survive more than one downfall, but the Dudleys survived two – the execution of Edmund Dudley as an overzealous servant of Henry VII, and the treason of his son Northumberland, who had so nearly dragged the whole family with him to the block. But despite his rehabilitation certain men regarded Lord Robert with intense suspicion, first on account of his ancestry, then because of his over-familiarity with the new Queen. Norfolk, the natural spokesman of the ancient nobility, saw Dudley as a *parvenu*, ambitious and unprincipled, while Sussex from his deathbed in 1583 would warn friends to 'Beware of the gipsy, for he will be too hard for you all. You know not the beast as well as I do.' Much of the abiding antipathy to the favourite was to be set down years afterwards in a singularly vituperative tract, *Leicester's Commonwealth*, and there his disdain of 'all the nobility of our realm, how he contemneth, derideth and debaseth them' was overshadowed by an even baser characteristic, his insatiable lust for women. Because it was Dudley's masculinity that had won him his unique place at court it was distorted by enemies into a vicious trait, so that he was portrayed as a compulsive adulterer: 'seeking pasture among the waiting gentlewomen of Her Majesty's Chamber he hath offered £300 for a night,' ran the improbable tale.

The emergence of a favourite necessarily shattered the unity of the court. So long as Dudley held the Queen's affections he could do no wrong and would remain a power to be reckoned with, although he was not yet a Privy

Mary Queen of Scots and her first husband, Francis II of France: drawings made in 1559 and 1560 by François Clouet.

Councillor. As an outsize character few could remain neutral about him and so factions began to form. Cecil, seeing his own position as chief minister undermined, was out of his depth where Elizabeth's affections were concerned. He desperately hoped that the affair would pass like midsummer madness and urged serious consideration of a Habsburg prince, not yet as an end in itself but as an instrument of diplomacy. The unexpected death of Henry II from a wound in the tiltyard brought to the French throne Francis II, whose wife was already Queen of Scots and claimed to be Queen of England. Never had the 'Auld Alliance' threatened England so seriously. Discussions about the possible betrothal of Elizabeth and the Archduke of Austria had opened in very different circumstances, yet they seemed to Cecil in particular the one lifeline against England's isolation in a hostile

Europe. At the same time the Earl of Arran, son of the Duke of Châtel-herault, heir presumptive to the Scottish throne, came to England: the Lords of the Congregation north of the border had put forward the suggestion that he might marry Elizabeth. Arran enjoyed a series of discussions with the Queen, but she found as little favour with him as with his plan.

De Quadra, the new Spanish ambassador, under strict orders from Philip II to promote Elizabeth's interest in one of the Emperor's sons, had quickly dropped Ferdinand, the elder, for his brother Charles, since the Queen knew enough about Ferdinand to assume he was a bigoted *devote* and said he was fit only for praying for his own family. She felt the idea of the Archduke Charles worth pursuing, however, and asked countless questions about him. Was it true that he had an enormous head, far bigger even than Bedford's?

Did he ride superbly, dance well and delight in music? It was no good the House of Austria offering her a man 'who sits at home all day among the cinders'. The Archduke's chamberlain, Baron von Breumer, came over to sing his master's praises, but Elizabeth wanted a sight of Charles himself. She told the envoy that he had better talk with her councillors, since she was quite undecided whether to marry. Soon the English ambassador in Augsburg was required to answer a detailed questionnaire about Charles's personal qualities – his physique, complexion, habits, education, religious views and 'whether he hath been noted to have loved any woman, and in what sort'. The results were unhelpful, and three months later de Quadra, still as mystified as ever about Elizabeth's intentions, tackled both Lord Robert and his sister, feeling that they knew rather more about the Queen than anyone at court. Lady Sidney told him not to take Elizabeth's refusals too literally, as 'it was not the custom here for ladies to give their consent till they were teased into it,' while the favourite assured him that in the end the Queen would accept the Archduke's proposal. Later in the year she wrote a diplomatic letter to tell the Emperor that she had no intention of marrying as yet, though she was conscious of the honour paid to her by Charles, who was the best possible husband for her. 'God will direct the future,' she wrote, leaving the door open for future approaches.

The same autumn Dudley was welcoming another proxy suitor, Duke John of Finland, who came to plead the cause of his brother, Crown Prince Eric of Sweden, a persistent author of passionate love letters in Latin. Her 'most loving Eric' was 'bound by an eternal love towards her', yet still did not know whether she reciprocated his intense feelings, so he had sent his brother to obtain a 'favourable answer'. Duke John was lodged in the Bishop of Winchester's house on the south bank, but could not keep away from the palace, forcing his company on the Queen at the slightest chance, scattering largesse wherever he went in London and drinking very freely.

There was a delightful comedy while negotiations on behalf of Prince Eric and Archduke Charles were being conducted concurrently. 'Here is great resort of wooers and controversy amongst lovers,' wrote Cecil, already weary of a masquerade that in effect had scarcely begun, though Elizabeth revelled in the drama of being wooed from so many quarters, charmed by 'so many loose and flighty fancies'; yet of the 'ten or twelve ambassadors competing for her favour' it was the Swedish and Imperial proxies who led the field, 'courting at a most marvellous rate'. The Imperial ambassador ridiculed the Swede whose father, he said, was 'only a clown who had stolen his kingdom' from the Danes, provoking Duke John into uttering murderous threats, so that the Queen took care they should not meet in the palace, 'to avoid their slashing each other in her presence'. De Quadra became alarmed in case she should suddenly accept Eric's proposal on the spur of the moment, since she was 'only a passionate, ill-advised woman', and when the Crown Prince summoned his brother home, accusing him of philandering with Elizabeth himself instead of playing the true servant, the Spaniard was greatly relieved. Eric still held out hopes, sending another envoy with presents of money and piebald horses, vowing he would cross the North Sea to lay his heart at her feet, but he never came. While the farce was being played out, courtiers came to agree with Bishop Jewel that however Elizabeth acted, she was 'thinking of an alliance nearer home'.

When Norfolk returned to London at Michaelmas he quickly grasped that proxy wooing was of little significance compared with Dudley's enhanced status and he bitterly complained about the Queen's 'lightness and bad government'. He had it out with the favourite, warning him that if he did not abandon his 'present pretensions and presumptions' he would not die in his bed. 'I think his hatred of Lord Robert will continue,' reported de Quadra to Philip II, after a conversation with Norfolk, 'as the Duke and the rest of them cannot put up with his being King.'

Dudley had no intention of heeding the warning, and a sign of the Queen's continued infatuation with him was his appointment as Lieutenant of Windsor Castle. Norfolk spoke to him again in the plainest terms and let him know he warmly supported the proposals for Elizabeth to marry the Archduke. When Lord Robert retorted that he was 'neither a good Englishman nor a loyal subject who advised the Queen to marry a foreigner,' the Duke left in a temper. To oppose Dudley, Norfolk had come down in favour of the Habsburg match, and allied with him were Arundel, his uncle Howard of Effingham and Sir John Mason, at this time the most ardent Imperialist. Others, like Bacon and Parry, who were mistrustful of Cecil's handling of relations with Scotland, regarded a marriage treaty with the Holy Roman Empire as much less of a threat than a declaration of war against the French north of the border, towards which the Secretary was heading.

Open intervention in Scotland was strenuously opposed by Bacon, Arundel and Mason in particular, yet Cecil had deftly won over Pembroke, Clinton and Howard, all veteran soldiers who saw a display of force as the most powerful diplomatic weapon in preserving England's national security, and it was Admiral Clinton who spoke out clearly that no good Englishman could ever consent to France having the upper hand in Scotland. The Queen remained lukewarm about the operation, retracting her decisions, to the Secretary's dismay, by pandering to the 'weak-hearted men and flatterers'; she blew hot and cold on the campaign between one set of instructions and another. When the time came for negotiating a peace treaty, Cecil knew that he must himself travel north to lead the discussions in Edinburgh and he feared that while he was away from court his reputation would be at the mercy of detractors. 'My friends abroad,' he wrote, 'think I am herein betrayed to be sent from the Queen's Majesty.' Of course he would have a far freer hand than if the peace conference were being held in London, where Elizabeth might keep changing her mind between sessions, but he was well aware that to leave court for two months was to put his whole career at risk. He trusted Pembroke and Clinton to look after his interests and was relieved to have a letter from the prickly Mason before he left, making clear his continued opposition to the forward policy in Scotland, yet promising not to come to court in Cecil's absence.

With Cecil away as well as Norfolk there was no one left to stand up to the favourite and there was a disturbing rumour that Dudley was contemplating a divorce. He and the Queen, it was said, spent days shut up together, for she was completely under his spell, happily ignoring state affairs. 'Not a man in England but cries out, at the top of his voice this fellow is ruining the country with his vanity.'

In the north Cecil achieved all he had set himself, for by the Treaty of

Edinburgh the Scots recognised Elizabeth as Queen of England and undertook that their own Queen Mary, still in France, should relinquish her claims to rule in her place. The French troops finally left for home and, far from being at the mercy of the House of Guise, England was now secured against any threat from the north as the fresh understanding between the Protestant Lords of the Congregation with their English allies put an end to the Auld Alliance. The success of Cecil's policy enhanced his status with his fellows on the council, and he could reasonably expect his advice to be accorded a much greater authority by Elizabeth. She showed scant gratitude to him on his return, however, for, as he had predicted, his long absence from court had left him vulnerable – especially to the machinations of Dudley. The Secretary, who should have been the hero of the hour, was soon so despondent that he talked seriously about resigning and made tentative plans that Throckmorton, ambassador in Paris, should, if possible, succeed him, since under Dudley's influence the Queen was becoming intolerable. If she would not let him leave without a fuss he said he would risk making an incident, however awkward it might prove for him, even if it meant a sojourn in the Tower, anything 'rather than having to continue with a perpetual displeasure to myself and my foolish conscience'.

Friends who feared that Cecil really might retire from politics said that it would be more serious for them than the loss of half their lives. Early in September he poured out his troubles to de Quadra, warning him that because of Elizabeth's strange behaviour he had decided to withdraw from her service before the inevitable storm broke. The Secretary even hinted that Dudley might attempt to murder his wife, though he trusted God would never permit such a crime to be accomplished.

Later that week Amy Robsart was found with a broken neck at the bottom of the staircase at Cumnor House. The storm had indeed broken.

Lord Robert was with the Queen at Windsor when the news arrived, and she sent him away from court to his house at Kew until the coroner's inquest was over. Eighteen months of malicious gossip put Dudley, and even Elizabeth, under a high degree of suspicion and for the next few weeks gloom and uncertainty dominated those about the Queen. De Quadra, unable to get any coherent accounts from his contacts in the palace, predicted a revolution, with the Queen being sent to the Tower and the crown passing to the Protestant Earl of Huntingdon. Banishment played on Dudley's fears: 'I am sorry so great a chance should breed me so great a change, for methinks I am here all this while as it were in a dream and too far, too far, from the place where I am bound to,' he wrote to Cecil, imploring him to pay another visit to Kew and stand as his friend, for his world had been shattered. The jury at Cumnor brought in a verdict of accidental death, for the evidence was not in dispute; Lady Dudley had died from a broken neck in an empty house, as all her servants had been given a day's holiday. Her poor state of health was well known, but it was impossible for the coroner to link the malady of the breast from which she had been suffering with a broken neck, so while her husband was cleared by the law he remained morally under a cloud. (Only in recent years has a satisfactory explanation been offered for the mystery of Amy Robsart's death, since it has now been established medically that cancer of the breast in an advanced stage can cause a spontaneous fracture of the spine.)

No one had expected Amy Robsart to live for long, which itself made her

Theobalds, the Hertfordshire mansion built by Lord Burghley for entertaining the Queen and court on progress: drawing by John Thorpe.

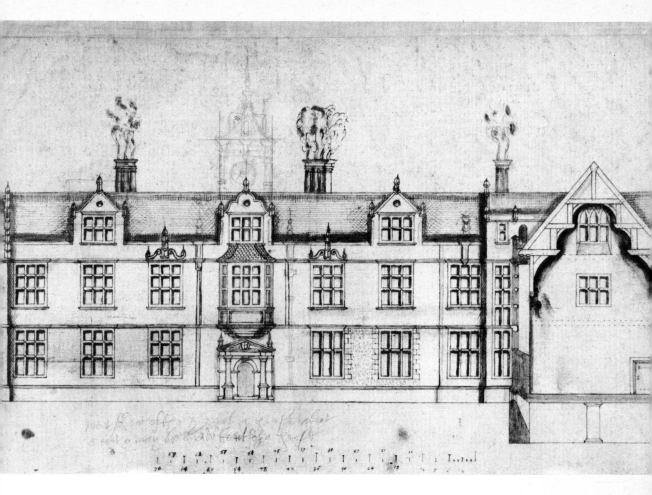

husband's neglect seem the more callous and Elizabeth's complete monopoly of his company cruelly selfish, even if all affection in the marriage had withered, but the manner of her death twisted the whole position. Dudley's Catholic brother-in-law, Lord Hastings, writing what amounted to a letter of condolence, was wide of the mark in declaring that his bereavement must bring him from sorrow to joy, from care and trouble to rest and quietness. Had Dudley's wife died peaceably in her bed, leaving him free from all suspicion, the way would have been open for Elizabeth to marry him after a discreet period of mourning, but as things were the future was full of imponderables. The tense situation was not unlike the atmosphere of the Scottish court six years later, in the aftermath of Darnley's murder.

Reactions from foreign courts to the affair were alarming. In Paris Catherine de'Medici jibed that she heard that Elizabeth was to marry her horse-keeper, while Throckmorton, the ambassador, held his head in shame at the scandalous stories being circulated, 'for every hair of my head stareth out and my ears glow to hear'. Catholics at Catherine's court taunted him by asking 'What religion is this that a subject shall kill his wife and the Prince not only bear withal, but marry with him?' and Throckmorton warned that if Elizabeth married Dudley she would be utterly discredited abroad and her country 'reviled, undone and made prey'. It was such comments that pulled her up with a jerk, for despite her protestations to the contrary she was extremely sensitive to criticism from other sovereigns. Cecil, who had been talking of resigning, now found her responsive to his tactful handling. Most probably he did not pass on to her the unsolicited advice of Sussex in Ireland that she should 'love where and whom she list' and that if her affections settled on Lord Robert then she should marry him, for the maxim *omnes ejus sensus titillarentur* would ensure an heir of her body, which was properly England's priority.

A month after the Cumnor tragedy Cecil assured the Spanish ambassador that the Queen would not marry Dudley, for she had herself told him so, and it seemed as if the worst of the crisis were over. After an intolerable struggle reason overcame emotion. She had come to realise that marriage with the man she loved was incompatible with her position as Queen, for he was too unpopular in general and too controversial a personality to choose for a consort without irrevocably dividing her court; what she did not realise in the autumn of 1560 was that she would remain emotionally tied to him until his death.

Both Pembroke and Northampton had been supporting Dudley, but were now less committed, and Sir Thomas Parry, whom he trusted more than any man to help his return to favour, was sick unto death. In November Throck-

morton, at his wit's end, sent across his confidential secretary Robert Jones to relate the latest unsavoury gossip of the French court that could not decently be put in dispatches and to ask for guidance on how to refute these allegations. Jones had an audience of the Queen at Greenwich, who told him in a matter-of-fact way that the findings of the coroner's inquest touched 'neither Lord Robert's honesty nor her honour'. Killigrew, of late a staunch supporter of Dudley, told Jones that the favourite would 'run away with the hare and have the Queen,' though his hearer was not convinced since he noticed that talk about the marriage amongst courtiers had quietened down.

One thing became clear: marriage or no, Elizabeth felt lost without Dudley at her side and to proclaim his restoration to favour she decided to create him an earl. When the warrant for the patent was drawn up and brought for her signature, however, she had second thoughts and cut it in shreds with a pen-knife, apparently exclaiming for all in attendance to hear that the Dudleys had been traitors for three generations. Angry that her inability to control her emotions had lost him an earldom, Dudley pleaded with her not to abuse him in this way in front of other courtiers, whereupon she playfully patted him on the cheek, declaring 'No, no! The bear and the ragged staff [his crest] are not so easily overthrown!' Later she hinted that she would make him Earl of Leicester on Twelfth Night, but once again, though other favours were shown him, she changed her mind. It was still too soon to

LEFT Gorhambury House, Hertfordshire, the residence of Lord Keeper Bacon, who added the wing to the left for the Queen's visit in 1577: a watercolour painted in the 1730s. RIGHT Panels from an enamelled glass window at Gorhambury, put up by Bacon for the royal visit of 1577.

honour him in this way, for too many people would misinterpret her motives.

Thwarted of an earldom for the present, Lord Robert did not lower his sights from a consort's crown. He had been broadening the base of his followers, of whom Sir Henry Killigrew (Cecil's brother-in-law) was the most outstanding recruit; it was thanks to Dudley that Killigrew was appointed to an office in the Exchequer. He also counted on winning over the mercurial Pembroke. On the basis of his strong Protestant connexions, Dudley had used his ecclesiastical patronage to benefit those who had been exiled under Mary; now, mindful of the value of Spanish support, he put out feelers towards various Catholics through Francis Yaxley, a gentleman of the Privy Chamber. It was at this time also that he appointed as his chaplain Francis Babington, Vice-Chancellor of Oxford University, who had recently exchanged the mastership of Balliol for the rectorship of Lincoln College; Babington was to be deprived of his post in 1563 on religious grounds. Men such as Lord Montague and Sir Thomas Wharton, once Mary's councillors, had begun looking to Dudley for favours and he recognised their value to him.

At the beginning of 1561 Dudley arranged that his brother-in-law, Sir Henry Sidney, should open secret conversations with Bishop de Quadra to persuade Philip II to use his considerable influence with the Queen in supporting her marriage. The price to be paid for his support was a promise that Elizabeth would restore Catholicism and that Lord Robert would regard Philip as a vassal. This intrigue was not quite so fantastic as might appear, since Dudley felt sure that Elizabeth was still deeply in love with him and, providing she had adequate encouragement to overcome the political difficulties, would gladly marry him. Her councillors by and large were neutral, well aware that to come out strongly either for or against Dudley at that juncture would be to risk political suicide, yet after the events of the previous autumn the Queen herself was too cautious of following her heart without a show of confidence by these magnates of the realm; in the winter of 1579, when she was on the brink of marrying the Duke of Alençon, she was to find her council just as reticent and unhelpful.

Strong support for Dudley by Spain and the Emperor would make the pro-Habsburg wing of her councillors declare themselves at last, and it would also silence Norfolk. Promises about the restitution of papal authority were, of course, idle, but Lord Robert agreed to persuade Elizabeth to receive a papal nuncio who was to invite English participation in the resumed Council of Trent. The ambassador saw no little merit in Dudley's plan, even though in putting it to his master he voiced doubts about the Queen's ability to bear children. In February, when de Quadra praised the favourite to the skies in an audience, Elizabeth did not deny her continuing affection for him, yet she loved him, she said, for his good qualities and had decided not to marry him 'or anyone else', though every day it became even plainer that she would have to take a husband and her people hoped she would choose an Englishman.

Cecil, feeling himself at last back in authority and basking in his lucrative appointment as Master of the Wards in succession to Parry, told de Quadra that the Queen needed a letter from King Philip giving unequivocal support to her marriage with Dudley. Once it arrived she would summon a select group from each House of Parliament to secure their consent. This was not at all what the favourite had in mind, since being presented to Parliament as a Spanish candidate would put him in the worst possible light, so he urged Elizabeth to act decisively, freeing herself from the tyranny of her subjects. When matters ground to a halt he even considered giving the Queen an ultimatum, either to marry him or to allow him to leave England for service with Philip II. Cecil had warned Throckmorton to cease attacking the idea of a marriage with Dudley, for his pungent criticisms always provoked Elizabeth into an angry defence of the favourite and it began to appear as if quiet indifference was proving the surest way of killing the whole affair. Bedford noted with relief that 'the great matters whereof the world was wont to talk are now asleep, having had some fits, both hot and cold'.

Cecil's sudden arrest of various Catholics, including Sir Edward Waldegrave, Lord Hastings and Sir Thomas Wharton, who were shown to be in communication with the Spanish ambassador, the imprisoned Marian bishops and exiles in Flanders, created the scare of a grand popish plot which ended any possible chance of the papal nuncio being received in England and made de Quadra realise that the schemings for Philip's approval of a Dudley match were futile. Norfolk's feud with Dudley, always liable to erupt on the Duke's return to London, angered the Queen and after fighting broke out between the two peers' servants the favourite sent Norfolk a terse note in February 1561. Was it true that his retainers were declaring that he was the Duke's enemy? If so, Norfolk should punish the men concerned for idle, scandalous talk. So Howard sent his chamberlain, Sir Nicholas l'Estrange, to Dudley's house to make diplomatic apologies and patch up the affair. Yet de Quadra thought that the Queen was still furious with Norfolk 'and is determined to humble him when she can. . . . He on his side is full of boasts, although I do not know how it will turn out when he has to carry them into effect.' For the remainder of 1561 their quarrel simmered rather than boiled, largely because the Duke chose to stay in his county.

By Easter 1561 the Queen, Dudley and Cecil were at last achieving a *modus vivendi* as a matter of survival; she needed them both and could no more do without the brilliant political adventurer than the dull, cautious statesman. Neither could eliminate the other. Sir William, although entrenched in power over his colleagues in council and rewarded with one of the wealthiest of offices, could not feel secure and assured of recognition. Lord Robert still lacked his earldom and was still no nearer to becoming Elizabeth's husband, but he, too, was at last in an entrenched position at court, being not merely a favourite but a man who could do no political wrong in the Queen's eyes, sitting at the centre of affairs and answerable to no one except his sovereign. His influence was unprecedented, and those who feared that it would be useless to lobby the Secretary now naturally turned to him. The death of Amy Robsart was already being seen in perspective and in view of Dudley's charmed existence he looked hopefully to the future. At midsummer he gave a water carnival on the Thames in Elizabeth's honour and she invited Bishop de Quadra into her barge to watch the pageantry. On that gay evening, for the sheer fun of it, Dudley suggested that since the Bishop was with them he could perform their marriage that very minute, and Elizabeth elaborated the joke by doubting whether the Spaniard had enough English to perform the office. It was a different world from the previous September.

4 The Habsburg Match

The prolonged negotiations for Elizabeth to marry the Archduke Charles of Austria, which were to intensify divisions at court, sprang from her illness early in October 1562. As she lay seriously ill at Hampton Court it became painfully clear to those about her that on her life alone depended the peace and security of England, for the question of the succession remained unanswered. When smallpox was diagnosed anxiety increased, for six weeks earlier Bedford's countess had died of the infection.

According to the only account that survives of the hectic, informal discussions at Hampton 'there were nearly as many different opinions about the succession to the Crown' as there were councillors present, though no one openly espoused the cause of Mary Queen of Scots. Dudley favoured the title of his brother-in-law, Huntingdon, and was supported by Bedford, Pembroke and probably by Norfolk. Since the Suffolk claim had been upheld by Henry VIII's will, others, such as Bacon and Hunsdon, regarded Lady Catherine Grey as the most suitable Protestant candidate: moreover, she already had a son. Lady Catherine would have gained the votes of Bedford and Pembroke, had she not been in the Tower for her marriage with Hertford. Winchester spoke for a third group, favouring the Countess of Lennox and her son Darnley, but cautiously refrained from putting forward positive support. Instead the Lord Treasurer wanted to submit the rival claims to a panel of lawyers, in the hope that their Catholic sympathies would decide against the claims of Huntingdon and Lady Catherine and rule out the Queen of Scots, leaving the field free for Darnley and his mother, but most councillors found Winchester's plan too transparent. Cecil himself did not show his hand, since there was no clear-cut choice, but would have come down in favour of Lady Catherine Grey.

Before anything had been decided, Elizabeth began to recover and in her first hours begged the councillors round her bed in case of a like emergency to appoint Dudley Protector of the Kingdom with an income of £20,000 a year and a suitable title. This was a dramatic moment, and it was clear to Cecil that Lord Robert's admission to the council, foreshadowed by this royal pleading, must be balanced by the addition of Norfolk. The Duke and the favourite were both sworn councillors on 20 October and with the Queen daily growing stronger their personal animosity increased, even if outwardly they showed 'a close intimacy'. Lady Mary Sidney, mother of Sir Philip,

The Archduke Charles of Austria, brother of the Holy Roman Emperor, Maximilian II, with whom Elizabeth reopened negotiations for a possible marriage in 1565.

79

LEFT Lady Catherine Grey with Edward, her elder son by Edward Seymour, Earl of Hertford, born in the Tower in 1561.

RIGHT Tree of Jesse, showing the issue of the Lord Keeper, Sir Nicholas Bacon, by his two wives, Jane Farley and Anne Cooke. Anthony and Francis Bacon, who were to play an important part in the policies of the later years of Elizabeth's reign, are shown on the right.

had nursed the Queen devotedly and herself caught smallpox, her face becoming so disfigured that she asked for leave to withdraw from court and never reappeared in society.

Speculation about the twin problems of the succession and the Queen's marriage continued throughout that winter. A group of peers discussed them into the small hours at Arundel House, when Howard, the Lord Chamberlain, spoke out against Dudley's pretensions and said that he could never approve Huntingdon's candidature. He won round Norfolk to support the Suffolk claim, perhaps holding out the hope of a marriage between Lady Catherine's son and the Duke's little daughter, Bess. When Elizabeth heard about the meeting at Arundel's she upbraided her Lord Steward for daring to hold discussions on the succession in defiance of her prerogative. This augured ill for the Parliament summoned to meet in January 1563. At the opening service in Westminster Abbey Alexander Nowell, Dean of St Paul's, a Marian exile whose religious position made him think the Suffolk claim easily the most satisfactory, preached before Her Majesty: 'All the Queen's most notable ancestors, have commonly had some issue to succeed them but Her Majesty yet none.' Turning towards his sovereign he admonished her

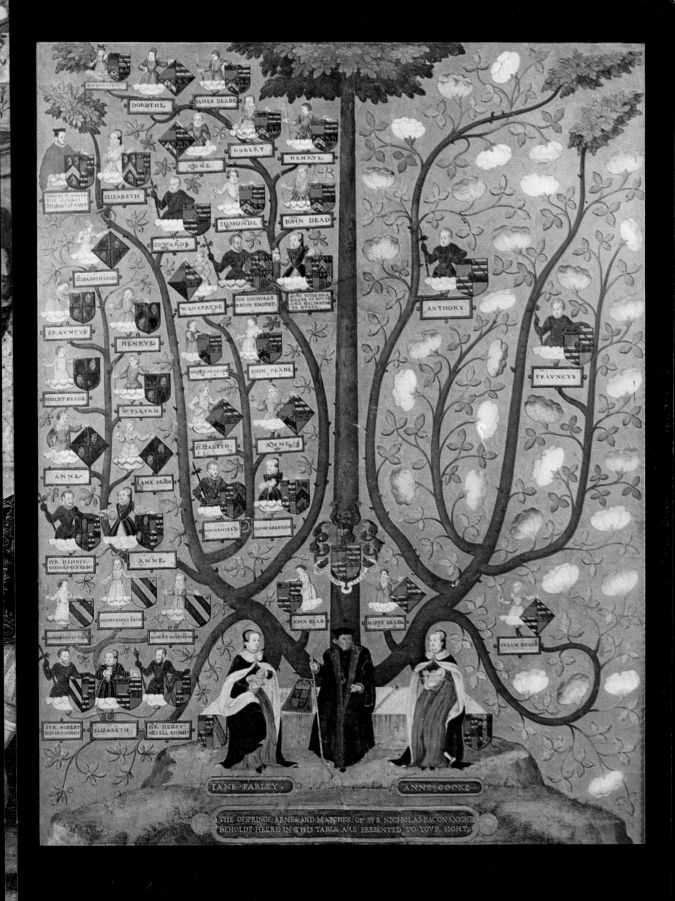

THE OFSPRINGE ARMES AND MATCHES OF SYR NICHOLAS BACON KNIGHT
BEHOLDE HEERE IN THIS TABLE ARE PRESENTED TO YOVR SIGHT

that her lack of a husband and child would plague the realm and rubbed this home by asking 'If your parents had been of your mind, where had you been then?'

In turn both Houses petitioned Elizabeth to marry; she told the Commons in an interim reply that 'though death possessed almost every joint' of her in her late illness, her primary concern had been for her people's safety, not her own life, assuring them that she would not neglect to take account of their wishes when she had reflected sufficiently on the great issues. The Queen was more outspoken with the deputation from the Lords, telling them that the marks on her face were not wrinkles but the pits of smallpox and even if she seemed an old maid to some of them God would send her children as he did to St Elizabeth. Someone introduced a bill in the Upper House to reduce the succession to four families, leaving it to the Queen to make her choice, with provisions for a committee of councillors to carry on the government until the succession was determined, yet the bill was dropped. At the end of the sessions on Easter Eve Lord Keeper Bacon read the Queen's considered reply to the Commons' petition, making them feel as if they had been intruding on her privacy. Her subjects were not to worry themselves about a successor before 'even hope of my fruit had been denied you,' while marriage was a personal matter and it was not at present opportune for her to make a statement.

Unknown to her confused and disappointed hearers, their debates and petitions on this ticklish matter had already goaded her into action. In March Mary's Secretary of State, Maitland of Lethington, had come to discuss with Elizabeth his mistress's claims to the English succession and, by implication, Mary's own search for a second husband. Maitland soon appreciated that Elizabeth would not name Mary as her successor and would do her best to thwart her marriage with Don Carlos, Charles IX of France, a Habsburg archduke or any other foreign prince, for such a union would threaten England's security; moreover for her to wed an English Catholic noble would strike at the heart of the country's peace.

Elizabeth now made the extraordinary suggestion that Mary should marry her own Dudley. There was no better consort living than the man Elizabeth knew so well, and if Mary agreed she would be prepared to endorse her claim to the English succession. The cost to herself would, of course, be excessive, for she would be losing her favourite to her rival, and yet the benefits of her self-sacrifice would be inestimable. Parliament and council would cease bullying her over the succession and her own marriage, and her great fears of being rushed into matrimony with an incompatible foreigner would be ended. Perhaps if she could be freed from the strain of facing the almost daily conundrum of the succession she could manage to live without Dudley at her side. By now, clearly, she had realised that she could not marry him herself, and for him to reign with Mary in Scotland, with their issue succeeding to the throne of England, was the next best thing. At the worst the very fact that negotiations were in train would buy time and could hamper Mary's search for a husband on the Continent.

Maitland was slow to react to the hints about Mary and Dudley, and Elizabeth had to instruct Randolph, her ambassador in Edinburgh, to suggest 'by indirect speeches' that Mary should choose 'some person of noble birth within our realm having conditions and qualities meet for the same'.

By the spring of 1564 Lord Robert had been named to Mary, who tactfully commented that she 'could have no misliking of him of whom the report by her good sister was so recommended'. It was during the visit of Mary's special envoy, Sir James Melville, to St James's that Dudley was created Earl of Leicester at Michaelmas 1564, to make the favourite more acceptable in Mary's sight. In the gardens at Whitehall a day or so before, Elizabeth had asked Melville how Mary had taken the suggestion, only to learn 'she thought little or nothing thereof'. Apparently Elizabeth told him that his mistress much underestimated Lord Robert, whom she esteemed 'as her brother and best friend, whom she would have herself married had she ever minded to have taken a husband. But being determined [as the Scot recalled her words] to end her life in virginity, she wished that the Queen her sister might marry him as meetest of all other with whom she would find in her heart to declare her second person'. Proud of her royal pedigree and of the brilliance of her first marriage to the Dauphin, Mary had no wish to stoop to marrying the cast-off favourite of her rival. For his part, though Leicester was anxious to keep in with Mary who, on the face of it, was the most likely successor to the English throne, he had no intention of being banished to the north. When subsequently commissioners from each country were appointed to discuss the topic, Dudley pleaded with Bedford not to press the matter. During Melville's stay Elizabeth continued to impress on him that all Mary's problems would be solved if she followed her cousin's advice and married Leicester, but to no effect. The Scot sensed double-dealing, convinced that Elizabeth and Leicester were 'inseparable'.

After Dudley's investiture as Baron Denbigh and Earl of Leicester, the Queen asked Melville what he thought of her new earl, a gorgeous figure, every inch a courtier. The ambassador was complimentary, but Elizabeth saw through him: 'Yet you like better of yonder lad (pointing to my Lord Darnley, who as nearest prince of the blood did bear the sword of honour that day before her). My answer,' recalled Melville, 'was that no woman of spirit would make choice of such a man, for he was handsome, beardless and lady-faced.' It was not a very successful lie, for once Melville had found out from the Spanish ambassador that there was no likelihood of Queen Mary being matched with Don Carlos, he went on his way to see Lady Lennox, Darnley's mother, as Mary had instructed him.

Lady Lennox and her husband had been imprisoned in the winter of 1561 for intriguing at the Scottish court and the Spanish embassy for their son to marry Mary, a union that would merge both Stuart claims to the English succession. After release, however, the Lennoxes were readmitted to royal favour and allowed to go to Temple Newsam, their Yorkshire home. Already, before Melville's arrival in London, the Earl of Lennox had been permitted by Elizabeth to travel to Scotland, ostensibly to attend to his estates there, but once in Edinburgh he was so lavish with his presents that there was 'a marvellous goodliking' of the idea of his son Darnley. Although Elizabeth made it abundantly clear that she would 'never willingly consent' to any of her subjects, save Leicester, becoming Mary's consort, the Queen of Scots had made up her mind about Darnley and asked her cousin to allow him to join his father. When the Queen refused, Lady Lennox pleaded with her, saying that Darnley would be there and back within a month, but she cut little ice; and then suddenly Elizabeth gave way.

Henry Stewart, Lord
Darnley, aged 17,
with his brother
Charles Stewart,
later Earl of Lennox,
aged 6. This double
portrait by Hans
Eworth was painted
for the boys' parents
in 1563.

THES BE THE SONES OF TF RIGHT HONERABLES TFRLLE OF LENOXE AD
TE LADY MARGARETZ GRACE COVNTYES OF LENOXE AD ANGWYSE.

1563

CHARLLES STEWARDE   HENRY STEWARDE LORD DAR̄
HIS BROTHER. ÆTATIS. 6,   LEY AND DOWGLAS. ÆTATIS. 17,

Leicester had added his pleas for Darnley's journey north, as an insurance against Mary taking Elizabeth's offer of his own hand seriously, and he advised her that Darnley's English possessions were sufficient guarantee for him obeying any summons to return. No sooner had Darnley crossed the Border than she bitterly regretted her decision and sent Mary an ultimatum: if she would take Leicester then her title to the English succession would be favoured, though Elizabeth would naturally delay holding a full enquiry into her claim until she 'be married herself or be determined not to marry'. Mary 'wept her fill' on learning this, for she was already madly in love with Darnley, 'the lustiest and best-proportioned long man' she had ever seen. Maitland was instructed to obtain Elizabeth's approval for their marriage but in an aside the Secretary suggested another Englishman as a possible alternative. This was the Duke of Norfolk, once more a widower, who was indeed the first in rank in the English peerage; the proposal was to be revived four years later with perilous consequences.

As a last-ditch action Elizabeth summoned her council on 1 May to sign a declaration warning Mary that marriage with Darnley would directly prejudice 'the sincere amity between both the Queens', and offering her a free choice of 'any other of the nobility in the whole realm, or any other place'. Leicester significantly did not sign the declaration, nor did Arundel, although Norfolk had been required to obtain the latter's signature. Throckmorton hastened north, pursuing Mary to Stirling, to use his considerable talents to try to prevent Mary from precipitate action, but young Darnley was already created Earl of Ross, a title for which he swore fealty as a Scottish peer, defying his English sovereign. Darnley and his father were outside her jurisdiction, but in a pique Elizabeth sent Lady Lennox to the Tower again. On 28 July Darnley was proclaimed King and the next day Mary married him. That marriage emphasised Elizabeth's own spinster state and her lack of any plans for the succession. The English Catholics, especially in the north country, rejoiced at the marriage, for it was the first ray of hope for them since the spring of 1559. Since the alliance of the two Catholic claimants to her throne was a dire threat to her safety, Elizabeth realised that her own marriage might become unavoidable on political grounds; death was a fate worse than marriage with a foreigner.

Meanwhile the Suffolk hopes to the succession had vanished amidst the Queen's fury at the publication, in the spring of 1564, of the injudicious *Discourse on the Succession*, which canvassed their claims. The author, a Chancery clerk called John Hales, was imprisoned, and Cecil found himself compelled to look afresh at the possibilities of the Queen's marriage abroad, and he persuaded himself that the Archduke Charles was far and away the most suitable candidate. In fact Elizabeth had already admitted this was the best match in Christendom, but she blew hot and cold on the suggestion as her fancy led her. Cecil's greatest success was in converting Norfolk to the Habsburg match, for the Duke was to be its most vocal protagonist. It would not only strengthen the old Spanish alliance, the cornerstone of England's commerce, but increase the Queen's standing by matching her with a prince of Europe's greatest House. As Charles was a younger son, England would not risk becoming junior partner in the marriage alliance, as had happened so disastrously with Mary Tudor's marriage to Philip. To pick up the threads of matrimonial diplomacy, Christopher Mundt, Elizabeth's agent in the Empire – there was no diplomatic representation at ambassadorial level in either country – was to broach the subject when he conveyed the Queen's condolences at the death of the Emperor Ferdinand I. The official wooing was to last a full three years. In opposition to the Habsburg match Dudley was supporting Catherine de'Medici's schemes for Elizabeth to marry into the House of Valois, though he was using the negotiations as a means of furthering his own suit.

The favourite's advancement to an earldom did not improve his relations

Thomas Radcliffe, 3rd Earl of Sussex (1526-83), Leicester's outspoken critic and opponent at court.

with Norfolk, for it made the Duke and the rest of the older nobility, all of them related one way or another to the House of Howard, conscious of what a *parvenu* he was. There soon occurred the incident in the royal tennis court where the rivals were playing together in front of the Queen: 'my Lord Robert, being hot and sweating, took the Queen's napkin out of her hand and wiped his face, which the Duke seeing said that he was too saucy and swore that he would lay his racket upon his face, whereup[on] rose a great trouble and the Queen offended sore with the Duke'. Norfolk was soon to receive welcome support from his kinsman the Earl of Sussex – Sussex's mother had been a Howard. In 1564 Sussex succeeded in laying down his difficult post of Lord Deputy of Ireland, which he had held since 1557. He had found it impossible to subdue Shane O'Neil, the rebel, and his long service in the field had affected his health. From Ireland the Earl had always regarded Dudley as an enemy and once he was back at court their enmity increased. As Cecil wrote, guardedly enough, to Dudley's brother-in-law Sidney, 'I wish that God would direct the hearts of those two earls to behold the harm that ensueth of small sparks of dissention betwixt noble houses – houses especially such as have alliances and followers.' He feared that the palace would become a battlefield.

Sir Nicholas Throck-morton (1515-71) painted by an unknown artist, *c.* 1562, when he was ambassador to France.

But Leicester had acquired one formidable ally, as the court divided into factions while the Habsburg marriage was being hotly debated. Sir Nicholas Throckmorton, a distant kinsman of the Parrs, had been disappointed at the distribution of posts on the accession. An ally of Wyatt's, he had wriggled out of an indictment for high treason on a technical loophole. In the last weeks of Mary's reign he had sent Elizabeth a memorandum on suitable appoint-ments, suggesting Cecil as *one* Principal Secretary and asking that the second secretaryship should not be allocated 'until I may speak with your Highness'. He hoped for the post himself, but Cecil had no coadjutor and Throckmorton waited for six months before being sent as ambassador to France. It was largely as a result of his representations that Elizabeth aided the Huguenots, intervening in the Wars of Religion in the firm hope of regaining Calais, but Throckmorton had been captured and seen his policy in shreds. Before he was replaced by Sir Thomas Smith he had asked Dudley to stand godfather to his son and on his return to England, identifying Cecil as his chief obstacle to promotion, he became Dudley's close confidant. This was a staggering realignment, for his outspoken comments from Paris about Dudley in 1560 had angered the Queen, but through the intermediary of first Bedford and then Sidney the two men had come together. Lord Robert was to find Throckmorton extremely valuable as a political adviser. His embassy in France had brought him in touch with both Catherine de'Medici and Mary Queen of Scots and it was these experiences that were to lead Dudley first to favour a French alliance in opposition to the Habsburg match, and then to pursue friendly negotiations with Mary in Scotland. Throckmorton wanted power, beginning with a seat on the council, and he understandably attached himself to Lord Robert's party. That so astute a politician as Sir Nicholas should have acted thus indicates the strength of the favourite at court in the mid-1560s.

When the threads of negotiations with the Archduke Charles were being taken up by Cecil, Leicester countered by throwing his weight behind a

91

bizarre suggestion that had come from Catherine de'Medici for a match between her eldest son, the fifteen-year-old Charles IX, and Elizabeth. But it was clear both to him and Throckmorton from the outset that there was not the slightest chance of success. What they banked on was that the French would throw all their support behind the favourite, once deadlock had been reached, as their principal chance of outwitting the House of Habsburg. This was the kind of situation in which the Queen of England revelled; the more proxy suitors to sing her praises the better, and Catherine de'Medici showered gifts on her, from a splendid coach to a train of camels. Leicester also had a shrewd suspicion that if the talks with the Archduke broke down, as he expected they would on religious grounds, the Spanish ambassador would shift his support to his own suit with the Queen. The balance of power in Europe was accordingly reflected in the partisan attitude of English courtiers, some of whom received presents from both sides.

Leicester did not enjoy the monopoly of the Queen's affections. The young lawyer Christopher Hatton, whose handsome figure had impressed Elizabeth when she watched him dancing in a masque at Gray's Inn, entered the select band of Gentlemen Pensioners in 1564, though it was not for another eight years, when he became Captain of the Pensioners, that he was regarded as a serious rival to the Earl. He subsequently remained until his death the ever faithful, ever hopeful bachelor, winning in the course of his wooing first Ely House and then the Woolsack. More unsettling for Leicester had been the emergence of Thomas Heneage in the summer of 1565. The Heneages had a pedigree of service to the Tudors – one had risen with Anne Boleyn, another had been Dean of Lincoln – and Thomas entered the Queen's service in 1560 as a gentleman of the Privy Chamber, where his abilities earned him gradual promotion first as Treasurer of the Chamber and then as Vice-Chamberlain in succession to Hatton.

Relations between Elizabeth and Leicester became strained in 1565, for she was in low spirits with the death of her much-loved Kate Ashley, and her irritation at failing to prevent Mary Queen of Scots from marrying Lord Darnley was directed at Leicester, since it was he who had persuaded her to allow Darnley to travel to Scotland. It was both more and less than a lovers' tiff. 'The Queen seemed to be much offended with the Earl of Leicester,' Cecil noted in his diary in August, 'and so she wrote an obscure sentence in a book at Windsor.' To teach him a lesson and find other consolation she took up with young Heneage, flirting with him quite brazenly, though in her eyes it was a harmless enough affair that would lead nowhere, since he was already married.

According to one account Throckmorton felt it essential for Dudley to discover whether the Queen would or would not one day marry him and, if he were not absolutely certain of success, to change direction and support the Archduke Charles as an insurance for continuing favour under a new regime. To test Elizabeth's affections he made advances to Lettice Knollys, Viscountess Hereford, 'one of the best-looking ladies of the court', and the Queen's cousin. This was to develop into a passionate affair, but he originally embarked on it to make Elizabeth jealous and he underlined this by asking for leave of absence from court, 'to go to stay at my own place as other men'. The Queen gave no answer, but after three days she summoned him to Windsor where there was a terrific quarrel. He complained that she had cast

RIGHT Queen Elizabeth at Wanstead House, the home of the Earl of Leicester; portrait attributed to Marcus Gheeraerts the Elder, *c.* 1585. The sword at her feet and the olive branch in her hand refer to justice and peace.

BELOW The Heneage Jewel, given to Sir Thomas Heneage by the Queen in 1580. This consists of a miniature of Elizabeth by Hilliard, surrounded by enamelled gold, rubies and diamonds. The lid is decorated by a red rose encircled by the device, '*Hei mihi quod tanto virtus prefusa decore non habet eternos inviolata dies*' taken from a poem, written by Walter Haddon, the judge, in 1567.

RD CHANCELLOR
ATTON 1589

TANDEM SI

him aside for another, and then she rated him before the whole court: 'If you think to rule here I will take a course to see you forthcoming. I will have but one mistress and no master.' After tears there was a reconciliation, but Leicester felt life could never be quite the same again. Heneage discreetly left Windsor, but not for long, and Elizabeth continued to show him favours.

Then passions cooled and, surprisingly, Heneage – like Hatton in his turn – succeeded in achieving cordial relations with Leicester. The warm friendship of the three men in later years was remarkable; perhaps they were too close to each other to keep up personal feuds on the score of the Queen's favour, and though she played one off against the others their devotion to her remained a powerful bond as they grew older, strengthened by the Protestantism they held in common.

An intruder into this charmed circle was Thomas Butler, tenth Earl of Ormonde, Lord Treasurer of Ireland, who came to court in 1565 for a spell, as an interlude in a lifetime spent fighting the Desmonds and O'Neils. Born in the same year as Leicester, 'Black Tom', as he was nicknamed, had been brought up in King Henry's household after his father had been poisoned. He had an Irish charm that quite captivated Elizabeth and he was much in her company. Archbishop Young of York, who looked to Leicester, felt moved in 1566 to admonish her for favouring Ormonde. She was greatly enraged, and Leicester with singular skill acted as peacemaker.

During the same summer in which Elizabeth tried in vain to prevent the Darnley marriage she was entertaining Adam Zwetkovich, the personal envoy of Maximilian II, the new Holy Roman Emperor. He had travelled to England to return the late Emperor's insignia of the Garter, though his chief concern was to find out how serious were Elizabeth's intentions towards the Archduke Charles. Maximilian had made plain to Zwetkovich that although his brother 'would be again prepared to woo the illustrious Queen, if he had clear indications of her intentions, he would not, as on the last occasion, suffer himself to be led by the nose'. He told Elizabeth that Charles had 'great desire to see her' and he was delighted that so many courtiers he met thought the suit would succeed. She suddenly put the envoy on edge by saying 'I have never said hitherto to anybody that I would not marry the Earl of Leicester' and asked him if Dudley was opposing the match. He assured her that the Earl was dealing very favourably towards him and termed him in his dispatches 'the most important originator and warmest advocate' of the proposals.

Elizabeth told Zwetkovich that she would have stayed single 'did not the Crown of England compel her to marry to the profit of England,' and vindicated herself against the slander of malicious tongues. The House of Habsburg, she said, would find she had always acted 'with due decorum'. The ambassador, indeed, made his own 'diligent enquiries concerning the maiden honour and integrity of the Queen', to find that there was not a shred of evidence against her virginity and royal honour and that all the aspersions were 'the spawn of envy and malice and hatred'.

What was anyone to believe about the Queen's intentions? The Imperialists felt that they were being hoodwinked, just as the French had been. One day the Archduke's chances seemed very high, the next Elizabeth was proclaiming her continued affection for Leicester, and the day after vowing she would stay a spinster. 'She is so nimble in her declining and threads in and out of the business in such a way that her most intimate favourites fail to understand her, and her intentions are therefore, variously interpreted,' noted one ambassador, anxious to prove that successive dispatches were from the same court and about the same individuals.

It was at this time that Cecil drew up a private memorandum weighing up the merits and disadvantages of the Archduke and Leicester as potential bridegrooms. He came down heavily in favour of Charles, providing the marriage treaty included certain safeguards, since no sovereign 'ever had less alliance than the Queen of England hath, nor any Prince ever had more cause to have friendship and power to assist her estate'. In his assessment of Leicester, Cecil drove home every point: 'Nothing is increased by marriage of him, either in riches, estimation, power. It will be thought that the slanderous speeches of the Queen with the Earl have been true. He shall study nothing but to enhance his own particular friends to wealth, to offices, to lands, and to offend others. He is infamed by the death of his wife. He is far in debt. He is like to prove unkind, or jealous of the Queen's Majesty.' The profile was not unjust. To Cecil, Dudley had from the start of the reign been the key trouble-maker at court and he would remain a potential danger until Elizabeth was safely married to someone else.

The affair of the Archduke proceeded all too slowly. The Duke and Cecil were anxious about the long-delayed reply from the Emperor and even more disheartened by the news that Philip of Spain was discouraging the match on religious grounds. While Cecil feared that the Archduke's intention of remaining a Catholic would prove a stumbling block, Norfolk was more hopeful. He was convinced that, despite the weight of French diplomacy being thrust in the scales for Leicester, Elizabeth would never consent to marry him; 'there is no one else but the Archduke whom she can marry,' he wrote. Anything was preferable to having the realm 'desperate both of marriage and succession,' and he continued to advocate this course for another two years as the only sensible solution to a difficult problem.

When Norfolk returned to London in January 1566 the feud broke out again, for he had been angered by Leicester's broken promises about abandoning his courtship of Elizabeth. He told the favourite plainly that he would stop at nothing to oppose him, and each marshalled his forces. To emphasise the divisions at court Lord Robert's supporters started wearing blue (or purple), and Norfolk's yellow. 'I am told that Leicester began it, so as to know who were his friends,' wrote de Silva, 'and the adherents of the Duke did the same in consequence of some disagreements they had with them about the aid the Duke and his friends had given to the Archduke's match.' Arundel, it seems, intervened to try to keep the peace; outwardly they were very friendly to each other, 'dissembling in the usual English way, but remaining of the same opinion as before'. Could it be otherwise? There is a tale, plausible enough, yet impossible of proof, that about this time an agent approached Amy Robsart's half-brother, Appleyard, to bribe him into denouncing Leicester as the murderer of his wife. He crossed the Thames at Hampton in his nightshirt to meet a man who suggested his joining those of the council 'who do mind to charge him [Leicester] with certain things . . .'. The atmosphere was as over-charged as ever, yet a truce was called for 24 January.

In the previous autumn, to cement Anglo-French relations following the Treaty of Troyes, Catherine de'Medici announced that her son wished to bestow the Order of St Michael on an English nobleman, an honour for which Elizabeth, as a woman, was ineligible. Smith, the ambassador in Paris, suggested Lord Robert and commented to the Queen how fitting it was that the letter should have come on the day on which he was created an earl. Elizabeth tartly replied that she did not approve of any subject wearing an insignia not held by herself and that if Leicester were offered it he should refuse for it would provoke jealousy and comment that he favoured French interests. After much haggling Charles IX was persuaded to invest two of her subjects and delegated the selection to her. She chose Leicester and Norfolk, who in the January became Knights of St Michael; at the same time the French King received the Garter by proxy. A joint investiture of the two contenders might help to end the dissensions between them. But the Duke had not been eager to accept the honour and, according to Sussex, had only done so in obedience to his sovereign. Accepting the Order, according to one shrewd observer, might well damage Norfolk's reputation for being a true Englishman, 'knowing that the populace were badly affected towards French Kings' – a traditional anti-Gallic prejudice that would persist for many reigns. Perhaps, as Sussex claimed, the Duke had even told his household of his dislike of the honour thrust upon him.

There was fresh trouble with Leicester. The whisperings of the rumour-mongers are unknown, still less has 'the budget full of pretty inventions' about the two peers been preserved; all we know is that there was 'a great contro-versy' between them. The Queen's attitude remained unpredictable. When the Duke asked her for her leave to return to Norfolk early in December, he spoke plainly to her about the necessity of marriage, to settle the succession and quieten the realm and once more extolled the benefits of a Habsburg match. Such, he said, was no personal whim, for he claimed to be spokesman 'of all the principal people in the realm who loved her and whose feelings on the subject he well knew'. He added that those of her council who had advised her to marry Lord Robert had done so because they imagined that was where her heart lay, 'not because they really thought the match would be beneficial to the country, or good for her own dignity'. Elizabeth did not lose her tem-per, but thanked her cousin graciously, though she refused to make firm promises. The same day Norfolk saw Leicester and reminded him that he had promised to drop his suit for ever, and it was with this assurance that his colleagues had reopened negotiations with the Archduke. Leicester, too, kept his temper and when the Duke left London he was prominent among the gathering of notables to speed him on his way, 'doing him all the honour in their power'.

Almost as soon as Norfolk reached home came a letter from Cecil telling of the latest developments with the House of Habsburg. Norfolk was 'well enough able to prick out both treble and bass', and in particular Cecil's hints that Leicester was still pressing forward with his suit. As spokesman of the majority of the council, he called on Dudley within a week of the investiture to have out with him the business of his continued intrigues. Now that they were friends, began Norfolk, he could be frank with him. In everything else he would do what he could to support Leicester, but over his renewed attempts to gain the Queen's hand he had no alternative but to stand in his way. Elizabeth, the Duke continued with assurance, did not intend to marry him, so nothing but trouble could be reaped from his schemes, and as he alone would be blamed by the entire country for further delays in the nego-tiations with Archduke Charles he would earn himself a fatal unpopularity. The only sensible course was for the Earl to join with the rest of his colleagues in promoting the Archduke's suit. Leicester characteristically replied that he would certainly do as Norfolk advised if he could so arrange matters that Elizabeth should not think that he was neglecting his suit out of distaste for her, as this 'might cause her, womanlike, to undo him'; and on this under-standing the rivals parted.

The Privy Council also debated whether they should collectively or indivi-dually approach the Queen on the same topic. Meanwhile Sussex lobbied de Silva, who promised to use his influence with Elizabeth; the Duke would have come and discussed tactics with the ambassador himself, but felt it might compromise him in the eyes of Leicester's party, and in any case he and Sussex 'were like one person' in their views. This series of confidential conversations, whose substance was soon the common knowledge of all the embassies, had an immediate effect, for when de Silva had an audience with the Queen at Candlemas, as they walked in the Privy Garden at Whitehall, she told him of Leicester's unselfishness in urging her to marry for her country's sake, her own sake, and even his, for he was being blamed for her single state. Leicester was away from court, and was advised by Sir Nicholas Throckmorton to delay returning, for the Queen was being difficult about the Archduke's religion, saying he must secretly undertake to forswear his Catholicism.

The Catholic Earl of Arundel took no part in these discussions. Some months before, in a fit of pique, he had surrendered his staff as Lord Steward of the Household, making 'sundry speeches of offence' towards Her Majesty, for which he had been confined to his residence. Now he decided to shut up Arundel House and Nonsuch Palace and leave for Padua to take a cure for his gout. Before leaving he told de Silva that he was sure the Archduke affair would come to nought and that his son-in-law of Norfolk was as a matter of principle pursuing the phantom of a Habsburg match merely 'out of enmity to the Earl of Leicester'. It was too harsh a judgment. Cecil, undiscouraged by the slow progress at the Imperial court, applauded the Duke's efforts. In March he wrote to Sir Thomas Smith in confidence that 'My Lord of Norfolk hath shewed himself a very noble man and wise,' throughout the affair. But Leicester's return to royal favour inevitably provoked fresh trouble with the Duke. He stayed away from court in a huff, even excused himself from the St George's Day celebrations at Windsor to avoid Leicester's company, and made a point of absenting himself from the royal visit to Oxford at the begin-ning of that month, where the Earl as Chancellor of the University would be playing the principal role. Even while he was away from court the ill-feeling between supporters of the two rivals increased apace, and there were high words between Lord North and Lord Clinton, now surprisingly behind Leicester. At the same time there was some measure of reconciliation between Throckmorton and Cecil, thanks to Pembroke's intervention. In front of Leicester, Throckmorton asked Cecil why he was being so unfriendly towards him and the Secretary gave his prepared answer – because Sir Nicholas was too fond of innovations in politics, too inclined to embitter affairs for the sake of faction and too much a Francophile. In his turn Throckmorton promised to act for the public good, but Leicester felt shamefaced.

During May 1566, Cecil's cousin Thomas Dannett, who had been involved in Hale's tract on the Suffolk claim, was sent as agent to Augsburg and Vienna to discuss affairs with the Emperor Maximilian II and the Archduke Charles. On the vexed issue of faith he reported that the Holy Roman Emperor 'seems not to be hard, but looks that the religion his brother was brought up in should be permitted him.' 'Something must be winked at by the Queen,' suggested the envoy, who for his part went out of his way to show the Imperial court that an Englishman was open-minded by accompanying the Archduke to evensong. More encouraging were his reports of the spouse proposed for Elizabeth, He was courteous, affable, liberal, wise, had a good memory, was popular, and liked vigorous outdoor sports. A recent attack of smallpox had not disfigured him; he was 'of a sanguine complexion and, for a man, beautiful and well-faced, well-shaped, small in the waist, and well and broad breasted; he seems in his clothes well-thighed and well-legged'. Because he stooped a little some might think him slightly round-shouldered, but Dannett added that in the saddle he was as straight in his body as any man alive. At last things were beginning to move, and soon Elizabeth would demand a portrait.

That summer the political situation at home was still uncertain, and rumours were rife. At a council meeting Leicester accused Sussex of responsibility for Shane O'Neill's rebellion in Ireland, and when Sussex retorted that it was his accuser who had himself formented rebellion by his letters to O'Neill the two nearly came to blows. Recent developments in Scotland began to cast a deeper shadow, and were linked inevitably with the problem of the succession. The consequences of Rizzio's murder at Holyroodhouse Palace in March had become a powerful factor in English politics. A spy of Cecil's in Edinburgh reported in June that Mary had told him of friendly letters she had received from Dacres of the Crooked Back, Sir Thomas Stanley and others, and that she hoped through them to win over Norfolk, Shrewsbury, Derby and the northern earls, 'for that she thought them all to be of the old religion which she meant to restore again with all expedition and thereby win the hearts of the common people'. According to Sir James Melville, who hastened from Edinburgh to Greenwich in July to announce to Elizabeth the birth of James Stuart, Norfolk and Pembroke had now declared they would support Mary's claim to succeed Elizabeth. Had he known it, they had been joined by Leicester, for late in 1565 Throckmorton had put out feelers urging Mary to do what she could to win the confidence of Protestants both north and south of the border. The birth of Prince James had made all the difference to Leicester and soon he, with Sussex, Norfolk and Pembroke, would be taking steps to worship the rising sun, ensuring their future by keeping open communication with Mary, who was nine years younger than Elizabeth and could be expected to succeed her.

Norfolk's third marriage, with the Catholic Lady Dacre, had made him an obvious supporter of Mary's claims, but the twists of English politics had brought him strange bed-fellows. To Secretary Cecil, by contrast, there could be no accommodation with Mary, because she was not merely a

The front of the Lennox Jewel, made for Margaret, Countess of Lennox to commemorate the death of her husband, Matthew, in 1571.

Catholic but a Guise. 'There are communications going on among the aristocracy here, which threaten a storm,' reported de Silva in the early autumn, 'and I think, considering that the winter is near, that they will not dare to make any open movement.' There was, indeed, an undercurrent of uneasiness both at court and in the country, and it was clear that when Parliament opened unprecedented pressure would be brought on Elizabeth to marry. Meanwhile on this troubled eve of sessions noblemen, knights and burgesses discussed the succession at the great houses all down the Strand.

The Parliament that had been prorogued for the last three years reassembled on 2 October in a militant mood, determined to proceed with the question of the Queen's marriage and the settlement of the succession. In 1563 the Commons had gone home with a promise from Elizabeth that she would answer their petition for action under both these heads, yet she was determined that they should not meddle. To prepare her for the storm that might break out at any time, the almost forbidden topic was broached round the council table, with the Queen herself present, on 12 October. As agreed with his colleagues, Norfolk began the discussion with a prepared piece: 'Madam, you know that I have taken an oath to Your Majesty as a Councillor, by which I am obliged to have regard to your well-being and that of your subjects. Pardon me, therefore, if I take the liberty of putting this matter before you.' He reminded her of the Commons petition, now three years old, which still awaited an answer, rehearsed the recent developments in England, Scotland and Europe, and begged her to allow these weighty matters to be discussed openly in both houses. According to the French ambassador, who has left the only account of this meeting, Elizabeth replied angrily that she had governed her realm well. Who succeeded to her throne was her affair, not Parliament's, not even her council's, and she had no wish by naming a successor to be 'buried alive'. As for her marriage, they knew full well the dealings with the Archduke and an alliance with him was not far off. A few words more and she had taken her leave of them.

This was an inauspicious start. The next week in the Commons, when the Subsidy Bill was moved, debate on the succession began in earnest, with tempers raised and, it seems, members even coming to blows. Neither Cecil nor any other member of the government could give the House a satisfactory assurance, and as a result a message was sent to the Queen, via the council,

The Garter ceremony of 1576, engraving by Marcus Gheeraerts the Elder, depicting the knights and officials of the Order in procession with the Queen, who is wearing her Garter robes. Windsor Castle is shown in the left background.

that the Commons' grievances must be redressed before taxation was approved. Utterly exasperated by this, Elizabeth poured out her heart to the Spanish ambassador. Two days later, on 22 October, the Lords sent their own deputation to Whitehall Palace, led by old Winchester, who politely pointed out that Parliament was wasting its time; she should either declare her will or dissolve Parliament so they could all go home. Others followed, but Elizabeth was undaunted. The Commons were rebels, she said, and not a man there would have dared to behave like this in her father's time. 'My Lords, do whatever you wish. As for me, I shall do no otherwise than pleases me.' She would seek the advice of the best lawyers in her realm about the succession, but Parliament was too feeble-witted a body to deal with so important a matter.

Next day the Commons sent a committee to discuss further with the Upper House, and in the end, overriding Winchester's senile vacillation, the Lords agreed to join with the Commons in a suit to Her Majesty, presenting a united front. Once again Norfolk was the spokesman. De Silva, in whom Elizabeth confided at this time, and with whom Sussex and the Duke were quite open, pieced together an account of this stormy audience:

The Queen was so angry that she addressed hard words to the Duke of Norfolk, whom she called traitor or conspirator, or other words of similar flavour. He replied that he never thought to have to ask her pardon for having offended her thus. Subsequently they tell me the Queen asserted that she addressed no such words to the Duke. The Earls of Leicester and Pembroke, the Marquess of Northampton and the Lord Chamberlain spoke to her on the matter, and Pembroke remarked to her that it was not right to treat the Duke badly, since he and the others were only doing what was fitting for the good of the country, and advising her what was best for her, and if she did not think fit to adopt the advice, it was still their duty to offer it. She told him he talked like a swaggering soldier, and said to Leicester that she had thought if all the world abandoned her he would not have done so, to which he answered that he would die at her feet; and she said that had nothing to do with the matter. She said that Northampton was of no account, and he had better talk about the arguments used to enable him to get married again, when he had a wife living, instead of mincing words with her. With this she left them, and had resolved to order them to be considered under arrest in their houses. This she has not done, but she has commanded them [Leicester and Pembroke] not to appear before her.

She later told the ambassador that being abandoned by all her council except Winchester had so angered her that she had railed at them. But in the end, on 5 November, she decided to address a committee of thirty members from each House, and her tongue lashed in turn Commons, temporal peers and the bishops for daring to discuss such matters. She would marry, she said, as soon as she conveniently could (hinting broadly at the Archduke Charles), and hoped to bear children. The succession in the interim was quite another thing, as experience of her sister's unhappy reign had convinced her of the lack of wisdom in naming a successor; once one was named he or she would become the focal point of every intrigue, thus uniting all her enemies at home and abroad. When after Christmas she came to Parliament for the dissolution she warned the Commons and Lords 'never to tempt too far a prince's patience'. But with the Queen of Scots as mother of a fair son, Elizabeth had no option but to follow up the Habsburg negotiations, if need be to the bitter end.

It was Sussex, the principal champion of the match, who was chosen to go to Germany to take further soundings at the Imperial court under cover of investing Maximilian II with the Garter, but there were interminable delays before he set out. The haggling about the size of what Elizabeth chose to call the Archduke's 'dowry' earned the Imperial reproof 'It is the future *wife* who provides the husband with a dowry *and* gives the husband a wedding gift.' The Queen stood on her dignity: 'It appears to me somewhat strange, Your Imperial Majesty, that five months should have elapsed without my receiving any tidings. I wrote in reference to Your Majesty that I was being fooled, or at least that there were many irons in the fire, so strongly did I suspect that I was being scorned, or being lured on in the expectation of something better.' Maximilian, in a private note to his brother, commented on the habit of 'our illustrious Queen' picking up and then discarding the threads of matrimonial diplomacy, 'for she seems to regard it as profitable to create delays somewhere or somehow in order to gain an advantage – and this we have some time suspected'.

It was not until the urgency for a marriage alliance had passed, with Mary Queen of Scots a captive of the Lords of the Covenant, that Elizabeth allowed Sussex to set out. By his instructions Sussex was to explain that Elizabeth could not allow the exercise of any but the established religion, but since there was 'a general toleration therein used to divers subjects living other-wise quietly', he would be given a certain latitude for his private devotions. When the negotiations began in earnest in Vienna this assurance appeared to Charles far too vague. His terms were that Elizabeth should allow him his own private chapel for Mass while he would publicly accompany her to Anglican worship. It was a reasonable request, but Sussex, anxious as he was for the success of his mission, dared not proceed without seeking further instructions from Whitehall.

At the end of October the Earl sent home Henry Cobham, younger brother of the Lord Warden, with letters asking for clear guidance. Leicester, anxious for the overthrow of his rivals' scheme, which would certainly bury any remaining hopes he had of becoming Elizabeth's consort, worked feverishly on Protestant passions, 'the like hath not been'. Some months before, Eliza-beth had rebuked Dean Nowell for preaching against images, but now public opinion had swung right round, largely as a result of the fate of the Calvinists in the Netherlands. Under Leicester's influence Bishop Jewel of Salisbury harangued the multitude at Paul's Cross to abhor trafficking with idolatry, and others drew a moral from Alva's militant Catholicism in the Netherlands.

The council were now equally divided on the question of the Archduke's religion, and Elizabeth asked Cecil to write to Norfolk, who was too ill to come to London, to send his views in writing. He counselled the Secretary to stand by the marriage at all costs, allowing the Archduke the terms which he had demanded. There was, he wrote, no prince of Charles's standing or understanding who would yield any further upon uncertainty. His was a most reasonable request, and if in the end negotiations foundered on other grounds than religion Charles would not have thrown away his principles. The danger of his being allowed his private Roman Catholic chapel was very small compared with the danger of an unsettled succession. Not all 'earnest Protestants' were like Leicester and his men who were 'making religion a cloak for every shower ... naming one thing and minding another'. To the

An allegory of the Protestant Succession painted on a wooden panel, 1572. Henry VIII is shown delivering the sword of justice to Edward VI, while Mary and Philip of Spain lead in Mars: Elizabeth in complete contrast joins hands with Peace and Plenty.

Queen the Duke wrote more guardedly: there was a risk of the Archduke as her consort becoming 'an open maintainer of papistry', which would clearly endanger the unity of the realm, and 'England can bear no more changes in religion – it hath been bowed so far that if it should be bent again it would break.' That said, it was important not to let the Archduke be frightened off. 'If this, then, should not take place, what present hope is there of any other, as delay of Your Majesty's marriage is almost an undoing of your realm?' Norfolk had cause to complain of 'mythical devices' and the efforts of Leicester's supporters to blacken his name, and lamented that he was 'nearly counted a papist'.

With so successful a propaganda campaign playing on men's nascent xenophobia, Leicester won the day and it is unlikely that had Norfolk and Sussex both been present at Whitehall the outcome would have been any different. Behind Leicester in council were Knollys, Pembroke and most probably Bacon, while Cecil could only count on Lord Chamberlain Howard, Admiral Clinton and the lightweight Comptroller Rogers. In her letter to Sussex in December 1567 Elizabeth finally closed the affair, refusing to concede the Archduke a separate Catholic establishment on the grounds both of the law of the land, 'which cannot be altered without the consent of the Estates of the Realm', and of her own conscience.

The despondent Sussex reckoned that it was Leicester who had principally thwarted him, since it was the favourite's own designs on the Queen that had ruined all efforts to forward the Habsburg negotiations. 'If God should ever put it into my dear mistress's head to divide the weed from the grain, she should reap the better harvest here,' he said, almost in tears, and his loyalty to her was more than tinged with a warm affection. Moreover during his absence in Vienna Sussex failed to secure the appointment as President of the Council of Wales, which he had been led to expect from the Queen. Dudley, by now a great landowner in North Wales, had promised his support but in the event deserted him to ensure that his brother-in-law, Sir Henry Sidney, increasingly indisposed through the stone, was continued in office. Sussex felt cheated by both Queen and favourite and even asked for leave to live in Italy. The following year, however, the death of Archbishop Young made way for the Earl's appointment as President of the Council in the North, a post of much greater importance than Sidney's presidency. The crisis in Scotland, following Darnley's murder, had brought Throckmorton to Edinburgh as a special ambassador to attempt a reconciliation between Mary and the Lords of the Covenant; it was an impossible task and he made little progress, asking for his recall, 'seeing I do nothing here but spend the Queen's money,' but later on he was convinced that it was his presence that preserved Mary's life after Bothwell's rout at Carberry Hill. It was the fate of Mary that was to polarise politics at the English court far more effectively than the Habsburg suit.

There were changes in Elizabeth's immediate circle of ladies. Kate Ashley had been succeeded as mother of the maids by Mistress Eglionby, who came from a Shropshire family and was probably introduced to court by the Earl of Shrewsbury. The five maids of honour, all in their teens, had been found places by the most influential peers: one was a daughter of Sussex; another, Mary Howard, was a grand-daughter of the Lord Chamberlain; Catherine Knyvett had made her début through Norfolk's influence; and Leicester had secured the appointment of Anne Windsor, while Dorothy Brooke came from the Lord Warden's family. Only four gentlewomen of the Privy Chamber were in post at the end of 1567 – the faithful Blanche Parry, widow of Sir Thomas, Elizabeth Knollys, Lady Stafford and Mrs Dorothy Bradbelt; the last, married to a London merchant who was to make a fortune from manufacturing soap, was rewarded with a smaller stipend than the others. Compared with the beginning of the reign there were no ladies of the highest rank among the gentlewomen of the Privy Chamber.

Though the Queen remained single there were notable weddings at court.

The Darnley Cenotaph, painted in London in 1567 for the Earl and Countess of Lennox to show the guilt of Mary Queen of Scots in Darnley's murder and her association with Bothwell. Darnley's effigy lies before the altar of victorious Christ, while the infant James VI,

the Earl and Countess of Lennox and their younger son, Charles Stewart, are portrayed kneeling calling for the revenge of Darnley. In the left-hand corner, there is an inset view of the encounter at Carberry Hill in 1567, with Mary's surrender.

Fresh alliances were being formed in the mid-sixties, some of them cutting across religious or 'party' lines. Henry Killigrew, for years a stalwart of Leicester's, now became a brother-in-law of Cecil, while Pembroke, firmly in the favourite's camp, now made an intricate family compact with the conservative Shrewsburys. Less surprising was the alliance of Dudley and Russell when Leicester's elder brother, Ambrose Earl of Warwick, a widower, married Bedford's daughter Anne. Leicester had perhaps worked unnecessarily hard to bring about this marriage, declaring 'I know not how much I might better show it than wishing him [Warwick] I love as I love myself, to be so allied with him that next is, as dear a friend as can be to myself [Bedford],' and he took it upon himself to secure the Queen's blessing. Sovereign and favourite made elaborate arrangements for the wedding festivities at Whitehall, and Bedford, anchored in Berwick, was content that it should be thus. Elizabeth permitted the marriage service to be celebrated in the Chapel Royal with the wedding breakfast in the Council Chamber, and there was also a tournament in the tiltyard with Leicester himself as a defendant. Little Lady Warwick was to become a great favourite with Elizabeth.

Within the circle of Elizabeth's own cousinage, Howard of Effingham's son married Hunsdon's daughter. A remarkable alliance was the marriage between the widower Norfolk and Elizabeth, widow of Thomas Lord Dacre in January 1567, which the Duke intended to fortify with future marriages between Lady Dacre's four children and his own. The rich Dacre patrimony, with lands in Cumberland, Westmorland, Durham and Yorkshire, brought Norfolk a direct interest in the north country, with tremendous political consequences. Perhaps the most significant match of all was the wedding of Walter Devereux, Viscount Hereford, to Sir Francis Knollys's daughter Lettice, which led to the birth of Robert, Earl of Essex.

For more than a decade Leicester's extraordinary position with the Queen enabled him to trump every other courtier's hand. Cecil may have held the balance in council, but he was never supreme; he was always dependent on Elizabeth's confidence and she in turn looked increasingly to Leicester for advice – advice not merely on filling posts but on the entire range of political issues. The Secretary, indeed, for all his patient paperwork and long hours in the council room, had no status outside his office; Sir William was a commoner and in his own eyes a man of modest means, who found it far from easy to rub shoulders with peers and magnates of the calibre of Norfolk, Howard of Effingham, Sussex and Leicester. Dudley led so charmed a life in his relations with Elizabeth that he still could not believe she would not marry him sooner or later. Any clouding of her favours made him despondent. In May 1567, with the Habsburg suit finally buried, he had ended his feud with Norfolk so far as to stay as his guest at Norwich, where their relations were as good as at any time since the accession, and this new-found tolerance of each other was destined to have profound effects on political alignments at court.

While on holiday with the Duke, Dudley received a letter from 'one whom it has always been my greatest comfort to hear from' – namely Her Majesty – and whatever she wrote to him upset him. He admitted to Throckmorton that he might 'have many ways offended' and was afraid his star had fallen. 'If my days' service and not a few years' proof, have made trial of unremoveable fidelity enough, without notable offences, what shall I think of all that past favour which in such unspeakable sort remained towards me, thus to take my first oversight, as it were an utter casting-off of all that was before?' (The method of expression might have been a Hatton or a Raleigh of later years pouring out his heart.) Leicester knew too well with whom he had to deal, and it was a relief to set his worries in perspective by writing to the faithful Throckmorton. The cause of this tiff with Elizabeth is unknown, but for a little while it affected him deeply. Perhaps he saw at last the significance of de Silva's acute remark that the Queen would like everyone to be in love with her, but would never be in love with any one person sufficiently to marry him. It was this psychological factor that was to give Elizabeth's court its unique character in the years which followed.

Anne Russell, Countess of Warwick, the daughter of Francis Russell, Earl of Bedford. She married Ambrose Dudley, Earl of Warwick in 1565 as his third wife: painting by the Master of the Countess of Warwick, *c.* 1569.

C. Derbeia	C. Wigornie	C. Rotelandie	C. Cumberlandie	C. Suthsexiæ	C. Huntingdonie	C. Bathonie
C. Warwici	C. Suthamptonie	C. Bedfordie	C. Penbrochi	C. Herfordiæ	C. Leicestriæ	C. Essexiæ
C. Lincolnie	V.C. Montacui	V.C. Bindon	D. Abergaunny	D. Audeley	D. Zouche	D. Wlughby de E.
D. Berkeley	D. Morley	D. Dacre	D. Cobham	D. Stafford	D. Grey de W	D. Scroope
D. Dudley	D. Stourton	D. Lumley	D. Montioy	D. Ogle	D. Darry. B	D. Sandes
D. Vaulx	D. Windsore	D. Wentworth	D. Borough	D. Mordaunt	D. Cromwell	D. Eure
D. Wharton	D. Riche	D. Wlughby de P	D. Sheffeld	D. Paget	D. Darcy de C	D. Howard de E
D. North	D. Chaundos	D. Hunsdon	D. Saint Iohn	D. Buckhurst	D. de la Warre	D. Burghley
D. Compton	D. Norreys	C. Hatton Can	F. Knolles Th	I. Croft Compt	T. Heneage Vicec	F. Walsingh. P.S.

5 The Fall of Norfolk

The turning-point in Elizabeth's reign came when Mary Queen of Scots succeeded in escaping from imprisonment in Lochleven in May 1568 and, after the defeat of her followers at Langside, crossed the Solway to throw herself on Elizabeth's mercy. If the problem of Mary as Queen Regnant of Scotland had bedevilled the English political scene for seven years, the problem of Mary as a captive in England was to pose unanswerable complications for a further nineteen. Her presence at once hardened existing divisions and provoked corresponding realignments among courtiers; holding her miniature rival court in a series of closely-guarded houses, her very person attracted men to conspire and rebel for her cause and the fragile unity of the kingdom was shattered so that the rift between Catholics and Protestants became unbridgeable.

The news that Mary had landed at Cockermouth swept through the north country, where men rejoiced that a Catholic Queen had come amongst them, for on her their hopes were pinned. Magnates and their near-feudal tenants in the 'inly working' north where the old ways died hard took Mary's advent as a sign for feverish activity and inveterate intrigue to settle scores with Elizabeth's regime. The ancient Border family of Percy, now ruling the north-east from Alnwick Castle, had managed in 1557 to recover the earldom of Northumberland, which had been usurped by John Dudley in 1551. To the west of the Border region, the Neville Earls of Westmorland had held supreme power since the end of the fourteenth century. Both were strongly Catholic and held themselves as aloof from court and capital as they could. Thomas Percy, Earl of Northumberland, no longer supreme in his old domain as his father had been, rode to Carlisle intending to take charge of Mary himself, but he was too late. Although Lord Scrope, the warden of the West Marches, was away at court, his deputy refused to surrender the Scottish Queen to the Earl; and Sir Francis Knollys, the Vice-Chamberlain whom Elizabeth had sent north to take Mary into his custody at Bolton Castle in Wensleydale, sent Northumberland packing. Knollys ordered him to journey to court himself to explain his conduct, but he returned in high dudgeon to Alnwick Castle.

The political power of the northern earls had already been effectively reduced, following the war with the French in Scotland in 1560, when Sir Ralph Sadler, an administrator in whom Cecil placed great confidence, was

Christopher Saxton's *Atlas of England and Wales*, 1579: a page showing the shields of the courtiers.

given special responsibilities for affairs of the Border. Subsequently Northumberland had lost his wardenship of the Middle Marches to his enemy Sir John Foster, and his post in the East Marches to the Earl of Bedford, already Governor of Berwick. Lord Dacre, warden of the West Marches until his death in 1563, was reckoned so unreliable in his allegiance that Elizabeth kept him at court; he was succeeded by Lord Scrope, a brother-in-law of Norfolk and one of the few northern peers who could be trusted. The triumvirate of wardens of the Marches were themselves aided by the President of the Council in the North, with much wider responsibilities in Cumberland, Westmorland, Northumberland, the Palatinate of Durham and North Yorkshire – an office held by Thomas Young, Archbishop of York, who was the first ecclesiastic to be appointed to an important civil post. When Young died in 1568 he was succeeded by the Earl of Sussex. With courtiers of the calibre of Sussex and Bedford resident in the north, the Earls of Northumberland and Westmorland felt themselves by-passed and cheated of their hereditary role. Their aim was to lead a counter-revolution that would put back the clock in administration no less than in religion, as their predecessors had attempted in the Pilgrimage of Grace, but their schemings were to go off half-heartedly in the rising of 1569.

Before Mary's escape, as we have noticed, there had been a change in the attitude of various prominent courtiers towards both her person and her claims to the English succession. In the aftermath of the breakdown of the Habsburg negotiations, Norfolk and Sussex had turned towards Mary as the obvious successor, joining forces with their recent adversaries of the match with the Archduke – Leicester and Pembroke. Now that Mary had arrived in England, the future for them (as for the supporters of the Stuart claim on religious grounds, such as Arundel) was fraught with uncertainty, and for the first time since the accession the whisperings at court took on the tone of high intrigue.

The crisis interfered with the established routine of the court and made the Queen limit her summer progress to the home counties, 'as she is careful to keep near at hand when troubles and disturbances exist'. After much heart-searching she decided to appoint commissioners to investigate the charges made against Mary by her Scottish subjects as a preliminary to further action. She nominated Norfolk, Sussex and Sadler, who were to confer at York early in October with delegates appointed both by Mary and by the Regent Murray, Mary's half-brother. Mary herself would not appear; indeed it was obvious that she would never acknowledge the authority of a tribunal that sat in judgment on her affairs. Norfolk and his fellows were first to hear the charges brought by Mary's delegates against Murray; they were neither accusers nor judges, but were investigating her case, which hinged on her complicity in Darnley's murder. Her future would depend on their findings and their instructions included advice on how she might return to her throne 'without danger of relapse into misgovernment'.

At York Norfolk was shown the Casket Letters and was convinced of their authenticity: 'the said letters and ballads,' he wrote in disgust to Elizabeth, 'do discover such inordinate love between her [Mary] and Bothwell, her loathsomeness and abhorring of her husband that was murdered'. A few days later he went hawking with Maitland of Lethington, whom he had come to know well at the time of the siege of Leith in 1560, and on their ride the

MARIA D·G· SCOTIÆ REGINA, GALLIÆ DOTARIA, MAII 17·1568· AVXILII AB ELISABETHA
PROMISSI SPE ET OPINIONE DESCENDIT IN ANGLIAM· VBI CONTRA IVS GENTIVM, ET
FOEDERIS IVRATI FIDEM, ANNOS VNDEVIGINTI RETENTA, TANDEM HOSPITIS
ELISABETHÆ PARRICIDIO CHRISTI   MARTYRIBVS ADDITA, SANGVINIS LI-
BERALITER EFFVSI TESTI-   MONIO DEI LEGITIMVM CVLTV,
ET ECCLESIÆ ROMANÆ   FIDEM PROFESSA, CORONAM
MERVIT IN CŒLIS, ILLIS   TRIBVS ILLVSTRIOREM,
QVARV VSVM VIOLENTE   AMISIT IN TERRIS· 18·
· FEBRVAR·   1587·

Secretary suggested that the best way of dealing with the intractable problem of his Queen would be for the Duke to marry her. Mary could in consequence be restored to her throne and in time she and their issue could reign at Whitehall. This match would save Mary from dishonour and carry the Anglo-Scottish alliance a stage further. It was the third occasion on which Norfolk had been suggested as a suitable husband for Mary, but for the present the thought of taking as his fourth wife a woman whom he was already convinced was both an adulteress and a murderess can have had little attraction for him. Nor can he have failed to recall the clause in his royal instructions as a commissioner which stated that anyone with whom Mary contracted a marriage, or anyone advising it, 'shall be *ipso facto* acknowledged as traitorous and shall suffer death'. Even so, the seed sown by Maitland was to germinate rapidly within a few months. Before Norfolk's secret talk by the Ouse, Knollys had suggested to him that an admirable way of dealing with Mary would be for her to marry his cousin George Carey, Hunsdon's son. Sir Francis was to mention this to Mary herself and understood that she did not 'greatly mislike' the idea.

Norfolk would come to ask himself, if George Carey was eligible, why not himself? Certainly, by the opening of 1569 he had determined that when opportunity occurred and Mary were free he would marry her. For once opposition from Elizabeth and Cecil provoked a strange boldness in him; he allowed himself to be compromised by schemes devised by bolder spirits, of which he knew few details, until he eventually reached the point from which he could not honourably withdraw. It would be for him a dynastic match in the old Howard tradition, like his two aunts' marriages to King Henry, and his ambition to sit on a throne was tempered by the conviction that such a marriage would both solve the Scottish conundrum and settle the intolerable uncertainty of the English succession. The monarchy had been elevated by the break with Rome and had now been given a new mystique by a young and masterful Queen; it was this that made people's preoccupation with the succession obsessive, and it was this that spelt Norfolk's downfall: by birth a thane of Cawdor, he saw in marriage with Mary the opportunity to be 'king hereafter'.

The York Conference became bogged down in procedural difficulties and ended in stalemate, for Murray would not produce his most telling evidence against Mary – the Casket Letters – unless Elizabeth would commit herself to giving judgment against Mary, and this she would never do. The Queen knew enough to suspect that Norfolk had been showing undue partiality towards Mary, and in London it was whispered that he was contemplating a marriage with her; indeed, before the end of October, the French ambassador had passed on this rumour to Elizabeth. She therefore decided to appoint a much enlarged commission to continue the investigations at Westminster under her nose. Put out at the whispers against him, which (as with any prominent courtier) always became more malicious during absence from court, the Duke expressed his 'vehement misliking of such a marriage'. After the Westminster Conference had itself broken down, the Queen asked him to his face about what she had heard. Though he now hated the idea of marrying Mary, perhaps in the future he could be persuaded to change his mind, if it were shown to be for the benefit of the realm and the safety of his

Queen? Norfolk knew he was being tested, and answered his mistress that 'no reason could move him to like of her that hath been a competitor to the Crown; and if Her Majesty would move him thereto he will rather be committed to the Tower, for he meant never to marry with such a person, where he could not be sure of his pillow' – an allusion to Darnley's fate. A politic answer, indeed, for by then the full horror of the Casket Letters, which Murray had been tricked into producing at the inquiry, had been brought home to him. Elizabeth herself was satisfied with this protestation; at any rate she had given Norfolk a broad hint. Ironically, it was hints such as this which played on his ambition and persuaded him to take the idea of the marriage seriously. It developed from a vague idea to a serious project.

Elizabeth wrote to Mary herself, congratulating her on so faithful and skilled a servant as the Bishop of Ross, but advising her most earnestly to answer the charges against her in writing so she could be delivered by the justification of her innocence. In fact, now that the Casket Letters had been produced, Elizabeth was in a very strong position, for she had ample evidence to justify her treatment of Mary to the courts of Europe. She would in truth never agree to meet Mary, but at least she would not rule out the possibility of her restoration, which might still be the best solution to the Scottish problem, for she made it quite clear that she despised the Regent.

Outside the conference room Norfolk discussed the problem of Mary with Murray, Maitland and others. Exactly what took place and what was said is uncertain, for the evidence of these conversations, most of it set down two or three years later, is conflicting, but the following is the most likely reconstruction. The Earl of Morton, determined to embarrass the Regent, had sent a servant to divulge to Huntingdon details of the agreement reached at York between Murray and Norfolk. As he had hoped, Huntingdon told Leicester, who told the Queen, though Elizabeth had long suspected this. Norfolk by all accounts was exasperated and we are told that to get his revenge on the Scottish commissioners he asked the Earl of Westmorland to intercept them on their way home to Edinburgh; how far he intended to go is conjectural and in the event he changed his plans and wrote to his brother-in-law to cancel the *coup*.

The idea may have been no more than to give Murray a scare and if this were so it served its purpose, for catching wind of the rumour that his throat might be cut on the way to the Border he decided to go in penitence to the Duke to patch things up. A rendezvous was arranged in Hampton Court Park and Sir Nicholas Throckmorton brought them together. Murray asked for Norfolk's pardon, blaming the intrigues of his associates for the way the conference had developed. Howard replied that 'he knew his gentle nature was abused by the craft and concurrence of some of the Council of England, who had joined with some about him' to overthrow the agreed plan of campaign. They agreed for the future to keep closely in touch and swore themselves to secrecy. The Duke again reminded Murray that he was resolved to marry Mary and hinted at the possibility of a match between the young King James and his own daughter: 'Earl of Murray,' he said, 'thou knowest that thing whereunto I will make none in England nor in Scotland privy, and thou hast Norfolk's life in thy hands.'

Norfolk was delighted at his new concordat with Murray, but Mary must have been alarmed when she had a letter from him announcing this resumed friendship, for she knew her half-brother could not be trusted for one moment. Before he left London he had related to Elizabeth the tenor of his secret conversations with the Duke: he did not in the least feel bound by his promises to Norfolk, for he had made them 'for fear of life'. Elizabeth agreed to support him as Regent and provide him with £5,000 to maintain his ascendancy in Scotland on certain conditions. There were other discussions, in which the Catholics Lumley and Arundel took part. Norfolk sent Lumley to Ross begging him to open official discussions with Elizabeth, to win her over to the idea of the marriage, then he understood that she had caught wind of his fresh dealings with Mary but reckoned 'he had satisfied her well enough'.

These were distressing days for Elizabeth, and her sorrow at losing two dear friends in quick succession affected those about her. Roger Ascham, her old tutor and Latin Secretary, had caught a chill working into the small hours of a cold December to finish a New Year poem in her honour, and the doctors could do nothing for him. Three weeks later her cousin Catherine Knollys died at Hampton Court at the early age of thirty-nine, while her husband was guarding Mary. She paid for a worthy funeral for Lady Knollys in Westminster Abbey. Certainty that her cousin Norfolk was behaving in a devious manner came as yet another cruel blow.

For the Duke, the temptation to marry Mary was irresistible. As the backstairs intrigues continued, they became entwined with further schemes and caught up others at court. In Elizabethan politics it was the duty of the opposition to intrigue, and at the beginning of 1569 the key issue was not Norfolk's matrimonial plans but the dominant position of Secretary Cecil, which seemed sinister to some at court. He was blamed for the embargo on trade with Spain and the Netherlands following the seizure of four Spanish treasure ships which had taken refuge in Plymouth Sound the previous November. The Secretary's unpopularity among city merchants was matched by a loss of confidence in him among colleagues in council who felt that with ten years' service behind him he should now be forced to resign. 'Many did also rise against his fortune, who were more hot in envying him than able to follow him, detracting his praises, disgracing his services and plotting his danger' – so ran a biographical sketch written while Cecil was still alive.

Chief among Cecil's opponents was Leicester, who had so systematically taken a stance against his policies that he might aptly, if unhistorically, be termed 'leader of the opposition'. In particular the favourite was convinced that it was Cecil who had prevented him from winning Elizabeth's hand. But he had many other opponents. Norfolk saw him as the arch-enemy of Mary Queen of Scots, whom he thought he was now committed to marry. Pembroke and Northampton disliked the policies that Cecil's Protestantism had led him to pursue, especially his aid to the rebels in the Netherlands and France and his support of the Suffolk claim to the succession. The Roman Catholics, Arundel, Lumley, Northumberland and Westmorland ascribed to the Secretary the severity with which the laws against recusants were being enforced since Mary's arrival in England and saw his dismissal as the essential preliminary to a re-establishment of their religion. Even old Winchester, in his dotage, could still sway with the wind. Many regarded Cecil, as Norfolk had once done, as the 'new man' bent on overthrowing the old

ABOVE Self-portrait by Nicholas Hilliard, painted in 1577 when he was thirty.

BELOW Queen Elizabeth's Second Great Seal: the obverse showing the Queen in Majesty. This seal, cast by Dericke Anthony from an initial design by Hilliard, was completed in 1586 and used until the end of the reign.

nobility in the power of the state. There were others, too, who viewed with alarm the growing estrangement from Spain, not solely on grounds of commercial prudence but also because they feared that England would be thrown into alliance with France, her traditional enemy, and anti-Gallic prejudice died hard in 1569. These were strange bed-fellows who joined forces to protest against Cecil's presumption 'to reign in the Commonwealth'.

Norfolk and Arundel made it their business at the end of February to contact the Spanish ambassador de Spes, who was confined to his house and under guard. They sent along the Florentine banker, Ridolfi, with whom each had had dealings in the past, and provided 'a safe cipher'. They assured de Spes that the treasure would eventually be returned to Spain, but that as yet they were not strong enough to resist Cecil; they were (as the ambassador managed to report to Alva) 'gathering friends, and were letting the public know what was going on, in the hope and belief that they will be able to turn out the present accursed government and raise another. ... Although Cecil thinks he has them all under his heel, he will find few or none of them stand by him.' Leicester seemed slow to declare himself. De Spes wrote again a fortnight later in much the same vein: the Duke and his friends dared not resist Cecil, he said, or even point out his failings to the Queen, 'until they have felt their way with the other nobles and with the people. This they have now done and have many sure pledges.' Unknown to the ambassador they had already moved.

They intended that in the Queen's absence Cecil, like Thomas Cromwell before him, should be charged at the council table with being an evil adviser, arrested and sent to the Tower. Once he were imprisoned 'means to undo him would not be far to seek'. Queen and Secretary caught wind of the design just in time. She immediately summoned a Privy Council meeting to quash the affair, but everyone who counted – even Leicester – made excuses. She had a further opportunity a day or so later, on Ash Wednesday. Cecil, Norfolk and Northampton were in her chamber before supper when in came Leicester, whom she rebuked for the unbusinesslike behaviour of the council. The Earl thereupon burst into an attack on Cecil, who in the eyes of so many people was ruining the State. She flew to the Secretary's defence, castigating Leicester, while the Duke at the other end of the room said to Northampton (not as an aside, but loud enough for Elizabeth to hear): 'You see, my Lord, how the Earl of Leicester is favoured so long as he supports the Secretary, but now that for good reasons he takes an opposed position, she frowns upon him and wants to send him to the Tower.' 'No, no, he will not go alone,' Northampton replied. 'I praise God that you, the first subject of the realm, are willing at last to show your quality. I am prepared to follow you and to support you in every way I can, for I have come to complain.' The Queen's comment is not recorded. This interview should have shown them all quite plainly that Cecil was not to be sacrificed by his mistress and that if they wanted a change of policy it would mean a change of sovereign.

The conspiracy against Cecil still went on, but it had lost its force. De Spes reported that on three occasions in April, when the others had steeled themselves to act, Leicester 'softened and said he would tell the Queen'. Delays gave Cecil the chance of uncovering the design and he begged his fellow councillors 'not to do anything scandalous', offering to come over to their wishes but saying quite firmly that they must present a united front to Spain.

One of their schemes, apparently, was a plot to accuse Cecil of having caused a book to be written attacking the nobility. Finding that they could not secure his removal, a number of the malcontents rallied round Norfolk to promote his marriage with Mary.

When he first heard of the estrangement between the two men Sussex had thought it the 'worst thing' possible and, although he knew not its cause, he implored Cecil to 'rip up this matter from the bottom with the Duke himself', offering to ride to London – 'yea to Jerusalem' – to act as mediator, if one were needed. A fortnight later, when news arrived of their resumed friendliness, Sussex was delighted, for he had always pinned high hopes on Norfolk as a statesman 'whom the world hath always judged to be void of private inclines'. The outward reconciliation had been achieved largely through Cecil's part in the affair of the Dacre lordship, decided in favour of the Duke. It is improbable that the Duke at this time took Cecil into his confidence, even in the most general terms, by mentioning his hopes of marrying Mary: tactics apart, it was not a matter which he was as yet in a position to reveal. Cecil may even have suggested in good faith that Norfolk should marry his younger sister-in-law, recently widowed; as de Spes put it 'the Duke would not listen to it, for he has his thoughts high, having fixed his eyes upon the Queen of Scotland'.

Following the crisis on Ash Wednesday at least three distinct, yet simultaneous, designs can be traced. There was in the first place the scheme, probably initiated by Maitland, for Mary to marry the Duke, which was now put by Leicester as the sure remedy for the body politic both in England and in Scotland. Throckmorton was the Earl's go-between with Norfolk and later with Pembroke. They discussed the matter with the Bishop of Ross and opened negotiations with the Regent Murray. The terms suggested were that Mary's abdication should be cancelled, Darnley's murder forgotten and a divorce from Bothwell obtained, so that she would be free to marry Norfolk. Once restored to her throne, Mary was to ratify the Treaty of Edinburgh, and the Parliament at Wesminster would then pronounce her heir presumptive to the throne of England. She was on no account to conduct an independent foreign policy, though she was to grant freedom of worship in Scotland.

Leicester later admitted that 'he would not have [Mary] if he might' and that the Duke was only persuaded to contemplate the match to benefit Elizabeth – 'if it was for her commodity he would sacrifice himself'. Ever since Mary had returned from France to Scotland there had been the question of a suitable husband for her. The suggestion now made solved the problem of Mary and her kingdom and also of the English succession at one stroke, for Mary already had a son. The attraction of the scheme for Leicester was just that. It would no longer be of prime importance whom Elizabeth married. The diplomatic manœuvres with Imperial archdukes and French princes would at last cease, to everyone's intense relief, and Dudley could himself marry the Queen and wear the crown matrimonial.

Norfolk hesitated out of discreet convention, but he had already made up his mind before Throckmorton approached him. There were but two obstacles: Cecil's known preference for the Suffolk line of succession, and Elizabeth's aversion to Mary. Leicester aimed at carrying the council with him and then forcing the issue with the Queen, in the face of Cecil's opposition, if necessary. As far as the Duke was concerned his allegiance to Elizabeth was not at stake; as he understood Leicester, he would undertake the affair with his own Queen's permission, even encouragement.

There was, secondly, a more desperate design, directed by Arundel and Lumley, which was supported by Northumberland, Westmorland, Leonard Dacre and the northern Catholics. This had as its objects the liberation and enthronement of Mary in Elizabeth's place and the restoration of Roman Catholicism, with Spanish aid. Mary was to marry Norfolk as a means to this end. At the outset Northumberland and others were suspicious of Norfolk's religious leanings; the best that could be said of him was that he had Catholic connexions, for while he most certainly did not appear as a champion of Protestantism he nonetheless seemed to them undeclared, and as such would be an unsuitable husband for Mary, to whose cause they were attempting to attract the full support of the powers of the Counter Reformation. They expected the Duke of Alva to bring over an army of seasoned troops from Flanders to aid the fifteen thousand men the northerners could put in the field, yet both Alva and Philip II were far too cautious to build on any such hopes. Norfolk was merely on the fringe of these negotiations, for neither Arundel nor the northern earls took him into their confidence until it was too late.

There were, thirdly, Mary's own negotiations with both sets of English conspirators and also with the Scots, which she conducted chiefly through the Bishop of Ross. Though she grasped at straws for her release and restoration she was shrewd enough to beware of dissipating her efforts. To her the cardinal feature of any plan was marriage with Norfolk, and she sought to work upon his ambition, his vanity, his sense of honour and his very real sympathy to bring him to collaborate in her designs. By the middle of May the two of them had exchanged tokens.

Elizabeth watched her courtiers uneasily as the storm gathered during the summer, conscious of the undercurrent of dissatisfaction with her government that might at any time burst into open revolt, especially in the north. As a precaution, she ordered musters of the militia to be taken in the shires. That July a group of friends met at Tattershall in Lincolnshire for a day's hawking on the Clinton estate, where Henry Fiennes, the Admiral's son, played host to Lords Scrope and Berkeley. The day's sport at an end, they all went to a tree and each pulled off a bough and, hand in hand, swore a solemn oath that they would again meet in the self-same spot a year later. As it happened none was able to keep his vow. A generation later Henry Fiennes, by then Earl of Lincoln, was cross-examined about the Tattershall meeting. In the aftermath of Essex's revolt, informers were hard at work and, grasping at old hearsay, they tried to implicate him in the conspiracy of 1569 and accuse him of underhand dealings with Norfolk. He easily cleared himself by assuring his accusers that there had been nothing sinister about the day's hawking or the vow under the greenwood tree: 'they did like the place of their hawking near my house so well that they all vowed to meet that day twelvemonth there'.

That summer the Duke stayed unwillingly at court. At this juncture he could not risk being out of touch with events and he was too troubled to go home to Kenninghall until the air had been cleared by securing Elizabeth's permission for the marriage. He feared she might hear of the plan from an unfriendly source, and after a merry evening with Leicester and Arundel at Bletchingley he returned to Howard House to learn that the Queen 'had been out of quiet'. Cecil, who was now told in confidence what he had long suspected, urged Norfolk more than once to make a clean breast of the affair, but the Duke was reluctant to act against Leicester's advice. The Earl had insisted that the proposal should come from Scotland, preferably at the hands of Maitland, who was daily expected in London. They waited in vain. Norfolk grew impatient with Leicester, who insisted that he must wait for the right moment to speak to Elizabeth to avert disaster. To test his strength Norfolk had asked a leading question of fellow councillors to Pembroke's rooms in Greenwich Palace while Cecil was away. He proposed that Mary should be set at liberty on condition that she married an Englishman, and this motion was passed by an overwhelming majority. Indeed 'the greatest in the land agreed in writing to stand by the Duke to carry this resolution into effect'. At last he and Leicester could confront Elizabeth with the fact that most of the council were in favour of the match, and the French ambassador was convinced that she dare not oppose it. Yet still they tarried.

In those critical days Norfolk missed the guidance of his closest friend, Sussex, and he had no one else to turn to for advice. His alliance with Leicester was first to last an uneasy one, a marriage of convenience in which the vows were taken in order to be broken. Pembroke lacked strength of purpose and was then under Leicester's domination. The Duke's relations with Cecil could never be the same after the intrigues of the past spring, and the wily Secretary

characteristically refused to commit himself until the Queen had made up her mind. Only Sussex could have steeled Norfolk's irresolution and made him stand up for himself against Leicester, only from Sussex would he have taken to heart a warning to stop playing with fire, and the latter rued the day he had been sent to York as Lord President and had thus been denied the opportunity of stopping Norfolk's folly.

At the end of July the court had moved to Richmond, and Norfolk followed a day or so later, even more anxious to have the matter settled. When he came across Leicester fishing in the Thames near his house at Kew, he learned that affairs had reached a critical stage: some women at court had babbled to the Queen, who became convinced that they were going to proceed with their plans for the marriage without consulting her – indeed, 'that the matter was already concluded'. Leicester had satisfied her, so he said, that such tales were false, but he made it clear to Norfolk that they must walk warily and pick their time most carefully for speaking with Elizabeth on the topic.

The Queen gave Norfolk a chance of speaking out himself a day or so before the court left Richmond on progress. He had just returned from a visit to Howard House and was talking in the garden when Elizabeth noticed him and called him to her side. What news had her cousin to tell her? The Duke replied that he knew of nothing. 'No!' she exclaimed, 'You come from London and can tell no news of a marriage?' It was a dramatic moment. Just then Lady Clinton came up, and rather than wait and say his piece when the lady withdrew, Norfolk took the opportunity of slinking off to Leicester's rooms. He was dumbfounded, yet determined after the Queen's broad hint

BELOW LEFT Greenwich Palace from the south east, showing the huddled roofs and towers of the Tudor palace with the river beyond: early seventeenth-century painting.
BELOW RIGHT Richmond Palace: a detail from John Norden's map of Surrey.

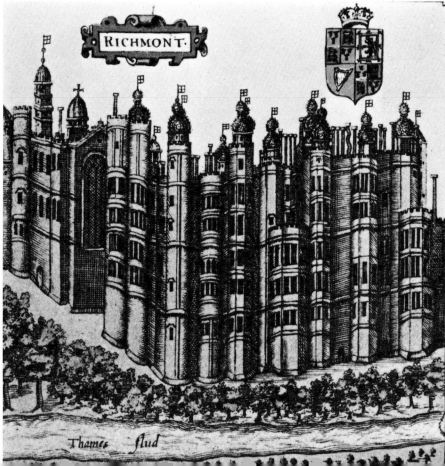

RICHMONT

Thames flud

to persuade the Earl to let him tell her himself. As luck would have it Leicester was out stag-hunting near Kingston, but Norfolk waited patiently in his rooms talking with Throckmorton until he returned. Dudley again insisted on secrecy until he had spoken with Elizabeth. As a result no steps had been taken to obtain the Queen's permission when she left Richmond on 5 August for her summer progress.

Norfolk was an unwilling member of the royal entourage, for a royal progress was for him the worst aspect of a courtier's life. He had hitherto avoided them by spending the summer on his estates, but in August 1569 he had to accompany the Queen to keep Leicester up to his promises. After a few days at the royal manor of Oatlands near Weybridge Elizabeth journeyed to Guildford and then spent two days at Loseley, the fine house in Guildford Park which Sir William More had finished building the previous year. The Duke again spoke earnestly with Leicester and the next morning (probably 12 August), as he was going into the room that was being used as the Privy Chamber, he found one of Sir William's children 'playing upon a lute and singing, Her Majesty sitting upon the threshold of the door, my Lord of Leicester kneeling by Her Highness'. Months afterwards the Duke vividly recalled that charming scene:

Her Majesty commanded me to come by, into her chamber. Not long after my Lord of Leicester rises and came to me, leaving Her Highness hearing the child, and told me that as I was coming, he was dealing with Her Majesty in my behalf; to which I answered, if I had known so much I would not have come up; but I desired to know how he found Her Majesty, when he told me, indifferent well, and that Her Highness had promised to speak with me at Thornham.

Thornham was Arundel's house in Kent, where they were due much later in the progress. Before then, in fact, Elizabeth had put out another feeler. At Farnham on 15 August she requested the Duke to dine alone at her table, but he still found himself unable to speak about the affair, partly out of timidity, partly for fear of upsetting Leicester's plans, and at the end of the meal she gave him a nip, saying 'that she would wish me to take good heed to my pillow' – an allusion to their interview nine months back. 'I was abashed at Her Majesty's speech,' Norfolk confessed, 'but I thought it not fit time nor place there to trouble her.' He had been given three opportunities of speaking in ten days and he had let all three slip by. There was no excuse for his behaviour and he had given the Queen abundant reason for concluding he had forfeited her confidence.

The progress continued at a leisurely pace but, after staying with the court for a few days at Southampton, the Duke returned to London. Both Leicester and, apparently, Cecil promised to speak with the Queen in his absence. While at Southampton he told Richard Cavendish that 'before he lost that marriage he would lose his life' and boasted about his ability to handle the affair, yet in London he was now desperate. He approved a plan for Northumberland and his old enemy Leonard Dacre to descend on Wingfield to rescue Mary Queen of Scots from Shrewsbury's custody once the Duke should give the signal, and Northumberland proudly claimed that 'the whole of the north' was at his devotion. After a fortnight away from court Norfolk was more at ease, and Pembroke wrote to him from the Lord Treasurer's house at Basing that Elizabeth dare not refuse her permission to the marriage as

ABOVE The Queen's bed-
room at Loseley House,
near Guildford, Surrey,
the home of Sir William
More. Elizabeth is
reputed to have stayed
in this room during her
visit to Loseley in
August 1569.

RIGHT Two 'maids-of-
honour' chairs, supposedly
worked by the Queen and
her ladies, now at
Loseley House.

there was not a person about her who dared to give her contrary advice. And then Cecil wrote a day or so later from The Vyne, near Basingstoke, warning him to hasten to court as the Queen had asked for him; Cecil's views about the marriage had hardened after a letter from Hunsdon, who spoke out against it most strongly, despite his affection for Norfolk.

Norfolk reluctantly rode south, but instead of seeking an audience straightway he bided his time, awaiting a summons to the presence. Leicester in the meanwhile had taken to his bed at Titchfield Abbey, the Earl of Southampton's mansion in Hampshire – a tactical sickness. He begged Elizabeth to visit him, and when she came to his bedside on 6 September, anxious and

Holograph letter written by Thomas Howard, 4th Duke of Norfolk, from his mansion at Kenninghall to 'Mr Secretary' Cecil, 31 August 1559.

full of sympathy as always, he for the first time revealed the full details of the plan for the marriage with Mary. Though he swore that his own loyalty was never at issue, he craved her pardon. That same day in the gallery at Titch-field she rated Norfolk, and in a temper, deciding that the time of friendly warnings was past, she charged him on his allegiance 'to deal no further with the Scottish cause'. To escape her wrath he promised to give over his preten-sions and told her he had 'a very slight regard' for Mary. Her position and fortunes if she were to be restored, were, he said, no attraction for him; indeed his own 'revenues in England were not much less than those of the Kingdom of Scotland ... and that when he was in his Tennis Court at Norwich he thought himself in a manner equal with some kings'. He could not put away his pride even in the act of penitence, but at last he knew where he stood. Elizabeth was as stubborn as he and had determined that in the light of the widespread political unrest the projected marriage would spell disaster for her. All the delays and lack of co-ordination in their designs had strengthened her position and made Leicester and his group look like whispering conspira-tors who would never come into the open. During those six tense weeks the Duke had constantly pressed Leicester to act as he had promised, yet he had shirked it and forbidden Norfolk to speak to the Queen on his own behalf. The Duke was slow to realise the way things had been going and slower still to grasp that Leicester had been deceiving him.

He did not at once escape from court, for such would have aroused the worst suspicions, but remained with the progress, uncertain of his plans. Courtiers began to shun him. 'I am right sorry,' he told Cecil, 'that no man can keep me company without offence. I never deserved to be so ill thought of. I hope time will bring her Majesty to like of them which wish best to herself and till then I must bear all overwarts with patience.' He still hoped that his mistress would change her mind, but the hope became daily much fainter. Each day he grew more uneasy. No other peer joined him at table, everyone was whispering about him, and, worst of all, Leicester treated him with cold disdain. At last he could stand it no longer and left, without seeking formal leave to depart from court. Instead he let it be known that he needed to be in London for some days to prepare for some law suits that were coming up in Michaelmas term. A servant of Arundel met him as he left Titchfield and suggested in all seriousness that they should take the Tower, but the Duke thought it a monstrous idea. On the way he called in at Wilton to talk matters over with Pembroke, who hoped that he could still influence the Queen, but Norfolk reckoned that persuasions were now useless. In London he found no peace of mind, for there were too many rumours about him.

Elizabeth was anxious now for her own safety, fearing that the withdrawal of her principal courtier was the prologue to a general rising which would bring under one banner all the opponents of her regime, rescue Mary from Wingfield and advance on London. Already there was an alliance between her two most formidable enemies, the religious malcontents in the north under Northumberland and the political malcontents among the ranks of the Privy Council, and the slightest pressure might plunge England into civil war. The Duke's great popularity and his hold over East Anglia made up for his lack of courage. Cecil as yet knew nothing about possible aid to Mary's cause from Philip II or Alva, but feared the worst. To surmount the crisis, the most dangerous moment since her accession, Elizabeth swiftly made her dispositions. Huntingdon was sent to Wingfield to supersede Shrewsbury, who was ill, as Mary's jailer, with orders to remove her for greater safety to Tutbury. The ports were closed and the militia alerted. Elizabeth would shut herself in Windsor Castle, prepared to stand a siege if need be.

But there was still the chance of calling Norfolk's bluff, and the Queen instructed Leicester and Cecil to write to him jointly, ordering him to repair to Windsor and submit. Norfolk pleaded an ague. He told Cecil that he did not wish to risk going about until the attack was quite over, but he hoped to be at Windsor by 26 September. Mary wrote from Tutbury to Fénélon, the French ambassador, asking him to warn the Duke of the dangers of imprisonment and another letter from Leicester petrified Norfolk when it warned him of the likelihood of being sent to the Tower. He rode from London to Kenninghall in great fear and, once home, wrote to Elizabeth: 'My enemies found such comfort of Your Highness's heavy displeasure that they began to make of me a common table talk; my friends were afraid of my company.' Overnight he realised that he had become 'a suspected person' and he saw the shadow of the Tower 'which is too great a terror for a true man'. He wrote telling friends that he had withdrawn himself 'to procure a remedy against indignant rumours which are always entertained at Court'.

When Elizabeth heard of his leaving London she did not realise that it was a retreat but imagined it was the signal for rebellion, and everyone at court assumed he had ridden north, not to Kenninghall. Arundel and Pembroke were ordered to keep to their lodgings under house arrest and Lumley was summoned to court. Camden, who later enjoyed Cecil's confidence, wrote that 'all the whole court hung in suspense and fear lest he [Norfolk] should break forth into rebellion; and it was determined (so the report went) if he did so, forthwith to put the Queen of Scots to death'. Letters were sent to all lords lieutenant to scotch rumours that Elizabeth intended to deal harshly with the Duke, 'Her Majesty being loath to have such a noble man abused with untrue reports', and Cecil anxiously awaited letters from Sussex on the state of the north. For eleven years there had been peace within the realm. It was almost unprecedented: Mary Tudor had had to face the supporters of Lady Jane Grey and of Thomas Wyatt; her brother's reign had seen the Prayer Book Rising in the West and Ket's Rebellion; even her father's position had been seriously challenged by the Pilgrimage of Grace. Twice in the last hundred years the Crown had been seized by claimants with far fewer influential supporters than Norfolk could command, far fewer troops than Northumberland could muster. Yet, instead of emulating Edward of York or Henry Tudor, Norfolk now astounded his countrymen by doing nothing.

Throughout the country men expected Norfolk to lead a movement which would put back the clock in religion and politics, a rising not so much against the Crown as against its 'evil advisers' – for long the formula favoured by English rebels. The Earls of Northumberland and Westmorland had promised him that if he could not achieve his purpose with Elizabeth's goodwill he could count on their assistance 'to the uttermost of their powers'. This was no idle promise, and there were plans to liberate Mary, murder her keeper and march on Windsor, once the Duke should set up his standard. He was popular in the country, had behind him the moral support of most of the nobility and could count on the overwhelming sympathy which so many felt for Mary. But instead of taking the field proudly as Surrey's son, Norfolk lay paralysed by fear for his own safety at Kenninghall. De Spes, who had strongly advised him to stay at his palace and rally his supporters, thought he would only be ruined by 'his own pusillanimity', and ruined he was. He ruled out flight abroad and after a miserable day and night, feeling desperately ill, he felt he could never lead a rebellion but decided to submit to the Queen. Before he was well enough to move she commanded him on his allegiance to repair to Windsor, and when he hesitated, the gentleman pensioner who was sent to him was ordered to remove him by a litter if need be, for his 'case was notorious'.

Within ten days Norfolk was in the Tower, but before he left Kenninghall he sent a message to the Earl of Westmorland, his brother-in-law, at Topcliffe, to call off the projected rising, for if he and Northumberland should rebel 'it should cost him his head'. When the messenger arrived Lady Westmorland commented to her husband 'what a simple man the Duke is to begin a matter and not to go through with it'. Four weeks later it was to be Lady Westmorland's words that swayed the wavering Earls to action, for it was more than she could bear to see her husband emulating her brother's timid behaviour. Elizabeth came to admire her spirit and after her husband, the last of the Nevilles, had fled abroad when the rebellion failed, the Queen allowed Countess Jane to live at Kenninghall and granted her an annuity; she lived on until 1593, but never came to court.

The arms of Thomas Howard, 4th Duke of Norfolk, England's sole Duke in the reign of Elizabeth, and hereditary Earl Marshal. His arms include the leopards of England, showing his closeness to the blood royal; it was for heraldic offences that Norfolk's father, the poet Surrey, was executed in 1547.

Norfolk's fall encompassed others before the northern rebellion had broken out. Throckmorton, the broker between Leicester and the Duke, was closely questioned in the Tower and then put under house arrest at his Carshalton farm. In February 1571 he was taken mortally ill with pleurisy at Leicester's London home, though Dudley's enemies insisted he had been poisoned. His mantle was to fall on Francis Walsingham. Southampton was charged with being privy to the marriage plans, as was Pembroke, the Lord Steward, who established his innocence and after a brief period of detention at court was permitted to go home to Wilton. Although Pembroke was back at court by the end of the year, he was to die the following spring. Arundel was, with justification, kept in custody for rather longer and then required to remain at Nonsuch. Leicester, however, went scot free. Cecil explained that, since he had revealed all he knew of the project for Mary's marriage, 'Her Majesty spareth her displeasure the more towards him,' though for anyone else it would have been the Tower.

More damning in the Queen's view than the evidence provided from the peers under arrest was the attitude of Sussex, Norfolk's great friend who held the key post of Lord President of the Council in the North at this critical time when the country was in ferment. Sussex was not the man to panic into believing all the rumours that were afoot of intended risings. Much more in command of the situation than Cecil imagined, he felt he could handle the Earls in his own way. He summoned both of them to York to require their assistance in scotching the rumours and sent them to their homes to be ready to deal with any hotheads. 'I trust the fire is spent with the smoke,' he reported to Cecil on 10 October – 'a great bruit of an intended rebellion, the cause of which is yet unknown, and which I think is now at an end' – and he placed his faith in temporising to avoid open action until the restlessness should die with the coming of winter.

Elizabeth was not satisfied with this policy. Sussex's close friendship with Norfolk had placed him under suspicion and she was not only convinced that he underestimated the gravity of the situation but also feared he must abuse the trust placed in him, at best to treat the Earls with more sympathy than they deserved, at worst to come down openly on their side. She intended to deal with Northumberland and Westmorland as she had dealt with the Duke, and on 24 October ordered Sussex to send for them without delay and in her name summon them to court. He was also to report to her all that he knew about the proposed rising, including the authors of the rumours, and at the same time the other members of his council were to write individually to Cecil about the disturbing recent events – an indication of the Queen's lack of confidence in the Lord President. Sussex told her that all his council agreed with him that it were best, for the sake of keeping the country quiet, to postpone an examination of the causes of the recent troubles and to delay sending for the Earls until dead of winter, but seeing her pleasure was otherwise he had now summoned the Earls to York once more and would command them to go to Windsor. His intelligence about who had been conferring with the Earls and the nature of their discussions was remarkably accurate, judging from Northumberland's later confession: 'the motives of their counsels seem of divers natures – some specially respect the Duke of Norfolk, some the Scottish Queen, some religion and some, perhaps, all three yet use my Lord of Norfolk for a cover to the rest'.

The Earls feared for their safety as Norfolk had feared for his, and his fate made it impossible for them to believe that submission would not mean the Tower. When they requested to be excused from attending on Sussex at York, pleading urgent business, the President sent a pursuivant to them on 4 November, demanding their immediate appearance. Northumberland temporised – he would come in a few days when his business was settled – but Westmorland sent a blank refusal: 'I dare not come where my enemies are without bringing such a force to protect me as might be misliked; therefore I think it better to stay at home and use myself as an obedient subject.' Sussex wrote again, warning them not to be frightened of their own shadows, but while his messenger was still at Topcliffe late on 9 November the bells of the church were rung backwards as a signal to raise revolt, and next day, under Lady Westmorland's goading, they rode with their supporters to Durham. From there they issued a proclamation stating that the object of Norfolk, Arundel, Pembroke, themselves and others of 'the ancient nobility' was to determine 'to whom of mere right the true succession of the crown appertaineth'.

Yet for the Earls the recognition of Mary's right was secondary to the restoration of Roman Catholicism. Their proclamation at Ripon, which they addressed to all members of 'the old Catholic religion' on 16 November, made this quite clear:

Forasmuch as divers evil-disposed persons about the Queen's Majesty have, by their subtle and crafty dealing to advance themselves, overcome in this our realm the true and Catholic religion towards God and by the same abused the Queen, disordered the realm and now lastly seek and procure the destruction of the nobility, we therefore have gathered ourselves together to resist by force, and the rather by the help of God and you good people, to see redress of those things amiss, with restoring of all ancient customs and liberties to God's church and this whole realm ...

Though Norfolk's fate was recognised in 'the destruction of the nobility', Mary's claims did not feature at all; nevertheless their plan of campaign hinged on her release.

Bypassing York they rode on south, from Ripon to Wetherby, Knaresborough and Cawood, to reach Selby on 24 November, where they were within striking distance of Tutbury. Sussex, with only the skeleton of local levies at his disposition, did not try to halt them. But on 25 November, when Mary was hastily removed to Coventry, the rebels were checked abruptly in their plans; to proceed further south was out of the question owing to the threat of Hunsdon's army, and as they withdrew north, intending to give battle to Hunsdon on their own ground, the heart was taken out of the rebellion. As the pace of the retreat quickened, their numbers melted away in the face of deteriorating weather and internal dissension, until they reached Brancepeth again. The foreign aid promised by Alva to Northumberland never materialised, even though the rebels had captured Hartlepool as a suitable port for him to disembark troops. At Durham on 15 December the Earls decided to flee before it was too late, and with a few horsemen rode from Hexham and across the Pennines, to Naworth and thence into Scotland. The following February Hunsdon defeated Leonard Dacre in a last-ditch action near Naworth.

Elizabeth was relieved that no other peers rode with the rebel Earls, for

❧ A Proclamation set foorth by Therle

of Sussex, the Queenes Maiesties Lieuetenaunt generall in
the North, declaring truely the falsehodes and
vayne delusions vvherby Therles of Northumberlande
and VVestmerlande, and their confederates, do abuse the
Queenes Maiesties subiectes, to mayntayn their
rebellious enterprises, the xxviii. of
Nouember 1569.

Here Therles of Northumberlande and westmerlande, with their confederates haue most vndutifully and vnnaturally conspired to leuie warre against their and our most gratious soueraine Lady the Queenes Maiestie, and therevpon haue entred into open and actuall rebellion, and to couer their wicked and detestable attemptes, haue abused and deluded many of her Maiesties subiectes in these partes, sometymes commaunding them in her highnesse name to repayre to them in warlike maner for the defence and suretie of her Maiesties person, when their intent of calling them was in deede to mainteine their horrible treasons, and therby to put in perill her most royall person, whom God long preserue, sometymes affirming their doynges to be with thaduise and consent of the nobilitie of this Realme, who in deede be wholly bent (as manifestly doth appeare) to spende their lyues in dutifull obedience against them and all other traytours, somtimes pretending for conscience sake to seeke to refourme religion, where in deede it is manifestly knowen many of them neuer had care of conscience, or euer respected any religion, but continued a dissolute lyfe, vntyll at this present they were dryuen to pretende a popishe holynesse, to put some false colour vpon their manifest treasons, directly against the commaundement of God in holy scripture, the lawes of this Realme, and the auncient prerogatiue of the imperiall crowne of Englande, sometymes declaring that they be dryuen to take this matter in hande, lest otherwyse forraine princes myght take it vpon them, to the great perill of this Realme: where in deede they not contented with the good quiet and publique administration of iustice, so long continued vnder the Queenes Maiestie, as the lyke was neuer before in any princes tyme, haue by all the wicked meanes they could, practised with forrayne princes to ayde them in this wicked enterprise, and thereby sought not only the manifest perill of our most gratious soueraigne Ladyes person, state, and dignitie royall, but also to bryng the whole Realme to perpetuall thraldome and miserie, vnder the subiection and slauerie of forrayne powers and potentates, hoping therby to satisfie some part of their licentious and dissolute myndes, and sometymes couering their naughtie intentes with a shewe of desire to preserue the state of the auncient nobilitie from destruction, prepared (as they say) against them: where in deede it manifestly appeareth, that in whole twelue yeres past the Queenes Maiestie hath had such care of the preseruing of that state, as from the beginning of her raigne to this houre there hath not perished one of that flocke, and they them selues who abuse the people with these slaunderous deuises, haue most gratiously and liberally tasted of her Maiesties fauour, good countenaunce, bountie, and familier vsage, more then others dyd of their equalles, and farre aboue their desertes, and of whom her Maiestie had conceaued so good opinion, as hardly coulde she of long tyme be induced to thinke that either such lacke of duetie coulde enter into their heartes agaynst their soueraigne, or such ingratitude against her that had so liberally dealt with them, and so louingly vsed them, although she manifestly knewe that some of them liued in daunger of her lawes, whereof she gaue them to vnderstande she had good knowledge, and dyd tollerate with them in hope of their loyalties otherwayes.

Proclamation by the Earl of Sussex, Lord President of the Council in the North, declaring that the Earls of Northumberland and Westmorland were traitors, 28 November 1569.

intelligence reaching Windsor had suggested otherwise. It was Sussex's unshaken loyalty that had been the overriding factor, even though his cousin Egremont Radcliffe had sided with the rebels. Ties of blood counted little, for though his daughter had married Northumberland, the Catholic Earl of Worcester did not move; and the Earl of Cumberland who had married Dacre's sister remained loyal – surprisingly, for he was completely out of sympathy with the new regime and had not been to court since Elizabeth's coronation. Northumberland's appeal to the Earl of Derby for support fell on deaf ears while the Catholic Lords Wharton and Monteagle stayed aloof. With other courtiers there was a closing of the ranks. The Queen had at once sent Cousin Hunsdon to York as her general, while Clinton and Warwick commanded supporting forces which included many men from court eager for action, greedy for plunder and hopeful of grants of traitors' lands when the fighting was over. Among the young men in arms were Cecil's ward, the Earl of Rutland, and his elder son Thomas. In case of an attempt to land foreign troops to aid the rebels, Bedford was appointed to command the West Country and Pembroke to defend the Queen's person. Huntingdon and Viscount Hereford were commissioned to move the Queen of Scots to Coventry and to guard her most closely, but Leicester was given no military role – he was to stay by Elizabeth's side at Windsor, and once the crisis had passed he went home to Kenilworth.

Gradually the estates of the Earls and their principal followers were distributed among fervent supporters of the Elizabethan regime, few of whom had any previous links with the north. Some properties, such as Raby, were kept in Crown hands for a number of years for strategic reasons, but most were parcelled out to the men who had sided with Hunsdon, Clinton and Sussex, and this redistribution of lands, much more extensive than the granting out of abbey estates a generation earlier, helped to break down the particularism of the north. The close ties binding tenant to feudal overlord for those who had known no prince but a Percy, a Neville, or a Dacre, were cut once and for all in 1570.

Three months after Hunsdon's victory the Bull *Regnans in Excelsis* was published, by which Pope Pius v deposed Elizabeth and absolved her Catholic subjects from allegiance to her. A price was put on her head so that she might be 'deprived of her pretended right to her realm'. This precipitate action, coming far too late to stiffen the resolve of potential rebels under the Banner of the Five Wounds of Christ, provoked a spate of penal legislation against English Catholics who at last had to make an effective choice between their sovereign and their Church. Thus began the drift of the faithful to exile in Flanders and Italy, since all who continued to obey the Queen were liable to the dreadful papal sentence of anathema.

The Rebellion had ensured that both Mary and Norfolk would be kept in close custody. Elizabeth, who had hoped to be able to charge the Duke with high treason, was shown to her dismay that he had not infringed the Treasons Statute, but she did not know how to deal with him, any more than she knew what action she could take against her other cousin. In time Norfolk was released from the Tower to his own mansion at the Charterhouse, once he had made a full submission and promised never to deal with Mary again. He now came under the sway of Roberto Ridolfi, the Venetian banker, who was convinced that the English were too inexperienced as revolutionaries to make their own plans. He won over the Bishop of Ross and the Spanish ambassador to his grand design for a general rising, with foreign support, to rescue Mary, enthrone her in Elizabeth's place and re-establish Catholicism. Ridolfi believed that every second Englishman most fervently desired to spring to arms in obedience to the Papal Bull and confidently listed various peers who promised to raise between them 39,000 men. An analysis of the English nobility he made with the help of Arundel and Lumley six months later put thirty-three peers as Catholics, sixteen as 'Heretics' and fifteen as 'Doubtful' or 'Neutral' – the last group including Leicester and Sussex. Thus as a militant crusader of the Counter Reformation Ridolfi began to weave the threads of the conspiracy bearing his name, which was destined to bring about Norfolk's final downfall.

By September 1571 the government knew sufficient details of the plot to send Norfolk back to the Tower. 'My Lord of Norfolk's causes filleth out daily more and more to the offence of Her Majesty,' wrote Cecil to Shrewsbury, 'whereof in respect of the honour and love I bear him I am right sorry.' Only now did the Duke begin to realise the seriousness of his offence; for three years he had been following a will-o'-the-wisp, strangely unaware that it was any but the most honourable path he had been treading.

While Elizabeth was thankful that at last the conspiracy had been laid bare, she took cold comfort in the fact that various of her nobles had to a greater or lesser degree been involved in Norfolk's schemings. Whom beside Burghley could she trust? By mid-October Lumley had been sent to the Marshalsea Prison; Southampton, another zealous papist, was again in the Tower; while Cobham was under arrest in Cecil House and Arundel placed under guard in Arundel House; as yet she knew nothing of the young Earl of Oxford's intrigues. Since Norfolk was connected by marriage to all the chief nobility, Elizabeth could not but feel there might be others sympathetic to his cause, and if tried by his peers what would their verdict be? At least one of Derby's sons and a stepson of Shrewsbury were deep in the plot, and over the water and north of the border there were others intriguing for all they were worth. Among courtiers even Christopher Hatton seemed uncertain in his loyalties. Cecil apart, Elizabeth could rely only upon Bacon, Knollys, Sadler and Hunsdon among the inner circle of her council; but none of these was popular, while Cecil, her greatest supporter, had earned much enmity up and down the land.

Despite the treacherous role Norfolk had played, there was still much sympathy in the country for the Duke, for the people loved him dearly. In the north and in his own East Anglia men could not believe that the Queen would not pardon him. When it was obvious that he could not possibly escape arraignment, could not possibly be acquitted, courtiers began to cast envious eyes on his lands and offices. Some had coveted his possessions as early as his first disgrace at Titchfield two and a half years before, but now the crows prepared to swoop in earnest. A week before Christmas Hunsdon openly told Burghley that he was hoping to be made Keeper of Howard House. 'I dare not ask it as a gift of the Queen,' he added, as it was too princely a mansion and he knew his sovereign too well.

In January 1572 Norfolk went before his peers in Westminster Hall, with Shrewsbury as Lord High Steward, and the verdict was a foregone conclusion. The Queen tarried so long over signing her cousin's death warrant that not a few courtiers expected she would pardon him. Elizabeth could not make up her mind whether or not to allow the law to take its course. She drafted orders, then hastily cancelled them. As Cecil told Walsingham, when the Queen thought of her own danger she was determined that justice should be done; next day, when she considered Norfolk's 'nearness of blood, of his superiority of honour, etc., she stayeth'. Lesser traitors received their sentences, yet Norfolk remained. Every ounce of evidence that he could supply

My lord me thinkes that I am more beholdinge to the hinder
part of my hed than wel dare trust the forwards side
of the same, and therfor sent to the Lieutenant
and the S. as you knowe best the ordar to
defar this execution till the hier furdar
and that this may be done I doute nothing
without curiocitie of any further warrant
for that her rasche determination upon
a very unfit day was countermanded by
your considerat admonition the cause that
moved me to this ar not now to be expressed
lest an irrevocable dede be in mene while
comitted. If the wyl nides a warrant
let this suffice all writen with my none
hand. Your most lovinge soveraine

Elizabeth R

Elizabeth's letter to
Lord Burghley, further
delaying the Duke of
Norfolk's execution.
He had been found guilty
by his peers on
16 January 1572, but was
not executed until
2 June following.
(Ms. Ashm. 1729. fol. 13r)

about Mary Queen of Scots had been squeezed from him and as a witness of
State he had outlived his usefulness. 'God's will be fulfilled and aid Her
Majesty to do herself good,' muttered Cecil, his patience almost at an end,
as his mistress delayed yet again.

When Parliament had met at the beginning of May, the demands for
Norfolk's head on a charger had grown to a deafening shout, but Elizabeth
had steadily resisted, and by the end of the month even Leicester could see
'no likelihood of her surrendering to the clamour'. Then at last Cecil persuaded his mistress that the sentence could be delayed no more. He saw the
Ridolfi conspiracy as a godsend, and intended exploiting it to the full to
consolidate his position. 'The adverse party must needs increase when they
see justice forbear against the principal, and him spared to set up the mark,'
Cecil had written early in April. For reasons of state traitors must go to the
block and that right soon; and he knew that unless he got his way over Norfolk

there would be no hope of persuading the Queen to bring Mary Queen of Scots to justice. Elizabeth could not indefinitely hold out against the logic of statecraft. She finally agreed to sign the warrant and not retract, but for years to come Norfolk's death would gnaw at her conscience and she would lay the blame for it on Cecil.

The fall of England's sole Duke left a void at court. Leicester, who under different circumstances would have profited most from Norfolk's removal from court politics and from Sussex's absence in York, had become isolated as a direct result of his schemings for the Norfolk-Mary marriage; the unnatural alliance between Duke and favourite early in 1569 now left Dudley without an ally in council, though he remained the most powerful influence with the Queen. It was Cecil who reaped the real benefit from Norfolk's treachery, since the failure of the Northern Rebellion was seen as an overwhelming vote of confidence in his style of government. In recognition of his unique role in political affairs Elizabeth had elevated him to the peerage as Baron Burghley, and on Winchester's death he succeeded as Lord Treasurer; he was no longer a *parvenu*. Leicester's flirtation with Catholic conspirators made it easy for Burghley in the months following the Bull of 1570 to appear (as he had always wanted to) in the role of champion of Protestantism which the favourite had tried to play, and he could count on the permanent backing of Knollys, Mildmay and Bacon. English Protestants had been deeply shocked at the fate of their co-religionists in the Netherlands during Alva's rule of blood and many identified their own creed more closely with Dutch Calvinism than Burghley thought politic, yet in the struggle with the forces of the Counter Reformation, whether at home or on the Continent, there could be no doubt of the Treasurer's own standpoint. Before long Leicester would be able to make capital out of Burghley's unwillingness to aid foreign Protestants or to press for root and branch reforms in the English Church, so that he himself could adopt a more radical stance and build up a party at court, finding as his chief ally Sir Francis Walsingham, Burghley's successor as Secretary.

Elizabeth's warm appreciation to Hunsdon on his victory over Dacre promised to increase his livelihood, nor was he disappointed in his desire for 'picking a salad' from Percy property. Warwick, too, received substantial land grants. A year after Cecil's elevation two other stalwarts of the 1569 campaign were promoted, for Admiral Clinton became Earl of Lincoln and Viscount Hereford who, with Huntingdon, had guarded Mary at the most critical time, became Earl of Essex. Besides these promotions there was a series of appointments in the early seventies which, taken together, mark the coming of age of a new generation of courtiers to replace others dead, disgraced or retired. Pembroke, who in 1569 had kept on the windy side of the law to preserve the estates he had clung to during four reigns, died the following March and after an interval was succeeded as Lord Steward by Lincoln. Northampton and Winchester, both of them survivors from the court of Henry VIII, died in 1571 and Derby the year after. Northampton had married as his last wife Helena Snakenburg, a Swedish girl who had come to England in the train of Cecilia, Margravine of Baden, and had been found a post among the maids of honour. Some years after Northampton's death she married Sir Thomas Gorges, a gentleman usher of the Privy Chamber, and

William Somerset,
3rd Earl of Worcester
(1526-89): portrait by
Hans Eworth.

the Queen granted them the old manor of Sheen, near Richmond Park in 1583. It was to Helena that Spenser dedicated his *Daphnaida*. Other links with the past had been snapped with the passing of Petre and Rich. The toll included Cumberland, who had so disdained the court, and Throckmorton, who would have liked to cut a greater figure there; the latter's post of Chief Butler of England went to Warwick.

The Queen's great-uncle, Howard of Effingham, now laid down his office of Lord Chamberlain and *honoris causa* the post of Lord Privy Seal was revived for him, though he held it for less than a year. Sussex left York with relief to succeed as Lord Chamberlain, glad to be able to continue the duel with Leicester at close quarters, and his place as President of the Council in the North went to Huntingdon, the Puritan Earl. Within the immediate circle of the court there were other changes. Sir Francis Knollys became Treasurer of the Household, while there was promotion for two courtiers in whom Elizabeth took especial delight, Sir Thomas Heneage, now appointed Treasurer of the Chamber, and Christopher Hatton who became Captain of the Gentlemen Pensioners or ceremonial guard. Knollys's Puritanism had not mellowed with the years and to balance him Elizabeth resurrected to the council Sir James Croft, who was known to hold Catholic sympathies, and possibly to be a pensioner of Spain. The Earl of Worcester, no less a Catholic by conviction than Croft, was now given the Garter and appointed to serve as deputy Earl Marshal. It says much for the Queen's tolerance and continued striving for a middle way in the face of the outcry against Catholics and their fellow travellers that Croft and Worcester were assigned responsible posts. Elizabeth's cousin, Sir Thomas Sackville, who had been created Lord Buckhurst in 1567, became a Privy Councillor four years later, an honour also accorded to Mary's custodian, Shrewsbury.

Amidst all these changes Leicester remained secure in his post of Master of the Horse, though with the promotion of Heneage and Hatton and the début of Oxford he could no longer reckon on a monopoly of the Queen's affections. Hatton made his supplications in heartbroken terms to his sovereign lady to keep him near to her and hold out to him some slight hope of attaining his elusive dream of happiness; for her sake he remained celibate to the end and would never cease reminding her of his unswerving devotion.

It was through a remarkable performance in the tiltyard before the Queen in 1571, that Edward de Vere Earl of Oxford, just twenty-one, made his mark at court and at once found himself in high favour. He had been bred for the court as a ward in Burghley's household from the age of twelve and had developed to a high degree many of the accomplishments that Castiglione had listed. Besides a thorough grasp of classical scholarship, he could play the virginals with enviable dexterity, his lyrics were far superior to the versifying of the average court poet and now he excelled on horseback with a lance. The exhausting time-table of his student days had begun with a dancing lesson at seven every morning, which seemed in retrospect a most valuable preparation, as Elizabeth was always dancing with the graceful lad with the brown hair and hazel eyes. Just when Oxford seemed set on a brilliant career he announced his engagement to Burghley's daughter Anne, aged fifteen, and their wedding took place in Westminster Abbey in the Queen's presence. It proved a disastrous match, for Oxford was soon as tired of Anne as of life at court. Despite more than one foolish incident he remained

Edward Vere 17th Earle of Oxford
Lord high Chamberlaine of Eng ld.
Married 1st Ann Daughter to
Wm Cecil Lord Burghley 2dly
Eliz Daughter to Thos Trentham
of Roucester in Com: Stafford
and died 24th of June 1604

the darling of Elizabeth, and Sussex pinned his hopes on Leicester's influence being reduced as a result of the young man's ascendancy. It was noted that the Queen 'delighteth more in his personage and his dancing and valiantness than any other. I think Sussex doth back him all he can. If it were not for his fickle head he would pass any of them shortly.' Fickleness was to be his undoing.

All favourites had been put on their mettle by fresh attempts to marry the Queen to a foreign prince. While Norfolk was spending his last summer in the Charterhouse, Charles IX had signed the Treaty of St Germain with the Huguenots to end the Third Religious War. A coalition of moderate Catholics and Huguenots was now in power, and for the first time significant concessions were made to French Protestants. There now returned to France two Huguenot aristocrats who had spent the last few years in England, where they had been much at court. One was Coligny's brother, Cardinal Châtillon, who retained his ecclesiastical title despite embracing the reformed faith and a wife, the other was the Vidame de Chartres. They saw the danger of Duke Henry of Anjou, the King's next brother, remaining in France, for he was a puppet of the Catholic Guise faction. Catherine de'Medici had long realised that unless Anjou were found a niche abroad he would continue to be a thorn in her side, a liability to the internal peace of France, and she agreed to Châtillon's suggestion that feelers should be put out to England for a possible marriage with Elizabeth. Cecil talked with the Queen and together they saw merit in pursuing the idea to counter Guise intrigues on behalf of Mary Queen of Scots and protect England against isolation in a hostile Europe. Reports from France suggested that unless Anjou were safely married to Elizabeth 'it will be most dangerous, as he will then turn to the Queen of Scots, since he *must* be provided for *somewhere out of France*'. Relations with Spain, estranged since the seizure of the treasure ships, were at their nadir and there was a great danger that France, free from internal strife, might join with Spain in an attempt to carry out the sentence in Pope Pius's Bull of 1570 to depose Elizabeth.

The arrival of a new ambassador, La Mothe Fénélon, had given an opportunity for improvements in Anglo-French relations, and to further the proposal Catherine sent over her personal agent, the Florentine Guido Cavalcanti, who began his mission by private talks with Leicester at Hampton Court. He knew the Earl was a firm Francophile, he said, and would rely on his judgment whether or not to carry the approaches further. Leicester replied that he had always been opposed to the Austrian match yet since Elizabeth was determined against marrying one of her own subjects he would not unwillingly sacrifice his own happiness in favour of Anjou's. A few days later, having prepared the ground, Leicester presented Fénélon to the Queen. For this audience she had dressed herself in her most resplendent clothes and began by talking about her former suitor, Charles IX's, recent wedding to Elizabeth of Austria. The ambassador parried by regretting he could not congratulate her on her own marriage, but she coyly admitted her regrets in not taking her want of posterity more seriously years before. If she did take a husband, she said, it should only be one from a royal House, of rank suitable to hers. Noting the hint, the ambassador suggested that the only possible candidate was the Duke of Anjou, brother of the French King, as 'the most

137

accomplished prince in the world and the only person worthy of marrying her'. Elizabeth understood that Henry of Anjou was in love with the Princess of Cleves, though she knew all about his excellent qualities. 'But I am an old woman and am ashamed to talk about a husband, were it not for the sake of an heir. In the past I have been courted by some who would rather marry the kingdom than marry the Queen, as generally happens with the great, who marry without seeing one another.' She and Fénélon went on bantering in this style for many more private audiences before proposals were properly launched. Catherine de'Medici had come to the conclusion that she did not intend to marry and, looking around for a suitable bride for Anjou, had wondered whether Elizabeth might name a female successor to whom he could be betrothed; the suggestion was a ridiculous one, but it had made Elizabeth think she might like Anjou for herself. She understood he had been brought up by a man 'not averse to the Protestant religion'.

Her sole concern, she told the ambassador at the end of January, was Anjou's age. Fénélon assured her 'he bore himself already like a man'. 'Yet he will always be younger than me,' she commented; and Leicester, who was with them, added with a smile 'So much the better for you.' Fénélon's advice was that any queen or princess who yearned for true wedded happiness with an ever-faithful consort should turn to the House of Valois, but this was too much for Elizabeth's sense of fun and she replied that tales of Madame d'Estampes and Madame de Valentinois – notorious mistresses of the French royal House – made her worry whether the man who honoured her as a queen would also love her as a woman. The arrival of Cardinal Châtillon at that moment, anxious to know if Elizabeth would really accept Anjou if he proposed, called the meeting to order. For France the prospect of such a match was indeed alluring and Charles IX was not overdoing the compliment when he referred to Elizabeth as '*la plus fine femme du monde*'.

Leicester became philosophical about it: 'I confess our estate requireth a match, but God send us a good one and meet for the parties,' he told Walsingham, the new ambassador in Paris, and asked him for a detailed description of the Duke. Sir Francis rated Anjou three inches taller than himself, 'his legs long and thin, but reasonably well-proportioned. What helps he has to supply any defects of nature I know not.' Opinions varied about his health, but he seemed somewhat sallow in the face of late and Walsingham thought it improper to be 'over curious'. A portrait could not be sent since it was against the law to publish portraits of the King and his brothers. The Puritan envoy was, indeed, as unfavourable as he dared be towards a match with Anjou. A Venetian ambassador had been more outspoken in his profile of the Duke he sent to the Senate: 'He is completely dominated by voluptuousness; covered with perfumes and essences. He wears a double row of rings and pendants at his ears . . . . He charms and beguiles women by lavishing upon them the most costly jewels and toys.' A Catholic French courtier wrote to Walsingham in much the same tone: 'He has conquered wherever he has cast his eyes and yet is ignorant of one hundredth part of his conquests'; but he added the telling sentences, 'You have been persuaded that he has a leaning to the new religion and might be brought to adopt it. Undeceive yourself. He was born a Catholic, he has lived the declared champion of Catholicism, believe me, he will live and die in the faith. I have, 'tis true, seen him with a volume of Marot's Psalms in his hands, and similar works, but he only perused

Catherine de' Medici, Queen Mother of France, with Henry of Navarre and the Court dwarf, watching a tourney: detail from a sixteenth-century Flemish tapestry.

Charles IX, King of France, 1560-74: portrait by François Clouet.

them to please a great Huguenot lady with whom he was in love.' Anjou's extravagant effeminacies were later to become a byword; he wore make-up and would go to a ball dressed as an alluring courtesan in a low-cut bodice. In time, as well, he showed himself to be absolutely under the thumb of the priests.

There is no doubt that Elizabeth initially intended to use the marriage negotiations as a diplomatic exercise, to be protracted for as long as possible and abandoned in due course, though if she were actually to fall in love with Anjou that would be different. In the early 1570s she still gave the strong impression of being very fond of suitors and most averse to husbands, and the more she learnt about the Duke the less promising it all seemed.

At the English court there was a good deal of idle chatter about Anjou, some of it instigated by Leicester. What a pity, said one of her ladies-in-waiting, that Monsieur were not a year or so older; but Elizabeth reprimanded her: 'He is twenty now and may be rated at twenty-five for his intellect and physique.' The Lord Chamberlain told a risqué story about Anjou visiting Rouen to see a beautiful Flemish girl, but the Queen minded this far less than suggestions of incompatibility on the score of age. She privately asked two of her most faithful ladies for their free opinion on the proposed match and Lady Clinton commended the project, saying she must not be put off by Monsieur's youth, 'for he was virtuous and Her Majesty was better calculated to please him than any other princess in the world'. Unwittingly, Lady Cobham was less tactful, for while approving of the marriage she added a rider that 'those marriages were always the happiest when the parties were the same age, or near about it, but that here there was a great inequality'. 'Nonsense!' broke in the Queen. 'There are but ten years difference between us' – it was, of course, nearer twenty!

Elizabeth quizzed Norris, then in Paris, very closely on the Duke's appearance and, well-satisfied that he was handsome, tried to hatch a scheme for him to pay a flying visit to England incognito. She would arrange to be on progress in Kent and he could easily slip across from France by the morning tide. If they took an unfavourable view of each other he need not prolong his stay but return the same night. Anjou was not prepared to fall in with these plans. Some hasty words of the Duke's, that he would never dream of marrying the Queen of England, 'for she was not only an old creature, but had a sore leg,' were duly reported to her and she was exceedingly cross, until Catherine de'Medici proffered a belated apology.

The Queen sent Lord Buckhurst to congratulate Charles IX on his own marriage and to open negotiations in earnest. Elizabeth, he said, was bent on marrying a foreign prince, yet it was unbecoming for a lady to seek a husband so openly and he succeeded in returning with a formal proposal on certain conditions, which made her tread warily. Walsingham was now to assure Catherine that the Queen of England was not dallying with her favourite son but could not be expected to give a precise answer until further talks had taken place, and she made a point of telling everyone that Leicester was 'ready to allow of any marriage that we shall like!'

By mid-February 1571, Leicester was writing to Sir Francis Walsingham, 'I perceive Her Majesty more bent to marry than heretofore she hath been.' After a long rigmarole about her natural preference for the single life and the many occasions on which she had been pressed by suitors, even in her father's reign, Elizabeth herself told Walsingham that she 'thankfully accepted' Anjou's offer and instructed him to put forward the marriage treaty of Philip and Mary as the basis for discussion. 'She could not prevent his exercising that form of religion in England which was prohibited by the laws of the realm,' but hoped for some *modus vivendi*. This was hardly an encouragement for a Roman Catholic no less staunch in his belief than the Archduke Charles. Burghley, reluctant to drop the Habsburgs for the Valois, had initially opposed opening negotiations with the chance of success so slender, but by now he had convinced himself of the importance of the marriage. 'If I be not much deceived,' he wrote to Walsingham, 'Her Majesty is earnest in this,' and he warned him to play down the religious differences in order to keep discussion open. Burghley, whose only way to justify a change of mind was to set down a lengthy memorandum, had concluded that Elizabeth would now marry for 'the benefit of her realm and to content her subjects'. There would be the strong possibility of children, the people would still hope the crown would remain in King Henry's noble line, and it followed that 'the curious and dangerous question of the succession would in the minds of quiet subjects, be, as it were, buried – a happy funeral for all England'. There would be difficulties enough, but England would be insured against a civil war and immune from the crusades of Catholic powers.

In April 1571 Guido Cavalcanti returned with a formal offer of Anjou's hand. He was stopped as he landed at Dover, and taken under guard to Burghley's London house for secret talks before he was allowed to go to the French embassy. Cavalcanti had been allowed to bring with him a portrait of the Duke and also brought one of the Princess of Cleves who might, he thought, be a consolation prize for Leicester. A wit at the French court even suggested that since Anjou was to wed Leicester's mistress the Duke should allow the Earl the honour of taking Mademoiselle Châteauneuf, his own latest conquest. The terms demanded by the French were that Anjou should be crowned King the day after the wedding and rule jointly with Elizabeth, he should be granted an income of £60,000 a year and be allowed with all his household the free exercise of the Catholic religion. The precedent of Philip's joint rule with Mary would allow for Anjou being styled 'King', and the income, too, Elizabeth was prepared to sanction, but the religious articles were out of the question. This was the point at which the negotiations with Archduke Charles had foundered, and since 1567 much had happened to harden her against Rome, for Anjou's Pope had deposed her for heresy. She might perhaps excuse a consort from attending Anglican services in public, but wider concessions were out of the question.

Reluctant to end the affair, she flirted with the idea of converting Anjou, as Helena had converted Constantine, and continued to woo him with words, imploring him to visit her. Cecil had understood from his Huguenot contacts that if Elizabeth held out on the score of religion the French would give way. But any pressure that Charles IX and his mother were, at Walsingham's instigation, able to bring to bear on Anjou so that he might win 'the rarest creature in Europe these 500 years' was nullified by the efforts of the Cardinal of Lorraine, and the rest of the Guises, backed by Spain.

By September 1571 the failure of the negotiations was obvious, but Elizabeth, awaiting the unravelling of Ridolfi's intrigues, dared not fall out with France. Meanwhile the latest intelligence from Paris showed how even Catherine de'Medici was falling more and more under the power of the Guises, the very House from which Mary Queen of Scots had sprung. Lorraine was adamant that the best match for Anjou was the captive Mary, while Catherine, ever a realist, was anxious for him to marry a Polish princess of impeccable orthodoxy. Elizabeth salvaged what she could of the affair, deftly picking her way through the threads of matrimonial diplomacy, but

Sir Thomas Smith,
(1513-77), scholar
and ambassador
to France.

the game could not last indefinitely. Sir Thomas Smith, the new ambassador
in Paris, was keener than his predecessor Walsingham to see a marriage
treaty signed, because the Queen, now thirty-eight, would each year become
less attractive; 'the more hairy she is before, the more bald she is behind,' he
commented to Cecil in his pithy style, though he quickly realised the impos-
sibility of making any progress with Anjou. When Catherine said that her
obstinate son insisted on practising his religion openly with its full ceremonies if he were Elizabeth's consort, Smith burst out 'Why, Madame, then
he may require also the four orders of friars, monks, canons, pilgrimages,
pardons, oil and cream, reliques and all such trumperies.'

Two days later the Queen Mother suggested that her youngest son, the
Duke of Alençon, might be a rather better proposition for Elizabeth, for he
was 'a much less scrupulous fellow' than Anjou. Smith at once saw the two
great advantages of Alençon: while his elder brother was rigidly orthodox,
he had for some years been attracted to the Huguenot party, so that negotiations ought not to founder on the religious issue, and secondly while Anjou
was heir presumptive to the French throne so long as Charles IX remained
childless, Alençon was outside the immediate line of succession. Anjou's suit
had lasted thirteen months, but Elizabeth was to woo his brother for a full
ten years.

6 The Threat from the House of Valois

The French marriage proposals were to run like a rogue's yarn through the politics of the Elizabethan court for a dozen years. The Duke of Alençon, rather than the Archduke Charles, was now regarded as the most favoured suitor. 'If she be disposed to marry,' said the judicious Sir Thomas Smith, who had the advantage of knowing the Prince, 'I do not see where she shall marry so well.'

Initially there were three doubts, none of which would be resolved until the Queen had actually seen him, touching Alençon's appearance, his age and his religion – in that order. Smallpox had scarred his face, but already there was promise of a beard that would hide the marks, and even if he grew no taller, it should be remembered that Pippin was short and yet fathered a Charlemagne. Alençon was less than half Elizabeth's age, yet his mother harped on his lusty, vigorous nature. Given the assurances about his affiliations to the Huguenot party, there seemed no insuperable problem about religion, compared with his bigoted brother Anjou. For the moment the primary objective of both countries was a treaty of alliance and with the changing French attitude to Mary Queen of Scots, following the unravelling of Ridolfi's conspiracy, the way for accommodation lay open. Charles IX now despaired of Mary – the poor fool, he said, would never cease plotting until she lost her head; he had intended to help her, but it was impossible. In April 1572 France and England signed the defensive Treaty of Blois, by the terms of which each undertook to aid the other in case of attack and France at last recognised the *status quo* in Scotland; at last, too, England could count on an ally.

The treaty of alliance made possible far more effective discussions of the match than had been possible with Anjou's candidature. The envoys sent to England and lodged in Somerset House were instructed to offer Leicester the hand of an unspecified Valois princess if he appeared to be obstructive, yet the Earl gave Montmorency and de Foix a lavish banquet and, in Burghley's view, throughout their stay they were entertained 'as never before in man's memory. The honour done them also by the Queen was such as she could do no more.' Yet now that Elizabeth had secured the defensive alliance the urgency for marriage faded and she delayed matters by asking for detailed reports about the Duke. Walsingham, then resident in Paris, wrote that he was about the same height as Lincoln, the Lord Admiral, was reputed to

François, Duke of Alençon – perhaps the most serious suitor for Elizabeth's hand: portrait painted by François Clouet when Alençon was thirty-one.

ANNO ÆTATIS SVÆ|31

have great courage but also was said to be somewhat feather-headed – a common fault, said the diplomat, with the French; he did not, however, enlarge on his appearance. Elizabeth began to wonder if the pockmarks were sufficiently ugly to enable her to ask for Calais as part of the Duke's marriage portion. But soon Alençon dispatched his personal representative, M. le Mole, to captivate the Queen.

Elizabeth, who was staying with Leicester at Kenilworth when the French envoys arrived, quickly warmed to their flattery. But, before le Mole was able to leave England with the Queen's professions of love, the grim news came through of the Massacre of St Bartholomew's Eve. On Catherine's orders, the Huguenot leader Coligny had been assassinated in Paris, where a great concourse had assembled for the marriage of Henry of Navarre with Margaret of Valois. This was a signal for spontaneous killings of Huguenots first in Paris, then in the provinces. It was the end of rule by the moderate centre party of 'Politiques', for the Guises regained power and the country was plunged into a fresh series of civil wars.

In England the Massacre was regarded as a wicked conspiracy by the powers of the Counter Reformation, and so the alliance with France, so recently concluded, was in jeopardy. After keeping the French ambassador Fénélon waiting for an audience at Woodstock to learn his version of the Massacre, Elizabeth required him to keep to his house until she was assured that her own diplomats in Paris were safe. She could not risk breaking the *entente* until relations with Spain had been put on a better footing, but all hopes of a marriage with Alençon faded. She subsequently agreed to become godmother to Charles ix's baby daughter, but considered conditions in France too dangerous to allow Leicester to represent her at the christening. Instead she sent the Earl of Worcester, who was plundered of the christening gift by pirates in the Channel.

Playing the role of *mauvais sujet* in the embittered French politics of the mid-1570s was a dangerous practice for Alençon, particularly after his brother Anjou had been elected King of Poland. When Elizabeth read his chivalric letters full of protestations of eternal love she suggested that he should slip away for a secret meeting at Greenwich, where she would be waiting for him alone at the water-gate; but any intention he may have had of keeping this romantic tryst was frustrated by his imprisonment at Vincennes for plotting with the Huguenots. Elizabeth made it plain to Catherine that she could not marry a man 'with irons on his feet' and though subsequently he was released, the death of Charles ix delayed further progress in the suit, for the Queen Mother kept him under her eye at court.

Lord North was dispatched to convey Elizabeth's congratulations to Anjou on his peaceful accession to the throne as Henry iii, and Catherine took advantage of the opportunity to remind him that the delays in the courtship were no fault of the French. In the festivities marking the accession Catherine had dressed up two female dwarfs in English costume in rather bad taste to mimic Elizabeth, which infuriated the Queen of England when she heard of it. Catherine based her apology on the grounds that Lord North's grasp of idiomatic French was at fault, otherwise he would have relished the buffoonery instead of regarding it a gross insult to his Queen. For a while Alençon remained surrounded by leading Huguenots and kept a rival court to his brother Henry III. Then, as the fifth Civil War ended, Catherine persuaded the King to grant him the rich duchies of Anjou and Touraine, provided he deserted the Protestant cause, and soon he was commanding a regiment against his former allies.

Elizabeth seemed to have forgotten Alençon entirely and gave the impression of becoming an embittered old maid – when Mary Shelton, one of the ladies of her Privy Chamber, married a Mr Scudamore without her leave, she let fly at the unfortunate girl, dealing 'liberal both in blows and words' so that 'no one ever bought her husband more dearly'. This was a dog-in-the-manger attitude towards matrimony, all tears and resentment. She sent to her godson Harington her speech to Parliament in 1576, in which she clearly expressed her dislike of marriage:

If I were a milkmaid with a pail on my arm, whereby my private person might be a little set by, I would not forsake that poor and single state to match with the greatest monarch. Not that I do condemn the double knot, or judge amiss of such as, forced by necessity, cannot dispose themselves to another life; but wish that none were drawn to change but such as cannot keep honest limits.

Yet for the sake of her realm she would dispose herself towards matrimony if the conditions were favourable and the suitor appealed to her. Those who heard her words must have concluded that the Alençon affair was quite dead.

Sir Francis Walsingham (1530-90), Secretary of State from 1583 until his death: portrait attributed to John Critz the Elder.

At court, Francis Walsingham was now at the hub of affairs as Principal Secretary. He had imbibed the strong wine of Protestant doctrine at Edwardian Cambridge, and on Mary's accession he had resumed his foreign travels, profiting by his exile to study civil law at Padua. He returned in time to take up a seat in the Parliament of 1559 which Cecil had found for him. Sir Walter Mildmay, the Chancellor of the Exchequer, had married his sister Mary, and Walsingham looked through him to Cecil for a suitable post. By the late sixties he had begun to provide the government with intelligence about the activities of Spanish and other spies in London. He seemed an obvious choice for taking custody of Ridolfi when he was under suspicion in 1569, and he came into his own with the dénouement of the Ridolfi Plot.

When a post worthy of his talents came his way – ambassadorship to Paris, in succession to Norris – Walsingham tried to excuse himself, for the whole ethos of Catherine de'Medici's court was anathema to him. He had to accept the post however, and was in Paris at the time of the Massacre. 'A most sharp maintainer of the purer religion', his fervour was a serious handicap to his embassy in the tortuous policy of the first stages of the Alençon marriage negotiations. To his great relief he was recalled and in 1573 became Principal Secretary of State, at first jointly with Sir Thomas Smith, but for most of the following seventeen years he was to bear the full brunt of that demanding office unaided.

Time and again Walsingham lamented the Queen's failure to hear the Gospel aright and her refusal to assume the role of champion of Protestantism, giving unequivocal aid to French Huguenots and Dutch Calvinists. In council he could count on the support of Leicester, Knollys, Mildmay and Pembroke, but it was the moderate Bughley who generally won the day, for Walsingham the fanatic never grasped the extent of Elizabeth's distaste for Calvinism or her wariness of becoming involved in the internal affairs of other states. He always wanted to anticipate an enemy's action by striking the first blow, whereas the Queen had a loathing for war. The Secretary's industry equalled that of Thomas Cromwell, and he would stay up half the night at Barn Elms, his house in Barnes, fighting the good fight as an armchair strategist to slay 'the bosom serpent Mary' and bring England nearer open war with Spain. Nothing pleased him so much as his daughter's marriage with Philip Sidney, the 'Shepheard Knight', who was the intellectual leader of the new militant Protestantism.

In 1573 Christopher Hatton became Captain of the Gentlemen Pensioners, and malicious gossip made much of the Queen's delight in him, for he was said to have 'more recourse unto Her Majesty in her Privy Chamber than reason would suffer, if she were so virtuous and well inclined as some noiseth her'. Hatton was a lawyer by training, but it was his skill as a dancer that originally caught the Queen's eye, though she soon came to appreciate his 'modest sweetness of manner'. But the label 'dancer' stuck, even when by sheer political ability he became Lord Chancellor. Leicester, alarmed that a younger, more serious rival than Heneage (who was safely married) should be thus fêted, asked Elizabeth if he might introduce her to a dancing master whose nimble footwork and elegant posture would put the new favourite's skill in perspective, but she was not to be drawn in this way: 'Pish. I will not see your man – it is his *trade*,' she snapped at the Earl.

Hatton was indeed well in favour; as a Gentleman Pensioner he had admired from afar, but his post as Captain of the ceremonial guard involved regular attendance on the Queen's person and he now believed that he was passionately in love with her. Alone of all her favourites he remained single, ever hopeful that his love would be returned, and Elizabeth did not disillusion him. When he had a serious kidney complaint, she not only visited his bedside daily but insisted, when he was well enough to travel, that he should go for a cure to Spa in the Low Countries under the care of Leicester's physician, Dr Julio. While away from court he penned a series of remarkable letters to her. Leaving her was a grief and never again would illness or fear of death persuade him to absent himself from her side for a single day. Away from her, 'I lack that I live by. . . . To serve you is heaven, but to lack you is more than hell's torment.' Only the opportunity of putting his thoughts about her on paper made her absence bearable:

I will wash away the faults of these letters with the drops from your poor Lydds and so inclose them. Would God I were with you but for one hour. My wits are overwrought with thoughts. I find myself amazed. Bear with me, my most dear sweet Lady. Passion overcometh me. I can write no more. Love me; for I love you . . .

'Lids' was Elizabeth's pet name for him, as 'Eyes' was her name for Leicester; 'Eyes' symbolising, perhaps, her own omnipotence, and 'Lids' her unfailing sense in knowing when to turn a blind eye. Both men used their nicknames in their letters to her, by means of symbols – the one drawing two circles each with a squiggle for an eyebrow, the other drawing two triangles for eyelids. In this age of puns and verbal conceits, Hatton also delighted in using a 'short-hand' signature; if the Queen could reduce her sign manual to 'E.R.' then her favourite could get away with drawing a hat crossed through with a letter X ('Hat-ten'). This was not so different from the punning valedictions in some of King Henry's letters to Anne Boleyn, and fitted

148

TEM: PVS

ACHESIS TRAHIT

DIALOGVS DE TEMPORE.

Cuius opus: quondam Lyfippi dic mihi quis tu: Tempus quidnam operæ
est tibi: cuncta domo, cur tam summa tenes: propero super omnia,
bimx, cur celeres plantæ: Me levis aura vehit cur tenvem tua dextra
tenet tonsoria falcem: omnia nostra secans redit acuta manus, cur tibi
tam longi pendent a fronte capilli: Fronte guiden facilis sum bene, posse
capi, cur tibi posterior pars est a vertice calva: Posterior nemo
prendere me poterit, talem me finxit quondam sytiomius hospes. Et
monitorem hoc me vestibulo posuit, pulchrum opus artificera laudat
pro Iuppiter o quam, debuit hoc pigros sollicita e viros.

in with the symbolic imagery of true lovers' knots. When Sir Christopher
built his prodigy house at Holdenby in Lincolnshire he dedicated it to the
Queen, for it was 'a shrine' for her to sit in and, unlike any other courtier, his
invitations for her to visit him were frequent and pressing. She sometimes
called him 'Sheep' or 'Mutton' in place of 'Lids'.

Hatton had long coveted Ely Place in Holborn with its fine gardens, but
Bishop Cox was determined to keep the 'harpies and wolves' from court at
bay. When he held out against the Queen's demands to lease his London
palace to Hatton she threatened to unfrock him and required Lord North to
knock some sense into his head. He was to throw off his 'stiff-necked determination' and yield to the Queen's 'known clemency'; 'wherefore, if you love
place, the preservation of your credit and the continuance of Her Majesty's
favour, conform yourself'. Richard Cox conformed, and the favourite was
installed in his Naboth's vineyard; the Bishop even agreed to pay for improvements to the house, though he retained the right to gather a bushel of roses and
a truss of hay each year from the gardens. Here, indeed, Elizabeth could claim
that she was putting into practice the precept of statecraft that Burghley had
advised earlier in that year; 'gratify your nobility and the principal persons
of your realm, to bind them fast to you ... whereby you shall cause all men
of value in the realm to depend only upon you yourself'.

Of all the correspondence Elizabeth received from admiring courtiers,
perhaps Hatton's missives alone come into the category of 'love letters' as the
term is generally understood. Others were expressions of courtly gallantry,
written by men who knew how Elizabeth fed on admiration and the choicest
flattery that the language allowed, but Hatton's had something more potent
than a mere sugary flavour – he was certain he was in love with her. When it
became clear that she would not respond to the passionate, physical love he
so desperately wanted, he did not react as Leicester or Raleigh and look for
fulfilment in marriage with someone else, but remained in love with the idea
of being in love with her, constant, dedicating his celibate life wistfully to the
dreams of what might have been. Even this was part of the masquerade of
Fair Oriana. Hatton wept freely when his star was not in the ascendant and
would go off and sulk in the country, anxious to find a go-between, like
Heneage, to act as messenger to take the Queen a present and bring back
the magic. Their relationship was to be a regular succession of teasings, tiffs
and reconciliations.

Hatton was, however, made to feel insecure by the arrival of the young
Earl of Oxford at court. Apart from de Vere's undoubted accomplishments
as dancer and in the tilt, age was on his side and he had the inestimable
advantages of noble birth and a powerful patron in Burghley. For a brief
season Elizabeth made him the idol of her court, even though he was married
to Burghley's daughter, and delighted 'more in his personage and his dancing
and valiantness than any other'; she named him 'Boar', and in time the
Queen took to heart the jealous Hatton's advice that she should reserve her
most gracious favour 'to the Sheep: he hath no tooth to bite, where the Boar's
tusk may both rase and tear'.

Oxford, yearning for action, departed for the Netherlands, perhaps to fight
in Alva's army, but when he was ordered to return on his allegiance, he
obediently came and satisfied the Queen that he had behaved with circumspection towards Westmorland and the other rebels in hiding in Flanders.

151

All might be well, thought Burghley, if he submitted unreservedly and was not subjected to 'the malice of some discontented persons wherewith the court is overmuch sprinkled'. Oxford, though forgiven, remained a square peg – 'by no means he can be drawn to follow the court' – yet many 'cunning devices' were attempted to wean him from his wanderlust until, in 1575, he succeeded in extracting the Queen's permission to travel abroad. Painfully aware of his spendthrift nature, his father-in-law made him arrange a suitable allowance for his Countess while he was away, but said there would be savings from it since she was sometimes at court, where food and fuel were provided; she was in fact eventually to die at Greenwich Palace.

The Earl returned home after many months, having 'sent his patrimony flying' in buying new-fangled luxuries in Italy, such as the perfumed leather jerkins he now wore and the embroidered gloves, trimmed with tufts of coloured silk and fragrantly scented, that he gave to Elizabeth. There was no present for his wife, from whom he remained estranged until 1582; he would never go to court unless he was assured that she was not in attendance and to the end of her unhappy days he treated her shabbily, falsely accusing her of infidelity yet himself enjoying affairs, keeping her short of money yet lavishly supporting indigent poets and promising actors. It took another favourite, Walter Raleigh, to reconcile Oxford with his sovereign who, despite his faults, still found something appealing in his eccentric, dissolute ways. It was her continued favour towards this worthless aristocrat that produced the wild story that they were lovers and that the Earl of Southampton was their offspring!

But, by 1580, Oxford was in disgrace yet again. First he became a Roman

RIGHT Lettice Knollys Countess of Essex, who secretly married the Earl of Leicester in 1579; portrait attributed to George Gower, *c.* 1585.

BELOW Illustrations from Giacomo di Grassi, *His True Art of Defense*, published in 1594. Left: 'Of Paces. The Agreement of hand and foot'. Right: 'The means how to defend'.

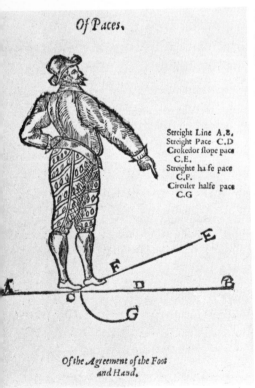

Of Paces.

Streight Line A.B.
Streight Pace C.D
Crokedor slope pace C.E.
Streighte hafe pace C.F.
Circuler halfe pace C.G

Of the Agreement of the Foot and Hand.

LONDINVM FERACISSIMI AN-
GLIAE REGNI METROPOLIS.

Hæc est Fregia illa totius Angliæ ciuitas LONDINVM, ad flu-
uium Thamesim sita, Cæsari, ut plures exsistimat, Trinobantum
nuncupata, multarum gentium comertio nobilitata, exculta domib. ornata te-
plis, excelsa arcibus, claris ingenijs, uiris omnium artium doctrinarumq, gene-
re præstantibus, percelebris. Denuq, omnium rerum copia, atque opum excellentia
mirabilis. Inuehit in eam totius orbis opes ipse Thamasis, onerarijs nauibus per
sexaginta millia passuum, ad urbem præalto alueo nauigabilis.

The Spitel fielde

Grenewiche orchard

THE TOWRE

Beere house

STILLIARDS) Hansa, Gothica dictio, conuentum, vel congregationem sonans, multarum ciuitatum est confœderata Societas, tum, ob præfita Regibus, ac Ducib. beneficia: tum, ob securam terra, marique, mercatura tractationem, tum denique, ad tranquillam Rerumpub. pacem, &, ad modessam adolescentum institutionem conseruandam, instituta: plurimor. Regum, ac Principum, maximè Angliæ, Galliæ, Daniæ, ac Magnæ Moscouiæ, nec non Flandriæ, ac Brabantiæ Du cum priuilegijs, ac immunitatib. exornata fuit. Habet ea quatuor Emporia, (untores quidam vocant, in quibus ciuitatum negotiatores resident, suasque mercatus exercent. Hor, alterum hic Londini, domestica œconomia niter, habens domum Gildchalla Teutonica, quæ vulgo Stilliard, nuncupat.

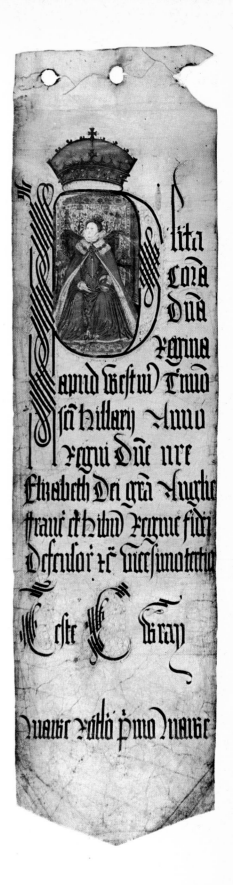

Catholic and then reported to Elizabeth the names of various recusant courtiers with whom he had been associating, such as Lord Henry Howard and Charles Arundel. They were placed under house arrest, while Oxford lost much credit and was 'abandoned by all his friends and by all the ladies of the court' – including the Queen.

However, Elizabeth's displeasure had less to do with Oxford's new-found religious scruples than his amours, for he had been much in the company of Ann Vavasour, a maid-of-honour with a reputation for promiscuity – a 'drab' was the word men used to describe her, the equivalent of a common tart. In March 1581 Mistress Ann gave birth to a son in the maidens' chamber

RIGHT Ann Vavasour, one of the Queen's maids-of-honour, who bore the Earl of Oxford a son: portrait attributed to John de Critz.

PREVIOUS PAGES LEFT Map of London by Braun and Hogenberg, 1572. RIGHT Illuminated portrait of Elizabeth from the first membrane of the Plea Roll of the Court of Queen's Bench for Hilary Term, 1581.

LEFT ABOVE Portrait of an unknown youth, epitomising contemplation and melancholy, by Isaac Oliver.
FAR LEFT Sir Walter Raleigh, a miniature by Nicholas Hilliard, c. 1585.
LEFT Young man amongst the roses, miniature painting by Nicholas Hilliard. It has been suggested that this portrait might be of Robert Devereux, Earl of Essex.

and Oxford acknowledged paternity, giving her £2,000 and speedily settling property on the infant. Next day Ann was committed to the Tower since 'Her Majesty is greatly grieved by the accident'. It was thought that the Earl would try to escape the Queen's wrath by fleeing abroad, but he was soon himself in the Tower for a spell. Later he had a prolonged, violent feud with Thomas Knyvet of the Privy Chamber, who regarded himself as Ann Vavasour's 'patron' and planned to kill Oxford. They fought a duel in 1582, in which both were wounded while the fight was continued by their servants. Knyvet's men wounded two of the Earl's retainers in Lambeth Marsh, and there were plans by the other faction to murder Knyvet as he stepped ashore at night at Blackfriars Stairs.

This gang warfare between courtiers entered a more serious phase when Knyvet himself killed an Oxford supporter. Fearful of the legal consequences, he entreated Elizabeth to persuade Lord Chancellor Bromley to have the case heard *in camera* during vacation. When Bromley refused to have the matter hushed up Hatton told him, 'My good lord; it is very necessary you take care to please the Queen in this case.' At the coroner's inquest Knyvet secured a verdict that he acted in self-defence, but it was not the end of the affair, for a month later Oxford's men murdered Long Tom, one of their number who had gone over to the rival faction. Oxford, now in deep disgrace, was required to consider himself a prisoner in his own house. Feeling subdued and penitent, he agreed to take back his wife, but Burghley was unable to move the Queen to relent and turned to Raleigh, then the reigning favourite. The latter felt with justification that he would be helping to cure a serpent that would later turn on him, yet he agreed to use his considerable influence. As a result, when Elizabeth was visiting Theobalds in May 1583 she summoned Oxford before her and after 'bitter tears and speeches' fully pardoned him and permitted his return to court.

Meanwhile, Leicester, jealous at Hatton's rise to favour, had begun his notorious liaison with Lady Douglas Sheffield, a daughter of Lord William Howard, the Queen's great-uncle. Leicester cuckolded her husband during a royal visit to Belvoir Castle, but Douglas carelessly mislaid a compromising letter, and Lord Sheffield set out for London in 1568 to begin divorce proceedings. Before he had made any progress, however, he became ill and died, leaving Douglas a widow at twenty-four. Leicester's enemies later accused him of poisoning Lord Sheffield, but it would have been a pointless crime, for he had no intention of marrying Douglas.

In 1573, after their father's death, there was much speculation about Leicester's relations with the widowed Lady Douglas and her unmarried sister, Frances: 'There are two sisters now in the court that are very far in love with him, as they have been long, my Lady Sheffield and Frances Howard,' wrote a court gossip. 'They, of like striving who shall love him better, are at great wars together, and the Queen thinketh not well of them and not the better of him.' Later in the year there was a rumour that the Earl and Lady Douglas had contracted to marry and the latter claimed rather dubiously that she had married him at Esher. Certainly in August 1574 she bore him a son, Robert Dudley, whom Leicester did not disown, but the father was not to be trapped into matrimony. He continued his flirtations first with Frances and later with Lettice Knollys, Countess of Essex.

Much was kept from the Queen so that the Earl might still pay homage as a suitor, but his relations were becoming increasingly complicated, while Hatton's remained transparently simple. Leicester addressed Lady Douglas as 'My good friend', signing himself 'Yours as much as he was, R.L.', yet despite his love for her, marriage was out of the question, he said. He was not 'void of conscience toward God, nor honest meaning toward my friend, and having made special choice of you to be one of the dearest to me, so much the more care must I have (to give you advice)'. He knew that for his sake she had been rejecting suitors who offered marriage, but she should think of herself, since for him 'to carry you away for my pleasure, to your great and further grief, were too great a shame for me'.

In the hot summer of 1575 Elizabeth stayed for a fortnight at Kenilworth as Leicester's guest during her progress in the Midland shires. The host, alas, could not supervise the final preparations, for he was with the Queen at Grafton, but he had taken infinite pains in arranging a series of entertainments, not least in obtaining the services of an Italian skilled in firework displays. At the castle gate the Queen was greeted by the porter in the garb of Hercules and then the royal party proceeded to the lake, where she was fêted by the Lady of the Lake and her nymphs who appeared to be walking upon the water. Over the main courtyard there had been constructed a

The Earl of Leicester's arms, the central portion of a tapestry which was made to be hung in the Queen's bed chamber on her visit to Kenilworth in 1575. It is probably of Flemish work.

temporary bridge, with seven pairs of pillars, adorned with votive offerings for her delight, each guarded by gods and goddesses; these decorations included two rugged staves hung with armour and two bay trees bearing musical instruments.

The Italian had wanted to send in fiery orbit live cats, dogs and birds but he was persuaded to be less ambitious; as it was there was a 'blaze of burning darts flying to and fro, gleams of stars coruscent, streams and hails of fiery sparks, lightning of wild fire, a'water and a'land'. In the hall Leicester had staged a series of banquets, masques and dramatics, including a performance of the Coventry Hock Tuesday play. Out of doors there was hunting and bear-baiting and an encounter with the rustic folk hero 'Wodwose', a savage dressed in leaves and moss, though the oak branch he carried made the Queen's horse shy. The climax of the revels was a water pageant, 'The Delivery of the Lady of the Lake', in which Proteus rode on a dolphin, inside which was concealed 'a consort of music'. Throughout these allegorical entertainments, rich in symbolism, the Queen was idealised as a gracious lady of matchless beauty and divine majesty.

There was soon yet another luminary at court in the person of Philip Sidney, son of Sir Henry, the President of Wales and hammer of the Irish. He was in attendance at Kenilworth for the Queen's visit and soon afterwards was appointed a royal cup-bearer.

Philip II of Spain was his godfather, for Sir Henry had been on the embassy to Spain which had brought home Mary Tudor's consort, and his son was given the name Philip as a matter of etiquette. After Christ Church, Oxford, Philip had been sent on a grand tour to complete his education. The tour began at Paris, where his father's friend Walsingham was ambassador, and continued through Germany, Austria and Italy. Visits to foreign countries were on a different plane from mere sight-seeing – 'if you should travel but to travel, or to say that you have travelled, certainly you shall prove a pilgrim to no saint,' wrote Philip, who grasped that the educational value lay in careful observation of the political and social scene in each country and in the opportunity of talking with statesmen and men of letters. The young Sidney made a remarkable impression and in France 'was so admired by the graver sort of courtiers that when they could at any time have him in their company and conversation, they would be very joyful, and no less delighted with his ready and witty answers than astonished to hear him speak the French language so well'. He met Peter Ramus, Ronsard, de Baïf, Tasso and other literary lions and at the same time won the respect of both Charles IX and Henry of Navarre.

Sidney left France a matter of days before the Massacre of St Bartholomew, but news of it had a profound effect on him and as he continued his travels he saw the political importance of forming an international Protestant League, directed from England, to push back the tides of the Counter Reformation. His mentor Hubert Languet, the Huguenot writer and diplomat, advised him on his return home to cultivate Burghley and Walsingham and to remember that the man wishing 'to live above contempt in the courts of powerful kings should moderate his pretensions, digest many injuries and avoid quarrels'.

Sidney had great advantages over most 'prentice courtiers, for apart from his parents' record of service to the Queen – which counted for much – he had the whole-hearted support of his uncle Leicester. Tradition has it that he was in the royal party when the Queen visited Chartley, the home of the Earl of Essex, and that Philip first met there Penelope Devereux, who was later to inspire some of his finest verse. Soon Elizabeth was using him on minor diplomatic missions, to the Emperor Rudolph II and to the Count Palatine John Casimir. While abroad he continued to develop his idea of a Protestant League; he met William the Silent, and there were even rumours that he might marry Orange's sister. Walsingham was delighted with his concept of militant Protestantism, but the Queen was alarmed, for his activist outlook ran counter to her cautious foreign policy. Leicester asked him to write a pastoral drama, *The Lady of May*, which was presented to the Queen in the gardens of Wanstead in May 1578, and this trifling work in some measure helped Sidney's rehabilitation. The next year Edmund Spenser dedicated to him *The Shepheardes Calendar* and readers were quick to identify Sidney with the character Philisides, the Shepheard Knight, depicted as the hero of Protestant action. It was not altogether fortuitous that this poetic cycle, with its obvious political undertones, should be published at a crucial stage in the French marriage negotiations.

Two of Philip's sisters died in infancy, a third, Ambrosia, endured a long illness and died in 1577. In offering her sympathy to Sir Henry, away again in Ireland, Elizabeth invited their surviving daughter, Mary, aged fourteen, to court. Here, the girl quickly made a remarkable match, becoming third wife to Henry Herbert, Earl of Pembroke. Their house at Wilton, near Salisbury, now became a second home for Philip, and Pembroke's support of Leicester grew closer. The Earl of Essex hoped to arrange a match between Philip and his daughter Penelope Devereux, but nothing came of it, and on the Earl's death the girl was placed in the care of the Countess of Huntingdon until, in 1581, she came to court. The Countess succeeded in making for her the best possible match, for she married young Lord Rich, who had just succeeded to his title and considerable property; the marriage was to prove disastrous. By contrast Sidney's marriage with Walsingham's daughter Frances in 1583 was to be supremely happy.

John Lyly, just down from Oxford and hoping to make capital out of his reputation as a wit, had looked for preferment to Burghley – 'this noble man I found so ready, being but a stranger, to do me good' – and this early patronage enabled him to write *Euphues, or the Anatomy of Wit* (1579), the earliest English novel, which won him golden opinions at court at the age of twenty-six. Begone dull care in the 'crabbed studies of logic and philosophy', for Lyly set out to entertain, not to instruct, and his romance was addressed to 'the gentlewomen of England', not to staid councillors; he would, he said, rather see his book 'lie shut in a lady's closet than open in a scholar's study' and he would not mind at all if it were kept merely as a bedside tale.

The polished style of *Euphues* and of its successor, *Euphues and his England*, created the vogue of 'Euphuism' in English prose, both written and spoken. This was a florid manner of speech, rich in simile – especially in successions of similes drawn from natural history and mythology – full of alliteration, careful in the balance of its phrases, Ciceronian in its choice of cadences and making significant use of rhetorical questions; a contemporary, William

Webbe, described it as a combination of 'singular eloquence and brave composition of apt words and sentences, in fit phrases, in pithy sentences, in gallant tropes, in flowing speech'.

Elaborate, like the shape and texture of an intricately patterned ruff, the conceit of Euphuism became overworked after a generation, a self-defeating piece of verbal extravagance, but in the 1580s and 1590s it dominated the language of courtiers. Those who 'could not parley Euphuism' felt as out of fashion as if they were appearing in the wrong garb, and the Queen herself, as her letters and reported speeches show, was an adept Euphuist. Shakespeare was to mock the euphuists in *Love's Labour's Lost* where Holofernes, the pedagogue, had 'a rare talent' for verbal gymnastics. As the schoolmaster confessed, this was 'a foolish extravagant spirit, full of forms, figures, shapes, objects, ideas, apprehensions, motions, revolutions: these are begot in the ventricle of memory, nourished in the womb of *pia mater*, and delivered upon the mellowing of occasion. But the gift is good in those in whom it is acute, and I am thankful for it.'

Lyly had hoped to become Master of the Revels and when the post went to Edmund Tylney he was led by Elizabeth to expect the succession. To fit himself for the office responsible for staging court entertainments, he deserted romances for the drama, especially 'court comedies', beginning with *Woman in the Moone*, acted by the children of the Chapel Royal. In 1585 he wrote *Endymion*, an allegorical play on Leicester's passions. The Earl, in the character of the shepherd Endymion, adored his heavenly mistress 'Cynthia, the Moon' (the Queen), but was also entangled in an earthly love for 'Tellus' (Lady Sheffield) and was attracted by another beauty, 'Floscula' (Lettice Knollys). The play was popular at court, but if tackling so *risqué* a theme did Lyly no harm, it did nothing to forward his claims to royal patronage.

Waiting for dead men's shoes was a dispiriting business and Master Tylney was in fact to survive John Lyly; Burghley had long since lost interest in his protégé and there was no likelihood of another post at court. He boldly petitioned the Queen: 'After ten years' tempest, I must at the Court suffer shipwreck of my times, my hopes and my wits,' and he asked for some small recompense to enable him to settle in a country cottage to 'write prayers instead of plays, prayers for your long and prosperous life and a repentance that I have played the fool so long'. The author of court comedies went unrewarded and in 1593 he petitioned Her Majesty again, in stronger terms:

Thirteen years Your Highness' servant, but yet nothing. Twenty friends that though they say they will be sure, I find them sure to be slow. A thousand hopes, but all nothing; a hundred promises, but yet nothing. Thus casting up the inventory of my friends, hopes, promises and times, the *summa totalis* amounteth to just nothing.

Spenser, waiting for noble or royal patronage, was to be no less disillusioned than Lyly. In *The Teares of the Muses* the poet who had dedicated every product of his pen to a distinguished courtier surprisingly lamented the meagre rewards that the great bestowed:

> For noble Peers, whom I was wont to raise,
> Now only seek for pleasure, nought for praise.
> Their great revenues all in sumptuous pride
> They spend that nought to learning they may spare,
> And the rich fee which Poets wont divide
> Now Parasites and Sycophants do share.

Befriended by the young Philip Sidney, Spenser had been found a niche at Leicester House and at once became intoxicated by the magnificence of the court; this, he felt, was his milieu and he would be its special muse. He was in Leicester's train during the Queen's visit to Cambridge when he was presented to her, hoping that the Earl's backing would lead to congenial employment of his talents. But he forfeited his patron's support, as he revealed long afterwards in the publication of *Virgil's Gnat*:

> Wrong'd yet not daring to express my pain,
> To you (great Lord) the causer of my care,
> In cloudy tears my case I thus complain
> Unto yourself, that only privy are.

The reason for Leicester's coolness was Spenser's indiscretion in referring to Lettice Knollys (whom, as we shall see, the Earl had married in strict secrecy the year before) in his March Eclogue in *The Shepheardes Calendar*, published in 1579. The coming of Spring leads the shepherd boys to think of love:

> Then shall we sporten in delight
> And learn with Lettice to wax light,
> That scornfully looks askance.

Woodcut illustrating 'The March Eclogue' of Spenser's *The Shepheardes Calendar*, published in 1579: 'two Shepherd boys taking occasion of the season, begine to make purpose of love and other pleasance, which to spring time is most agreeable'. In the verses in this Eclogue, Spenser indiscreetly alludes to Lettice Knollys, Lady Essex, already secretly married to Leicester.

The glossary of archaic and rustic words that Spenser's college friend Edward Kirke provided at the end of each eclogue identified Lettice as 'the name of some country lass'; yet in 1579 there was only one Laetitia in the realm, the widow of Walter Earl of Essex, who had secretly married Leicester. Leicester, therefore, must have regarded the allusion as a gross impertinence. The April Eclogue was a pæan of praise for the Queen, but Spenser's prayer for patronage was answered in an unexpected way when he was banished to Ireland as secretary to Lord Grey of Wilton, the Lord Deputy whose task it was to restore order after Desmond's rebellion. Throughout his long years in Ireland the poet never ceased to hope for a place at 'Cynthia's court'.

Raleigh urged Spenser to cross to England to present the first three books of *The Faerie Queene* to Elizabeth in person in 1589, and Sir Walter commended the work by adding a preface of two of his own sonnets. Spenser dedicated it to the Queen, almost as a matter of course, 'to live with the eternity of her fame'. *The Faerie Queene* was an elaborate allegory which Spenser had planned as a poem in twelve books, though he never completed it. The primary aim of the work, he declared in a prefatory letter, was 'to fashion a gentleman or noble person in virtuous and gentle discipline,' based on the twelve moral virtues of Aristotle. Like Castiglione's, his was to be a 'Book of the Courtier', to instruct men in the ways of courtesy, but to avoid envy and suspicion, instead of singling out a contemporary hero (such as Philip Sidney) for readers to take as their model, Spenser chose King Arthur, the folk hero of England *par excellence*. A second aim was the glorification of his sovereign in her two personalities as Queen and as 'a most virtuous and beautiful lady', so that Fairyland became located in Elizabethan England, peopled with characters that many felt could be positively identified; Mary Queen of Scots was identified in the character of Duessa, while Elizabeth appeared in turn as Belphœbe, the virgin huntress, as the chaste Britomart and as Gloriana the Fairy Queen herself.

She subsequently awarded him a pension of £50 a year, but there was to be no post in her train for the court laureate who had written the finest

English poem since Chaucer's *Canterbury Tales*. Spenser dwelt on the miserable condition of the suitor for preferment in *Mother Hubberds Tale*, a fable of the Ape and the Fox which satirised the life of the court.

> So pitiful a thing is Suitors state!
> Most miserable man, whom wicked fate
> Hath brought to Court, to sue for had ywist,
> That few have found, and many one hath missed!

One magnate whose duties never permitted him to come to court was George Talbot, Earl of Shrewsbury, custodian of Mary Queen of Scots. His father had been a Catholic but he was sufficiently Erastian for Elizabeth to rely on his loyalty. When he took on his onerous duty as jailer to the Scottish Queen, Shrewsbury had just married, as his second wife, the redoubtable Bess of Hardwick. Bess had already buried three husbands and had consequently amassed the remarkable chain of estates whose chief jewel was Chatsworth, a windfall from her second marriage to Sir William Cavendish. Indeed, her own wealth well matched Shrewsbury's. Characteristically, so as to preserve

Woodcut from the 1590 edition of the earliest books of Spenser's *The Faerie Queene*. It was Sir Walter Raleigh's encouragement that secured publication of this masterpiece, dedicated to Queen Elizabeth.

this inheritance, she married off two of her Cavendish offspring, Mary and Henry, to Shrewsbury's heir, Gilbert Talbot, and his daughter Grace respectively. The Earl remained very much under Bess's thumb, as was abundantly shown in the matter of the alliance between her daughter Elizabeth Cavendish and Charles Stuart, the younger brother of Darnley.

Since Mary's captivity, Charles's mother, Lady Lennox, had come out of the shadows, but when Elizabeth heard rumours that she had become reconciled to Mary, she questioned her. The Countess denied the rumours, declaring that she could 'never forget the murder of my child', Lord Darnley. The Queen was not satisfied, refusing her permission to visit Mary in 1574, yet Lady Lennox, on her way home to Yorkshire with her son, stopped at Rufford Abbey, near enough to Chatsworth to meet Bess of Hardwick and her unmarried Cavendish daughter. Legend has it that Charles Stuart fell ill – he was certainly a sickly lad – and before he recovered he had fallen in love with Elizabeth Cavendish. Scheming mothers had stage-managed the romance very effectively. Lady Margaret Douglas marvelled at the thought of a Cavendish dowry, while Bess of Hardwick quickly assessed the value of her daughter's alliance with a boy who stood in the line of succession to both England and Scotland, and the couple were married the next month.

Directly Elizabeth heard, she summoned both mothers to London, where they were imprisoned until her anger had passed. The Earl of Shrewsbury made it plain that the marriage had been arranged without his knowledge; as he put it in a letter to Burghley, Bess, 'finding her daughter disappointed of young [Peregrine] Bertie, where she hoped, and that the other young gentleman [Charles Stuart] was inclined to love with a few days acquaintance, did her best to further her daughter to the match'. The birth of a female heir, Arabella Stuart, at the end of 1575 must have been as great a disappointment to both families as Elizabeth's had been to her parents. Charles died of consumption a year later and his widow when Arabella was seven, so that the child was brought up at Hardwick by her maternal grandmother. In 1610, soon after Bess's death, Arabella eloped with the grandson of Lady Catherine Grey, thus uniting the Stuart with the Suffolk lines.

Other marriages of these years that caused trouble with the Queen were those of the children of the Duchess of Suffolk. On the very day that Elizabeth had been born, fourteen-year-old Catherine Willoughby d'Eresby had been married to Charles Brandon, Duke of Suffolk, the Queen's uncle. After some years of widowhood Catherine had married her steward, Richard Bertie. As zealous Protestants they had lived in Germany and Poland during Mary's reign, so that their son Peregrine was born in exile. It was through Burghley, always a loyal friend of the Duchess, despite her outspoken Puritanism, that Peregrine had been introduced to court. Here he fell in love with Oxford's sister, Lady Mary Vere, and they made a runaway marriage to flout the wishes of the Queen, the Duchess and Oxford, who all thought them incompatible. Peregrine was to model himself on Sir Philip Sidney, and was never so happy as when he was fighting Spaniards or Frenchmen; he was proud of his service in the field and hated the appellation 'courtier', saying 'he was none of the *Reptilia*'.

The Duchess of Suffolk had applauded the growing force of Puritanism in the country, in Parliament and even in Council, where Walsingham now

ABOVE LEFT Bess of Hardwick (1520-1608), who married George Talbot Earl of Shrewsbury as her fourth husband. She had a passion for building which she indulged at Chatsworth and Hardwick.

ABOVE RIGHT Lady Arabella Stuart (1575-1615), the daughter of Charles Stuart, Earl of Lennox, and Elizabeth Cavendish. Arabella was orphaned at the age of seven and was brought up by her formidable grandmother, Bess of Hardwick. This portrait by an unknown artist shows Arabella at the age of 23 months.

amplified the voices of Knollys and Mildmay. Yet the Queen resisted all attempts at root and branch reform of the Church. The last years of Archbishop Parker's primacy were overshadowed by the burning at Smithfield of Dutch Anabaptists as heretics and by the first real clashes between the Establishment and the Puritan movement. Earlier disputes about vestments were of small moment compared with the new dynamism of 'the precise believers', whose tenets were given an intellectual basis by Edmund Cartwright, the Lady Margaret Professor of Divinity at Cambridge, leader of a movement for Church reform based exclusively on scriptural authority.

An integral part both of Cartwright's campaign and of his blueprint for the new Jerusalem it would achieve was the practice of prophesying. Prophesyings took the form of public questions and answers between clergy and laity (much on the lines of a 'teach-in'), and while they promoted Biblical study they gave too many opportunities for airing doctrines that cut at the heart of the royal supremacy. The Queen was quick to recognise that here was a challenge to 'kingly rule'; the threat of the prophesying movement was serious, for several of her bishops were wholehearted supporters of it. Edmund Grindal, Parker's successor, had proved weak as Bishop of London in dealing with the early separatists, but his rule as Archbishop of York was relatively peaceful, since nonconformity in the northern province was exclusively Catholic. On Burghley's advice, the Queen had Grindal translated to Canterbury, but she soon regretted her decision, for instead of exterminating the prophesying movement as she had instructed, he defended it on the grounds of scriptural authority and its beneficial effects on educating clergy and laity. Grindal reported that the Bishops of London, Bath, Lichfield, Gloucester, Lincoln, Chichester, Exeter and St David's applauded the use of these exercises and that only his successor at York and the Bishops of Ely, Hereford and Winchester disapproved. 'If it be Your Majesty's pleasure for this or any other cause to remove me out of this place, I will with all humility yield thereunto,' he told the Queen and roundly said, 'I cannot marvel enough how this strange opinion should once enter your mind that it should be good for the Church to have few preachers.' Elizabeth chose to make an issue of it; Burghley's support was not of the slightest use while Leicester, whose doctor had recently been sentenced by Grindal for a matrimonial offence, was widely believed to have relished the Archbishop's own disgrace. In May 1577 Elizabeth wrote to the various bishops ordering them to put an end to all prophesyings, and she soon afterwards sequestered Grindal from office for six months on the grounds of disobedience to his Queen 'in her supreme authority ecclesiastical'. In effect the Church was without its primate.

At the end of the six months, efforts were made to bring about an accommodation, and it was suggested that Grindal, if reasonably penitent, might make a personal confession of his faults before the Lords of the Council and ask members to intercede with the Queen. But she refused to pardon him, as she considered his letter to the Lords too much in the vein of self-justification and there was nothing in it about amending his conduct. To depose him seemed impolitic, so she left him sequestered, hoping that he might resign of his own free will, but he was slow to come to any decision and his sight was deteriorating. 'My case dependeth long,' he wrote in February 1579, 'and yet if a man may believe in court promises, I was at no time so near an end of my troubles as at this present.' Convocation petitioned for his restoration, but this made the Queen urge him to consider his resignation more seriously. The *impasse* was only ended by Grindal's death in 1583.

During the 1570s the Netherlands remained the most sensitive zone for English interests, and it was Alençon's intervention in the States that provoked Elizabeth to revive her courtship of him. In March 1572 she had expelled Count la Marck's bands of privateers, 'the Sea Beggars', who had used English ports as bases for attacking Spanish shipping in the narrow seas. Her motives for this remain bewildering, and she can hardly have predicted the results of her action. After a month's aimless cruising La Marck seized Brill in south Holland, giving the Beggars a base in their own territory, and marking the real beginning of the revolt of the Netherlands. Elizabeth employed 'all correct means' to allow Protestant refugees in England and well-wishers among her own subjects to pass over to the Netherlands to fight against Spanish repression, but at the same time she repeatedly offered to mediate between Philip and his rebellious subjects. Alva, Philip's Governor of the Netherlands, knew that even if Elizabeth broke faith with him and encouraged traitors like Orange there was 'a great difference between open action and underhand'. This accommodation with the Spanish Netherlands, coming on top of the Anglo-French *entente*, gave Elizabeth five years of peace and security such as she had not experienced since her accession.

When Alva had been replaced as Governor of the Netherlands by the milder Requesens, Elizabeth tried hard to mediate between him and William of Orange, on the basis of a return to traditional liberties. She blamed William for continuing what she now regarded as an unnecessary war for the sake of a religious toleration she could not understand. She desperately wanted a peaceful settlement, honourable to both sides, and could never bring herself to countenance rebellious subjects against their lawful sovereign.

William's Calvinism was just as repugnant to her as his rebelliousness, a point of view which Walsingham never grasped, and she was determined to hold the reins of policy herself.

Elizabeth was so distressed at her inability to mediate at this time that she had a series of sleepless nights and even beat 'one or two of her ladies in waiting'. In August 1575 she openly proclaimed the Prince of Orange as a rebel and later threatened that she would aid Philip to restore the province of Holland to his obedience. In fact Elizabeth was free for the first time from pressing problems and could luxuriate in procrastination, to the dismay of her councillors. Sir Thomas Smith, her Secretary of State, complained:

> This irresolution doth weary and kill her ministers, destroy her actions and over-come all good designs and counsels – no letters touching Ireland, although read and allowed by Her Majesty, yet can I get signed. I wait whilst I neither have eyes to see or legs to stand upon. And yet these delays grieve me more and will not let me sleep in the night ...

Between Requesen's death and the arrival of his successor, Don John of Austria, in the Netherlands in 1576, the Spanish forces mutinied for lack of pay, sacking Antwerp in their fury and sending tremors throughout Europe. The States-General concluded a treaty with Holland and Zeeland, known as the Pacification of Ghent, which recognised William of Orange as Stad-holder of those two provinces. William appealed to Elizabeth to mediate with Philip of Spain for the confirmation of the Pacification, and also asked her for a loan. She acted with promptitude and firmness, dispatching Sir John Smith to Madrid and Edward Horsey to Don John, threatening to aid the States-General with money and men if Spain refused to recognise the settlement. Indeed, she had already sent the States £20,000 for immediate needs.

Her intervention persuaded Don John to accept the States' terms by his 'Perpetual Edict', and she therefore achieved the settlement she wanted: a united Netherlands, self-governing, with the liberties they had enjoyed under the Emperor Charles v, still under Spanish sovereignty but free from the tyranny of a Spanish army. Yet there were no satisfactory guarantees that Holland and Zeeland would enjoy liberty of worship, and William of Orange cold-shouldered the new Governor. Don John had his own ambitions, for once the Netherlands had been pacified he intended embarking his troops for an invasion of England, where he would rescue and marry Mary Queen of Scots and oust Elizabeth from her throne. When Elizabeth caught wind of these plans she countered by insisting to the States-General that the Spanish soldiers should be sent home by the land route, and in a panic Don John seized Namur in July 1577. Again Elizabeth acted swiftly, offering the States a loan of £100,000 and promising to send troops if the Duke of Guise came to Don John's aid, as was feared. Soon war was renewed in all its horrors in this cockpit of the Reformation, and when Alexander Farnese, Prince of Parma, arrived with a Spanish army, Protestant princes offered further aid. Elizabeth agreed to loan money on the security of her own jewels to enable John Casimir of the Palatinate to bring in a force of eleven thousand German and Swiss mercenaries, providing her name was not divulged. What-ever the Puritan hotheads said, she could not risk openly challenging Spain to war.

The Catholics of Artois and Hainault turned for help to the Duke of Alençon. Catherine de'Medici and Henry III were delighted to have the adventurer out of France, and felt it was most advantageous for him to carve a French duchy out of the southern Netherlands. He was elected 'Defender of Belgic liberty against the Spanish tyrant', and for England the prospect of French conquest of the Low Countries became far more alarming than continuing Spanish domination. To her councillors' consternation Elizabeth decided on controlling Alençon – something his mother and brother had never succeeded in achieving – by the expedient of reviving the marriage project. He quickly warmed to the idea, for Elizabeth was in a position to provide him with money for his troops as well as a consort's crown.

In 1578, Elizabeth made a progress to Norwich, and visited many of her courtiers in East Anglia. While she was staying at Long Melford in Suffolk with Sir William Cordell, Master of the Rolls, she received two of Alençon's envoys, M. de Bacqueville and M. de Quincy, whom she was anxious to impress. The chronicler of the royal visit to Suffolk certainly praised Cordell's efforts at entertaining, for he did 'light such a candle to the rest of the shire that many were glad, bountifully and frankly to follow the same

Elizabeth I gives audience
to two Dutch ambassadors
in the Privy Chamber.
In this painting by an
unknown artist, the Earl
of Leicester and the Lord
Admiral are among the
councillors in the
background.

example'. Alas, the scribe has glossed over a most awkward incident. Elizabeth asked Oxford to dance before the envoys, but he was petulant, saying that he hoped Her Majesty would not order him to dance 'as he did not want to entertain Frenchmen'. Sussex brought a further request across to him, but Oxford was adamant; no, he would not perform for the benefit of the French. No doubt Leicester had put him up to this, to show Alençon's ambassadors how unpopular they were. The same week Leicester had nervously written to Walsingham about the Queen's marriage: 'no man can tell what to say; as yet she has imparted with no man, at least not with me, nor for aught I can learn with any other'.

At Christmas 1578 Alençon sent Jean de Simier, his Master of the Wardrobe and a close friend, to woo Elizabeth by proxy. Simier had his own private troubles, for having discovered that his brother had been having an affair with his own wife, he had him murdered just before coming to England, and the wife subsequently took poison. Elizabeth had no inkling of this darker side of his character; she reckoned him 'a perfect courtier' and gave the impression of being swept off her feet by his typically French gallantry. His success was gauged by the speed with which he acquired a royal nickname – 'Monkey'.

Simier had brought with him jewels worth 12,000 crowns to distribute at court, which made Leicester outwardly affable, and the Queen gave a ball in his honour during which there was a masque between six ladies who surrendered themselves to six lovers. She wrote in haste to the Duke, telling him that his own words of love should be engraved in marble, not merely written on parchment, and vowed eternal friendship, assuring him she had *never* broken her word and 'since constancy is rare among royalty what she was offering him was almost unique'. M. Jean was a thorough ladies' man – 'a most choice courtier, exquisitely skilled in love toys, pleasant conceits and court dalliances'. He even raided the Queen's bedroom to carry off a nightcap to send as an illicit love token to Alençon; while Elizabeth went so far as to visit him in his lodgings before he was fully dressed, so that he had to see her 'with only his jerkin on'.

Leicester and Hatton were understandably put out. Leicester in bad faith advised Simier that Alençon should visit England while Parliament was sitting, when he would himself gladly move the House of Lords to demand the marriage, but the envoy saw through his schemes. Then Leicester accused him of using 'love potions and other unlawful arts' to entice Elizabeth to his master. When one of the Queen's ladies spoke up for Leicester, she railed at her, 'Dost you think me so unlike myself and unmindful of my royal majesty that I would prefer my servant whom I myself have raised, before the greatest prince of Christendom, in the honour of a husband?' She revelled in this fantastic game of love, was loath to be out of Simier's company and would have not a word of criticism of his behaviour. 'He has shown himself faithful to his master, is sage and discreet beyond his years in the conduct of the case,' she told Sir Amyas Paulet, her ambassador in Paris, adding the snub, 'we wish we had such a servant of whom we could make such good use'. There was an awkward tug between heart and head for those who, like Walsingham, were opposed to the marriage on religious grounds, yet felt that the international situation called for such an alliance.

Great preparations were made for Alençon's visit, with courtiers buying new clothes for themselves and their wives. Leicester asked Davison in Flanders to buy for him 4,000 crowns worth of velvet, silks and satin, as well as gold and silver tissue 'or such-like pretty stuffs'. Simier had asked for a coronation for the Prince immediately following marriage, an income of £60,000 a year and the right to make various appointments. The Queen stayed at Leicester's house at Wanstead in April while her councillors discussed these terms into the small hours, but no conclusion could be reached. When the court returned to Whitehall the new Lord Chancellor, Bromley, waxed eloquent on the unpopularity of the match and of the dangers of admitting Frenchmen, traditional enemies of long standing, to share in the government; they did not understand English law and institutions any better than they spoke the language. All present agreed with him, save Sussex, who was convinced that the marriage would frighten Philip II into making a settlement in the Netherlands that would be advantageous to English interests. When Simier was called in and told of the council's views he fled from the room in a rage and rushed to the Queen who was in the Privy Garden. Elizabeth vowed to him that she would marry Alençon despite her council's opposition, forgetting for the moment her standing proviso that she would never commit herself in advance to a suitor she had not seen. Subsequently she let the French know that outstanding disagreements in the draft treaty could be happily left to informal discussion between the two of them.

Once Elizabeth had signed Alençon's passport for entering the country, Leicester retired to bed at Wanstead, feigning illness. As always, the Queen felt that she must visit him in case his condition were serious, and while he was still away from court sulking a member of the sovereign's guard fired on Simier in the grounds of Greenwich, where he had been assigned a suite. Three weeks earlier there had been a scare when the royal barge, taking the Queen, Simier, Leicester and Hatton down the Thames, had been shot at, and most people assumed that Simier had been the intended victim. The second attack Simier regarded in a different light. Knowing Leicester's hatred of the proposed marriage, he concluded that the attempt on his life in the palace gardens had been plotted by the Earl; alarmed as much for his own safety as for the success of Alençon's visit, he brought out the sharpest weapon in his armoury. With a flair for winning confidences and winnowing truth from fanciful rumour, he had uncovered the greatest secret at court – that Leicester was married. In September 1578 Leicester had actually taken Lettice Knollys, widow of the Earl of Essex, as his wife twice over, for her father, Francis Knollys, insisted on a second ceremony which he could himself witness, fearing that Leicester might otherwise disavow her, as he had rejected Douglas, Lady Sheffield. There had been rumours enough of the Earl's trifling with Lettice Knollys, but nothing to suggest that they had become man and wife.

This revelation hurt Elizabeth more than anything since Norfolk's treachery. This was worse than Amy Robsart's death, worse than the bastard son born to Lady Sheffield. Her own Robin, to whom she had just lent £15,000 she could ill afford, whose protestations of adoring love she had always regarded as sincere, had deliberately deceived her. She could condone flirtations but she could never forgive him for contracting a marriage without her leave. Here he was, posing as a lone, forlorn widower, counselling her very strongly against plighting her troth to Alençon, while he was in fact a married man himself. In a burst of anger she ordered him to be sent to the Tower, and he would have gone had it not been for the persuasive reasoning of Sussex, who, despite his own abiding dislike of Leicester, knew that the Queen must be prevented from striking an angry blow that would do untold harm to her dignity.

Instead of the Tower of London, the Earl was lodged in a tower in Greenwich Park, and it was announced at court that he was taking physic and would see no one. After a few days he retired to his house at Wanstead, debarred from the Queen's presence until her fury had abated. She called her cousin Lettice a 'she-wolf' and forbade her ever to appear at court. The Earl wrote to Burghley, tearfully complaining of the Queen's 'very strange humour' towards him. 'I have lost both youth, liberty, and all my fortune reposed in her; and, my Lord, by the time I have made an even reckoning with the world, your Lordship will not give me much for the remainder of my twenty years' service; but I trust still, she that hath been so gracious to all, will not only be grievous to me. . . .'

Once Leicester's marriage with the Countess of Essex was public knowledge, Lady Douglas and her sister saw that there was no further merit in spurning the many proposals that each continued to receive at court. Douglas settled on Sir Edward Stafford, the English ambassador at Paris, whom she married in November 1579. Stafford's maternal grandmother had been a Pole, while his paternal grandfather, Buckingham, had been executed by Henry VIII for his nearness to the throne, so Sir Edward came of quasi-royal lineage. Elizabeth subsequently needed assurances that there was no impediment by an earlier marriage ceremony between Douglas and Leicester and spitefully said that if there had been a legally binding contract then the Earl should honour her with marriage 'or rot in the Tower', and his union with Lettice would be annulled. It fell to Sussex, a cousin of Lady Douglas by marriage, to cross-question the lady, who could produce neither document nor witness to back her statement that Leicester had plighted his troth to her in 1573. By now her hatred of him was intense, so she remained Lady Stafford and became a convert to Catholicism.

The marriage of Lady Frances Howard was in its way even more dramatic, for in 1582 she married the Earl of Hertford. With the death of his first wife, Lady Catherine Grey, Hertford was able to reappear at court and sink his roots in Wiltshire; his two sons, born in the Tower, probably spent their early years in Burghley's household. Lady Frances stayed as lady of the Privy Chamber, largely because the secret of their marriage had been well kept; the earliest evidence for the Queen chiding Lady Hertford about her indiscreet wedding was in 1593.

When the Queen's 'Frog' at last arrived at Greenwich on 17 August 1579 her first impressions were most favourable. She need not have worried about his face or his height, for Alençon was an utter charmer, a young romantic with considerable sex appeal, and her vanity was satisfied that a princely suitor had come in person to plead his own passionate cause. What transpired during his twelve-day stay is conjectural, for his visit was supposed to be a hushed secret; the Queen had assured the Spanish ambassador that the Duke had *not* come to her, and when she caught two ladies of the court gossiping about the Duke she placed them under arrest until he had left.

On their first evening, she dined alone with him in Simier's room, while on another night she let him eavesdrop at a ball where she was resplendently dressed and danced constantly. Alençon left convinced that he had won her heart and from Boulogne he sent her 'a little flower of gold, with a frog thereon, and therein Monsieur his physiognomy, and a little pearl pendant'.

Protestant horrors of St Bartholomew's Eve were still vivid and pressing, and the deep-seated prejudice against France that would in a later generation be summed up in the cry 'No Popery and no wooden shoes' flared up. Englishmen had not forgotten the loss of Calais and the treachery of the House of Guise, even if Elizabeth chose to put them out of her mind. In August, perhaps while Alençon was at Greenwich, the Puritan John Stubbs gave vent to the fears of half the nation in a forceful tract against the match, *The Discovery of a Gaping Gulf Whereunto England is like to be swallowed by another French Marriage if the Lord forbid not the Bans by letting Her Majesty see the sin and Punishment thereof.* Stubbs did not pull his punches. The Queen was too old to be contemplating marriage, and was at the most dangerous age of all for child-bearing, as her most faithful physicians could tell her; and as for Alençon, he was not merely a cunning French debauchee but 'the old serpent himself in the form of a man come a second time to seduce the English Eve and to ruin the English paradise'. Here was 'an imp of the crown of France to marry with the crowned nymph of England', and his manner of courting by paying Elizabeth a personal visit *incognito* was highly deplorable – 'an unmanlike, unprincelike, French kind of wooing'. Under the guise of his private chapel the Roman Mass would be restored in the land.

From the pulpits came virulent phrases about the daughter of God being corrupted by the son of Antichrist, and to silence this criticism Elizabeth issued a proclamation to be read by the bishops to their clergy, defending herself and the character of the Duke, while a preacher at Paul's Cross praised the achievements of the government and assured the multitude that their Queen would live and die in Christ. Stubbs' *Gaping Gulf* was castigated in the proclamation as a lewd, seditious book, showing true regard neither for the realm nor for the Queen, and all copies were to be seized and burnt. Author, printer and publisher were speedily sent for trial and sentenced under a statute of Philip and Mary to lose their right hands and undergo imprisonment. Elizabeth pardoned the printer, but Stubbs and his publisher had to endure the barbarous law. As soon as Stubbs' right hand was off he 'took off his hat with the left and cried aloud "God Save the Queen" '. He then fainted and was taken off to the Tower, where he spent the next eighteen months. Lifting up his bleeding arm, the publisher told the crowd, 'I left there a true Englishman's hand.' Elizabeth's popularity was at a very low ebb.

Only a year before, Oxford had refused to dance before Alençon's envoys at Long Melford, but now – perhaps under Burghley's influence – he had swung round to become an enthusiastic supporter of the match, while Philip Sidney remained an outspoken opponent. When these two young courtiers met, the effect was electric, and before Stubbs had been sentenced occurred the incident in the tennis court at Whitehall, where Sidney was playing when the Earl entered the court and, uninvited, joined in the game. Sidney objected, and as the Earl ordered all the players to leave, remonstrated with him. Oxford shouted that he was a puppy and Sidney, controlling himself under great provocation, remarked 'Puppies are gotten by dogs and children by men' but his opponent stalked off. Sidney felt that honour required him to challenge the Earl to a duel, but the Queen forbade the fight and required him to apologise to Oxford, because of the latter's high birth. This was anathema to the poet; instead of sending an apology he withdrew from court for a season, while the vengeful Earl made plans to murder him and was with difficulty persuaded to abandon what he thought was a fool-proof method of assassination.

At the request of Leicester and Walsingham, Sidney had already written a long letter to the Queen, speaking out against the marriage on behalf of all English Protestants, 'your chief, if not your sole strength', whose loyal hearts would be 'galled, if not alienated, when they shall see you take a husband, a Frenchman and a papist, in whom, howsoever fine wits may find further dealings or painted excuses, the very common people well know this: that he is the son of a Jezebel of our age; that his brother made oblation of his sister's marriage [to Henry of Navarre], the easier to make massacres of our brethren in belief'. All true believers would abhor such a man as consort and 'diminish much of the hopeful love they long held you in'. Elizabeth wept as she read this, and though she did not punish Sidney, he realised she had taken his letter in bad part and left court for a full year, staying mainly with his sister at Wilton, while he devoted himself to writing.

Did the Queen really want to marry Alençon in 1579, assuming that the religious and constitutional knots could be undone, and, if so, did she really expect still to bear children? While Alençon was twenty-three, she was exactly twice as old and at a difficult age. Her emotional instability was never so marked as in the middle and last acts of her protracted courtship with the Duke; she loved him, she loved him not; she would marry him straightaway, she lost all interest in the negotiations; she desperately wanted a baby, she dare not face the shock of consummation and the dangers of childbirth. All the signs are that at forty-six she was reaching or had perhaps even reached the menopause. At any time in the last fifteen years, news of Leicester's marriage would have wounded her womanly pride deeply, but coming at this crucial time in her life, it tore at her affections. Since Leicester had deserted her, Alençon gave her what she knew was her last chance of fulfilling herself as a woman, and she accepted his advances with relief.

Burghley had not the slightest doubt about her ability to become a mother, as he penned in a memorandum for his eyes alone in March 1579:

Considering the proportion of her body, having no impediment of smallness in stature, of largeness in body, nor no sickness, nor lack of natural functions in those things that properly belong to the procreation of children, but contrariwise [and this is significant] by judgment of physicians that know her estate in those things and by the opinion of women, being most acquainted with her Majesty's body in such things as properly appertain, to show probability of her aptness to have children, even at this day.

Many women even older and with a less suitable physique had given birth to healthy babies, and without impairing their own constitutions. The best medical opinion, Burghley noted, gave her as much as another six years in which to bear children: moreover sexual relations and the processes of conception and childbearing, far from endangering her health, would improve her general condition. Though Sussex, Leicester and Walsingham did not write elaborate memoranda on the topic, they were no less certain that Elizabeth was capable of bearing children. For them to have kept up an elaborate and prolonged pretence to the Queen herself on this delicate matter is one thing, but they could hardly have refused to have faced the facts realistically in their strictly private correspondence if marriage and issue had been quite out of the question. The frank opinion of Burghley, arrived at through discussion with the Queen's physicians, makes nonsense of all the old wives' tales that Elizabeth was barren. Some have thought her conduct in courtship could be explained rationally only on the supposition that she had a physical defect precluding hopes of issue, but all the evidence points the other way. In 1579 Elizabeth was convinced that a marriage with Alençon could be fruitful and desperately wanted it to take place. The shock of Leicester's marriage to Lettice Knollys had finally erased any lingering doubts, and driven her into Alençon's arms.

Had she been a free agent she would have accepted Alençon's proposal without more ado, but she was always sensitive to public opinion, and outbursts such as Stubbs' *Gaping Gulf* made her uneasy. Instead of giving way to her heart she turned to her council for advice, and decided once again to prorogue Parliament. If the council gave her the support she needed and expected (for they had been urging her to marry since her accession), she would do so and share the responsibility with them. She expected that Burghley, the great protagonist of the match, would carry the day.

The council debated the issue on 7 October, from 8 a.m. to 7 p.m. 'without stirring from the room, having sent the clerks away'. Every aspect was considered at length, except the Queen's personal feelings. By evening, Burghley found himself in a minority, for of the twelve present seven were against the marriage, including, as expected, Leicester and Hatton; but the Lord Treasurer managed to persuade them to give an open verdict. He went with Leicester, Sussex and Lincoln to tell the Queen that they could make no positive recommendations until they knew her own mind. This came to her as a calculated insult, and she told them as much, 'not without shedding of many tears'. It was insufferable that they should doubt the wisdom of her marrying and having a child 'to inherit and continue the line of Henry VIII'. She rued her decision to allow them to meddle in her affairs and later in the day she recalled the four senior councillors for a painful audience. Elizabeth marvelled 'that any person would think so slenderly of her as that she would not for God's cause, for herself, her surety and her people, have so strait a regard thereto as none ought to make such a doubt as, for it, to forbear marriage and to have the crown settled in her child'.

The council, wise after the event, worded an appropriate message of unanimous assent to the marriage 'if so it shall please her'. This was hardly encouragement; if they could do no better than that, she did not think it meet to tell them whether or not she would take Monsieur as her consort. In November, according to Mendoza, she again told her council that she was determined to wed and they 'need say nothing more to her about it, but should at once discuss what was necessary for carrying it out'. A quorum of councillors, excluding Leicester, talked terms with Simier, but Elizabeth made him agree to a moratorium of two months in the marriage treaty during which she would attempt to gain popular support for the match. By then, in effect, she had decided to proceed no further. Soon Simier, as well as Alençon, had left England and with Leicester permitted to be in regular attendance she began to lose interest in them both.

As the Catholic powers became more menacing Elizabeth decided that she must revive the Alençon affair, to 'keep him in correspondence'. Simier wrote to her:

> As for your Frog, his flame is immortal and his love towards you can never end, either in this world or the next. By God, Madame, lose no time. Take counsel with yourself and those whose faithful attachment is known to you for your *own* sake rather than *their* advancement. Let Monsieur again soon approach your charms – that is the daily prayer of your Monkey who, with all humility, kisses the shadow of your footsteps.

Elizabeth went to Deptford on 4 April 1582 to honour Sir Francis Drake, who had returned home in the late autumn from his remarkable voyage round the world in *The Pelican*, now aptly renamed *The Golden Hind*, 'fraught with gold, silver, silk and precious stones'. Elizabeth's own share of the booty, as a private investor in the voyage, was in the region of £160,000 – as much as a normal Parliamentary grant – since each of the backers enjoyed a return of 4,700 per cent. The chests of rich booty plundered from the *Cacafuego* had been sent to the Tower, as Elizabeth had steadily refused to listen to Mendoza's pleadings that these prize goods should be restored to Spain. So Drake's investiture aboard *The Golden Hind* was rather more than a domestic event, and the Queen planned to make as much political capital from it as she could. She slyly told him that she had a gilded sword to strike off his head for turning pirate, and then handed the sword to the Seigneur de Marchaumont, who was Alençon's special agent in London, asking him to perform the ceremony for her, which he gladly did. This alone foreshadowed an Anglo-French league against Spain.

While she was boarding Drake's ship, one of the Queen's purple and gold garters slipped down, and de Marchaumont claimed it as lawful prize, intending to send it as a keepsake to Alençon. Elizabeth asked for it back, 'as she had nothing else with which to keep her stocking up,' promising to surrender it to him on returning to the palace. So the garter followed the nightcap and the other trophies pocketed by Simier. Drake's present to her on this great day was an ornament of diamonds, and some said it was in the shape of a frog. 'This and all other signs seem to indicate a real intention to effect the marriage,' wrote Mendoza in alarm.

Within the fortnight the French commissioners for arranging the marriage treaty arrived, led by Francis of Bourbon; among the lawyers present was Jean Bodin. The entertainment of five hundred and fifty Frenchmen at court for some weeks, when feelings undoubtedly would run high, caused many headaches. A proclamation called on all Englishmen to show special honour to the distinguished visitors and forbade anyone to draw a sword within the court or to provoke a quarrel, on pain of death. The French were welcomed by Pembroke and Cobham, the Lord Warden, at Dover and taken by carriages to Gravesend, then by barges to Somerset House, which was to be their headquarters.

Elizabeth was determined to impress the commissioners with *fêtes galantes*,

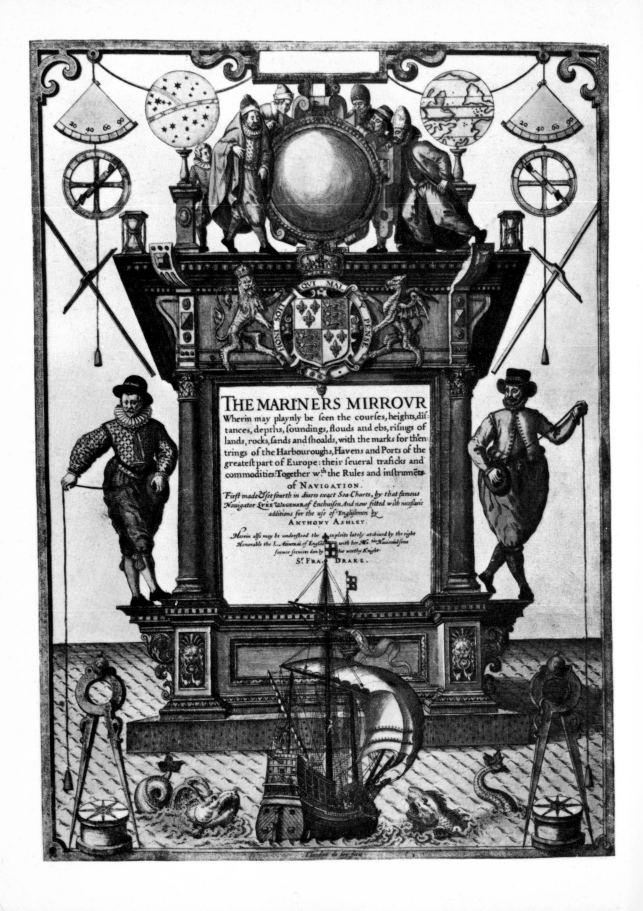

THE MARINERS MIRROVR

Wherin may playnly be seen the courses, heights, distances, depths, soundings, flouds and ebs, risings of lands, rocks, sands and shoalds, with the marks for the entrings of the Harbouroughs, Havens and Ports of the greatest part of Europe: their seueral traficks and commodities: Together w.th the Rules and instrumēts of NAVIGATION.

First made & set fourth in diuers exact Sea-Charts, by that famous Nauigator LVKE WAGENAR of Enchuisen. And now fitted with necessarie additions for the use of Englishmen by ANTHONY ASHLEY.

Heerin alss may be understood the exploits lately atchiued by the right Honorable the L. Admiral of England with her Ma.ties Nauie and some former seruices don by that worthy Knight S.r FRA. DRAKE.

Waghenaer's *Mariner's Mirror*, 1586. This manual on navigation, which included details of Drake's most recent voyages, was dedicated to Sir Christopher Hatton. LEFT Engraved frontispiece by Theodor de Bry. RIGHT 'A moveable compass for the stars', one of the detailed drawings.

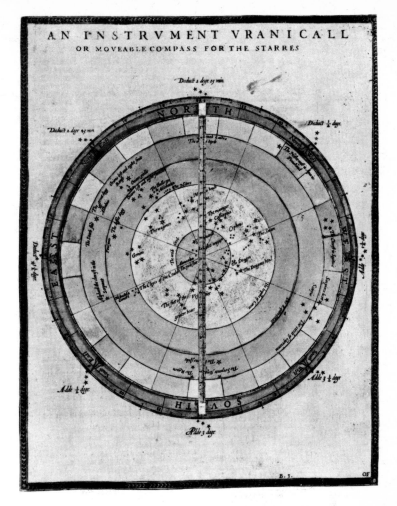

AN INSTRVMENT VRANICALL
OR MOVEABLE COMPASS FOR THE STARRES

and for the occasion a special banqueting-house was constructed of wood and canvas in the gardens of Whitehall, three hundred and thirty-two feet long and nearly as broad, with the canvas walls painted outside to resemble stonework, and with ninety-two windows. The inside was 'most cunningly painted' with impressions of the heavens, while great baskets of bespangled greenery and greengrocery decked out the roof. The highlight of the festivities was a Triumph in the tiltyard on 15 May, where the setpiece was the 'Fortress of Perfect Beauty', which was assailed by Desire and his foster children, courtiers led by Philip Sidney – an incongruous role for one who had been so outspoken against the marriage in its earliest days. Cannons were fired with scented powder and toilet water for ammunition, and there were frolics with 'pretty scaling-ladders and then footmen threw flowers and such fancies against the walls with all sort devices as might seem fit shot for Desire'. This elaborate pageant, with its enormous cast in dazzling costumes, was an allegory on the royal courtship. In vain did messengers address the Queen herself at intervals in the battle, asking her to surrender her perfect beauty to virtuous desire. An angel spoke for the defenders of her maidenly citadel: 'Sir Knights, if in besieging the sun you understood what you had undertaken, you would destroy a common blessing for a private benefit. ... Will

you subdue the sun? . . . We are content to enjoy the light, you to eclipse it.'
Long into the evening the performance lasted, until the challengers gave up
the unequal struggle. Virtue was too strong for Desire, and the Fortress of
Perfect Beauty was 'to be reserved for the eye of the whole world'.

The message cannot have been lost on the French embassy, yet the significance of the two months' merrymaking, the splendid dinners and costly
pageantry must have impressed the rest of the diplomatic corps. The marriage
negotiations might founder yet again, but here was the firm foundation of an
entente cordiale much more far-reaching than the Treaty of Blois, a power to
challenge the might of Spain. Elizabeth appointed a committee to discuss
details with the Prince Dauphin, confident that they would never agree; of
the six, only Sussex was heart and soul in favour of the marriage, while
Leicester, Hatton and Walsingham were opposed to it, and Burghley and
Bedford neutral. Protracted discussions on the marriage treaty made little
progress, even though the form of wedding service to be followed was agreed
upon. At the end of it all Elizabeth made it quite plain that whatever document the commissioners signed, the application of its clauses would depend
on a definite agreement between Alençon and herself. The affair was as much
in doubt as it ever had been, but she wrote warmly to the Duke, embedding
a diamond in the wax with which she closed the letter.

To encourage her suitor Elizabeth complied with his urgent request for
funds, and the £30,000 she sent helped him to pay his troops after forcing
Parma to raise the siege of Cambrai. After putting his soldiers in winter
quarters, Alençon finally arrived at the end of October and was most warmly
received. He was assigned a house near the palace at Richmond, where his
comforts were to be looked after by Lord Henry Howard and his nephew,
Philip, Earl of Arundel (Norfolk's eldest son). Elizabeth had herself super-
vised the furnishing of his rooms and said that he might recognise the bed!
She told him he was 'the most deserving and constant of all her lovers', and
counted on being able to prolong the preliminaries. To appease Protestant
critics she even persuaded him to accompany her to St Paul's Cathedral and
gave him a kiss in front of the congregation as a reward.

The climax of their affair was a scene in the gallery at Whitehall on her
accession day, celebrated that particular year with especial pomp. She told
the French ambassador that he could write to Paris with the news 'that the
Duke of Alençon shall be my husband,' and then turning to her suitor 'kissed
him on the mouth, drawing a ring from her own hand and giving it to him
as a pledge,' while Alençon gave her a ring of his in return. Then she called
her principal courtiers and the other ambassadors from the Presence Chamber out to the gallery and repeated her pledge. The Duke was 'extremely
overjoyed', Burghley praised the Lord that his Queen had at last arrived at
a decision, but Leicester fretted and Hatton was in tears. Even if she wanted
to marry, Hatton said, she should consider the grief she would bring to the
country and it was on her people's affections that her security always
depended. Leicester, more outspoken, dared to ask her if she were still a
virgin; he was again using Protestant preachers to work upon their listeners'
fears.

Few realised that the Queen's performance in the gallery at Whitehall was
no more than a clever piece of acting, carefully premeditated and rehearsed.
The story goes that the same evening her ladies, prompted by Leicester and

Hatton, 'wailed and by laying terrors before her did so vex her mind with argument' against marriage that she had a sleepless night. The following morning she sent for the Duke and told him that two more such nights and she would be in the grave, but in the long silent watches, torn between her duty as a Queen and her feelings as a woman, she had decided to sacrifice her own happiness for the welfare of her people, though her great affection for him was undiminished. When he later asked leave to depart the court she bade him stay – she would marry him, she said, at a more propitious moment, but at present her own feelings were too disturbed. So Alençon obediently and hopefully stayed on for another three months, fêted, courted and slow to realise he had outstayed his welcome. The 'wailings' of her women certainly had something to do with her uneasiness, but they did not now quite suddenly 'terrify her from marrying' as Camden suggests. Elizabeth used their warnings on the perils of childbirth as an excuse for jilting her Frog, but in fact her mind had been made up eighteen months earlier, when she saw the deep opposition of her council. After a feverish night she stayed in bed, sending for Sussex to do his duty in curbing her 'insolent favourites', and at the council meeting later in the day Burghley had to intervene to stop Sussex from striking Leicester.

Now that the Queen wanted to be rid of Alençon, his departure from England was reduced to hard bargaining on a cash basis. At last, on 1 February, the Queen left London with the Duke on the first stage of his return journey to the Netherlands and wept diplomatic tears at Canterbury when she bade him farewell and told him that she would be unhappy until he came back to her. He took with him £10,000 in cash with a firm promise of £50,000 more when he finally went aboard *The Discovery* at Sandwich, attended by Leicester, Hunsdon and other peers who were to escort him to Antwerp. But for the bad weather Elizabeth would have gone right to the coast with him. Leicester tried to excuse himself from the trip, but Elizabeth would not hear of it; he would suffer penalties if he failed to show true respect to the person 'she loved best in the world', and in any case the Earl was to take secret instructions to William the Silent to detain Alençon in Holland so that he could never return to England. (Sussex for his part was urging Alençon to detain Leicester in the Netherlands.)

Once the Duke had gone, Elizabeth was melancholy and wrote verses in the style of Petrarch on *Monsieur's Departure*. After the opposition to the marriage in the late summer of 1579 she knew that it would be impossible to go through with it, but kept up the pretence and continued to regard her Prince with great tenderness. Now he was too busy in the field to think of wooing her afresh and his tender missives became begging letters. She had wept at his going because their lengthy courtship had been her last; she was now an old maid. When he died of a fever in June 1584 she wrote to Catherine de'Medici: 'Your sorrow cannot exceed mine, although you were his mother. You have another son, but I can find no other condition than death, which I hope will soon enable me to rejoin him.'

7 The Shepherds of the Ocean

The 1580s were the years of Raleigh's prime. Compared with Hatton his rise was meteoric, and so incidents were invented by later generations, such as the affair of throwing his cloak in the mire for the Queen to walk upon, to account for his remarkable career. A rank outsider to the court, with no hint of noble birth, Raleigh was soon regarded by Elizabeth as 'a kind of oracle, which nettled them all', and he enjoyed a lease of Durham House in the Strand on very favourable terms, though he had to wait until 1585 to be knighted and a further two years for a court office. He probably owed his successful début in the winter of 1581 to the fact that his mother was a Champernowne, so that both Kate Ashley and Lady Denny had been his great-aunts.

The occasion of Raleigh's coming to court had been to report on the Irish wars where his service, following a season swashbuckling in France, had made him something of an expert. The Queen at once took to the tall, West Country adventurer, nineteen years her junior, and refused to let him return to Ireland. She soon appreciated his remarkable intellect and encouraged him to think himself in love with her. With Leicester married and Alençon marooned in Flanders, Raleigh made the most of his chances. Without specific training he showed that he possessed many of the qualities of the courtier that Castiglione had listed, but most of all it was his many-sidedness that appealed to the Queen and he was able to enliven her days with brilliant conversation. She once asked him as he hunted for favours, 'when will you cease to be a beggar?' and he capped this by replying 'when you cease to be a benefactress'.

Raleigh's greatest asset was 'wit', in the true Elizabethan sense of the term. Naunton (who in years to come was to be a member of King James 1's government that sent Raleigh to the block) provided a perceptive thumb-nail sketch of him; 'He had a good presence in a handsome and well-compacted person; a strong natural wit and a better judgment, with a bold and plausible tongue, whereby he could set out his points to best advantage.' Mocking his Devonian speech, Elizabeth nicknamed him 'Warter', but the poet in him soon drew from her other names. With his flair for maritime adventure, she dubbed him 'the Shepherd of the Ocean' and he responded that, since the seas were always ruled by the moon, she must be his 'Cynthia', the moon goddess of poesy. But if the Cynthia of allegory represented a cold, chaste creature, Raleigh's love for his Queen was more than platonic:

ABOVE Drawing of a Virginian Indian chief, from an account of the expedition sponsored by Raleigh to found Roanoke colony.

RIGHT Sir Walter Raleigh, Captain of the Gentleman Pensioners, in 1588: portrait attributed to the monogrammist 'H'.

My thoughts are winged with hopes, my lips with love,
Mount love, into the moon's clearest night,
And say, as she doth in the heavens move
On earth so wanes and waxeth my delight,
And whisper this but softly in her ears,
Hope oft doth hang the head and trust shed tears.

Tradition has it that in his first days at court, Raleigh wrote on a window pane with the diamond from his ring the words 'Fain, would I climb, yet fear to fall', to which Elizabeth herself added the line 'If thy heart fail thee, climb not at all.' Encouragement such as this was enough for any man of spirit to try his luck at the greasy pole of society. He spent a fortune with his tailor to be decked out in fineries that by comparison made Leicester seem almost shabby and Hatton soberly garbed; his jewelled shoes, it was said, were worth £6,000. Though he made a point of cultivating Leicester's friendship, he found rather to his surprise that he needed no patron, and his immediate success with the Queen made him 'the best hated man of the world'. With his lucrative wine licence and his revenues as Lord Warden of the Stanneries in Devon and Cornwall, he could live extravagantly. When Hatton eventually became Lord Chancellor, Sir Walter succeeded him as Captain of the Bodyguard and he capped his fortunes with a grant of the manor of Sherborne in Dorset. Raleigh remained a party of one, for most courtiers were rather scared of those intellectual qualities which had helped him win royal favour; they could not understand this man who professed to enjoy smoking tobacco, a strange mystic with topsy-turvy ideas about the deity and the universe, who was friendly with Edmund Spenser and Christopher Marlowe. Wanting him at her side, Elizabeth had refused to let him lead the expedition to the New World where he planned to found an English settlement, but she allowed his Roanoke colony to be called 'Virginia' after her. The Virgin Queen needed his adoration and his presence as hostages against loneliness and the passing of the years. A Jesuit pamphleteer, mistaking his role, called him 'the darling of the English Cleopatra', but Raleigh was not to be content with platonic love for a woman of fifty, even if she wore a crown. Her eyes, he wrote in a poignant verse, had fired his fancy, her hands had conquered his masculine desire:

O eyes that pierce our heart without remorse,
O hairs of right that wear a crown,
O hands that conquer more than Caesar's force,
O wit that turns huge kingdoms upside down!
Then Love, be judge, what heart may thee withstand!
Such eyes, such hair, such wit and such a hand.

From the turret of Durham House overlooking the Thames, with a view 'as pleasant as any in the world', Raleigh set down his innermost thoughts, but none of his verse was published in his lifetime. However devoted in his attentions, he could not for ever tread meekly the path of a Hatton, consecrating his life to an ideal of womanhood, harbouring a strange passion that could not be reciprocated, and after ten years of acting the part he had ceased to believe in it. He had been miscast as a courtier in the idylls of the Queen and when he discovered real happiness in his relationship with Bess Throckmorton, a lady of the Privy Chamber, he was banished. He was by

BELOW Aerial view of Longford Castle, Wiltshire, showing the triangular plan of the house, based upon the Holy Trinity.

BELOW RIGHT Lyveden New Bild, Northampton-shire, erected in about 1600 by Sir Thomas Tresham to symbolise the

ABOVE Detail of a cross from the triangular lodge at Rushton in North-amptonshire, also built by Tresham to symbolise the Trinity. The leopards of England are included in the decoration, implying that a Catholic resident could still be intensely loyal.

Passion. Tresham, a fervent Catholic, had been imprisoned in 1581 for harbouring the Jesuit priest, Edmund Campion, and was to be executed in 1605 for his part in the Gunpowder Plot, leaving his strange allegorical house incomplete.

then no longer dazzled by the Sun Queen and professed to have seen through the façade of the Presence Chamber, the ritual and trappings of regality, the hollowness of courtiers' words, the hypocrisy of ministers, the abject life of a favourite with no soul of his own and the falsehoods supporting the throne. The bitterness of the courtier fallen from grace comes out strongly in Raleigh's poem *The Lie*:

Say to the Court it glows,
And shines like rotten wood.
Say to the Church it shows
What's good and doth no good.
If Church and Court reply,
Then give them both the lie.

Tell men of high condition
That rule affairs of state
Their purpose is ambition,
Their practice only hate.
And if they do reply
Then give them all the lie.

Tell potentates they live
Acting on others' action,
Not loved unless they give,
Not strong but by affection,
If potentates reply,
Give potentates the lie.

Frances Sidney, Countess
of Sussex, the wife of
Thomas Radcliffe, the
3rd Earl: portrait
attributed to Steven
van der Meulen, c. 1565.
Under the terms of her
will, the Lady Frances
Sidney Sussex College
at Cambridge was
founded in 1596.

Spenser was thinking of Raleigh, the Shepherd of the Ocean who had helped launch the *Faerie Queen*, when he, too, came to paint the court in sombre colours:

> And, sooth to say, it is no sort of life
> For shepherd fit to lead, in that same place,
> Where each one seeks with malice, and with strife
> To thrust down other unto foul disgrace,
> Himself to raise ...

By 1590 it seemed to him that the most useful attribute of a courtier was 'a guileful hollow heart, wasted with fair-dissembling courtesy' yet such was too harsh on the Queen. However much Elizabeth fed on adoration she could readily distinguish between a fawning sycophant and a man of worth. Raleigh's sin lay in his own dishonest courtesy to his sovereign when he married Bess Throckmorton.

As Alençon's suit was withering, Elizabeth received enquiries for her hand from an outlandish quarter; Pissemsky, the Russian ambassador sent to England to conclude a treaty, had been instructed by Ivan the Terrible to sound the Queen on the idea of marriage. Uncharacteristically, she frowned on the idea from the first, but when the Tsar persisted in asking for an English lady with at least some royal blood in her veins, the name of Lady Mary Hastings, Huntingdon's third sister, cropped up. Elizabeth was little less enthusiastic about Lady Mary's proposal than about her own, and refused to allow a portrait of the lady to be painted, on the grounds that she had only recently recovered from smallpox. Eventually, in May 1583, the ambassador was allowed to see her, duly chaperoned, when he bowed obsequiously and kissed the ground in front of her, as homage to a Tsarina elect, but she became alarmed at reports of Ivan's proverbial cruelty and excused herself from the honour of marriage with him on the incontrovertible grounds that the Tsar already had a wife. To smooth out an awkward situation, Sir Jerome Bowes accompanied the envoy home on the Queen's orders to explain to Ivan that he must not pursue his plans, since Lady Mary's health was too frail for a hazardous journey and the rigours of a Russian winter. In fact the lady did not long survive the episode, but for a season enjoyed the nickname 'Empress of Muscovy' at court. The reputation of English ladies for beauty was by no means checked in Russia by this affair, for in 1601 Boris Godunov was to send an envoy bearing sables to prospect for a wife for his son, and there was some danger of Derby's daughter being banished to Muscovy.

Sussex followed the fashion in taking the waters of Buxton, but could find no relief for his worn-out body and died in his early sixties at his home in Bermondsey in 1583. As he died he warned those gathered about his bed to arm themselves against Leicester's wiles, now that his most forceful opponent was passing to another world. His widow, Lady Frances Sidney, subsequently founded Sidney Sussex College, Cambridge. He was succeeded in the earldom by his brother Henry, who had seen service in Ireland before settling down in Hampshire, where he was constable of Porchester and Portsmouth castles. Henry now found the third Earl's estates encumbered with heavy debts. He enjoyed the title for no more than ten years, to be succeeded by his son Robert Radcliffe, a man much in his uncle's mould as soldier and patron of letters.

These were, indeed, splendid years for the University of Cambridge, for Archbishop Parker had bequeathed to Corpus Christi his great collections of manuscripts, rich in Anglo-Saxon documents and medieval chronicles, and in 1584 Sir Walter Mildmay, Under-Treasurer to Burghley – himself Chancellor of the University – founded Emmanuel College as a bulwark of Puritanism. Mildmay looked to the ideal of a learned, preaching ministry and hoped that his college would furnish a succession of young men truly fitted to 'undertake the office of pastors'. There is a ring of truth in the tale that Elizabeth on hearing of his philanthropy remarked, 'Sir Walter, I hear you have erected a Puritan foundation,' to which he replied, 'No, Madam, far be it for me to countenance anything contrary to your established laws; but I have set an acorn which, when it becomes an oak, God alone knows what will be the fruit thereof.' With Edmund Cartwright lambasting the established Church from pulpit and lecture room, Cambridge was markedly out of favour with the Queen; her visit to the university, quite early in her reign, had been marred by protests from the young Protestants in residence, whereas Oxford, where Leicester was Chancellor, behaved itself and earned a return visit.

In the year following Sussex's death there appeared in print an anonymous vitriolic attack on Leicester, now familiarly known as *Leicester's Commonwealth* and believed to be the work of Thomas Moryson, the agent in France of Mary Queen of Scots. The tract took the form of a discussion, common in sixteenth-century writing, between a Gentleman, a Lawyer and a Scholar. Their speeches were larded with 'the very whisperings of the privy chamber', and old and new gossip were related with relish. Indeed, the pungency of the epigrams put the author in the first rank of political libellers; for Lady Sheffield and Lady Essex to be known at court as 'his Old and New Testaments', if not the truth, would be a brilliant invention, but the rest of the tract is a tissue of lies. The Earl is portrayed as a traitor, as well as a compulsive adulterer with an insatiable sexual appetite: 'his lordship changeth wives and minions by killing the one, denying the other, using the third for a time and fawning upon the fourth' (presumably her Majesty), while the death of his son, little Lord Denbigh, was taken as further proof of his continual infidelities, since 'the children of adulterers shall be consumed'. Nor was this all, for Leicester was branded as malicious, a tyrant, an embezzler and a coward. The book was suppressed, but such was the Earl's unpopularity that manuscript copies of it circulated freely, so that Elizabeth had to make a public statement, declaring the Earl's complete innocence of 'the most malicious and wicked imputations', while Philip Sidney sprang to his uncle's defence, though his rejoinder remained unpublished for many years. Leicester himself had been inured to jibes and slanders for over a quarter of a century, but so irrational and bitter an attack as was made in the *Commonwealth* grieved him by the depths to which the author had sunk to blacken his character.

At about the time of Raleigh's début, John Harington, the most notable of the Queen's score of godchildren, settled at court to amuse companions with lively conversation. This was Rabelaisian, perhaps, in comparison with

RIGHT Philip II of Spain; portrait by Titian.

OVERLEAF, ABOVE The Spanish Armada in battle with the English fleet in 1588. Elizabeth and her army is shown drawn up on the left of the picture, and the ship on the far right is the first Ark Royal in the Royal Navy. BELOW Elizabeth riding in procession to Tilbury Fort on 18 August 1588, to review the troops under Leicester's command. The upper part of the painting, reproduced on the left shows the Queen giving thanks to God for the victory over the Spanish Armada.

the favourite's sophisticated displays of wit, but it was the more appreciated for its directness. Harington's epigrams and pen-pictures of episodes in Elizabeth's last years were not to be published until the late eighteenth century. In the interval between studying law at Lincoln's Inn and marriage to the daughter of a neighbouring Somerset knight, John was in and out of Whitehall, cocking a snook at pomp, retailing gossip without malice, and finding to his surprise that the Queen took a liking to his 'free speech' and encouraged his poetry. There is a refreshing charm about Harington in that he realised his limitations and never traded on Elizabeth's affection for him by angling for preferment. He amused himself by translating into English the twenty-

ABOVE LEFT Armada portrait of Elizabeth, possibly painted by George Gower, c. 1588. In the background can be seen the victorious English fleet, while the Spanish Armada is destroyed by the 'Protestant Wind'. BELOW LEFT Sir Francis Drake, a miniature painted by Nicholas Hilliard in 1581.

RIGHT Thomas Cockson's titlepage for Sir John Harington's translation of *Orlando Furioso*, published in 1591. A portrait of Sir John is included at the foot of the page.

ORLANDO

FVRIOSO

IN ENGLISH

HEROICAL VERSE, BY

IOHN HARINGTŌ

Principibus placuisse viris non vltima laus est.

Horace

Tho: Coxonus sculp.

The frontispiece to Book 28 of Harington's translation of *Orlando Furioso*, 1591. This book, with its *risqué* tale, was translated by Sir John for circulation amongst courtiers, but when the Queen discovered her ladies reading his manuscript, she required him to undertake the labour of translating the entire poem.

eighth book of Ariosto's *Orlando Furioso*, which contained the slightly *risqué* tale of Giacomo. His manuscript circulated among the maids of honour, until the Queen wanted to know what the composition was that was of such absorbing interest to them. She ruled that it was an improper text for the young ladies in her charge, and when she discovered that her godson was responsible, she summoned him. As a punishment 'the saucy poet' was to stay away from court until he had translated Ariosto's entire poem – as an Italian scholar herself she knew that she was setting him a Herculean task.

194

Harington was not to complete his translation until 1591, when he arranged for its publication in a handsome folio; it was the first English book to be illuminated with copper engravings, thanks to the skill of William Rogers. John presented the Queen with a splendidly-bound copy when she visited him at Kelston, near Bath, the following year.

His next publication, *The Metamorphosis of Ajax*, which he presented to Elizabeth in 1596, caused no little offence, for it was a description of a water-closet (or 'jakes') he had invented at Kelston and advised the Queen to have installed in Richmond Palace. What troubled his godmother was not the earthy topic, which was tackled in a delightfully satirical vein, but the near-libellous allusions to contemporaries with which the work was peppered – not least the references to the late Earl of Leicester. Although a licence for printing the book was refused, Harington took a chance and three entire editions sold out within a year. He was required to make a second exile from court and during his absence, on service with the army in Ireland, all was forgiven. As his cousin Markham wrote to him, 'the Queen is minded to take you to her favour, but she sweareth that she believes you will make epigrams on her and on all her court. She hath been heard to say "that merry poet my godson must not come to Greenwich till he hath grown sober and leaveth the ladies' sports and frolics"'.' This was a reputation that John Harington rather cherished.

John Dee, scientist, mathematician and seer, had been introduced to Elizabeth by his cousin Blanche Parry. Throughout the reign he was frequently summoned to court to explain the significance of a new comet, to advise on combating the royal toothache or to discourse learnedly on a whole range of topics on which he was regarded as an authority. Dee made chemical experiments, advocated the reform of the calendar, had forthright views about the North-West Passage and could devise and break remarkable cyphers. He had been acquitted in the Star Chamber of practising sorcery against Queen Mary and had been called in to select the most fitting date for Elizabeth's coronation. A curious friendship developed between the two of them, and prominent courtiers such as Leicester, Hatton and Raleigh consulted him as the foremost astrologer and an ingenious interpreter of dreams. He was also able to empanel such godmothers for his children as Lady Walsingham, Lady Cobham, Lady Crofts and Mistress Scudamore, and he remained a close friend of that bizarre figure Mrs Tomasin, 'the Queen's dwarf'. Of his great learning there was no doubt, for through his foreign travel and his long list of miscellaneous publications he acquired a European reputation; Leicester and Walsingham once sent him to Germany to consult physicians there about the state of the Queen's health. Yet his dabbling in the occult brought unreasoning suspicions, and despite royal patronage he had to defend himself against those who termed him 'a companion of hell-hounds, a caller and a companion of wicked and damned spirits'.

Open intervention in the Netherlands, following the Treaty of Nonsuch, with the Dutch Provinces in 1585, brought courtiers flocking to the colours, for Elizabeth had undertaken to furnish an army of 5,100 foot and 1,000 horse to oppose Parma. Few had military experience, and even Leicester, 'the nobleman of quality' who was eventually nominated as commander of the army, had seen no fighting since his service in Mary's war against France in 1557. Robert Devereux, the young Earl of Essex, appointed by his step-father Leicester as a general of horse, spent freely in fitting out a train of followers, and provoked a reproof of 'wasteful prodigality' from his grand-father Knollys. Burghley's eldest son Thomas Cecil became governor of Brill, one of the cautionary towns to be handed over to English garrisons, while Sir Philip Sidney hoped to be made governor of another, Flushing. When his appointment seemed in doubt, Sidney escaped from court in disgust to join Drake in Plymouth for a voyage to the New World. Drake anticipated the Queen's fury at Sir Philip's behaviour. Moreover he had no room for an inexperienced sailor whose sole idea seemed to be that they should seize and hold a Spanish base in the Americas, so he warned Elizabeth of Sidney's plans and messengers hastened to Plymouth ordering his return to make preparations for taking the governorship of Flushing. At last there was to be action, and such was Sidney's personality that his presence in the Netherlands gave a great boost to morale in both the English and Dutch armies.

Leicester, by contrast, could not yet leave England, for the Queen, who was far from well, kept postponing his departure; she wanted him by her side, frightened that she had not long to live. Eventually, three months after the Treaty of Nonsuch had been signed, he managed to sail, and took up an awkward command with what he feared would be disastrously inadequate powers, for besides being tied by instructions from England he was to have his military authority limited by the Dutch council. Sidney and others, aware of the difficulties under which the English forces were struggling, intrigued to induce the Dutch to offer Leicester the widest possible powers. On New Year's Day 1586 a delegation arrived at the Earl's lodgings at The Hague to offer him, as Her Majesty's lieutenant, 'the absolute government of the whole provinces of Holland, Zeeland, Friesland and Utrecht', and he was foolish enough to accept the offer. Walsingham and other councillors privy to the plot had expected Elizabeth to be angry, but they hoped that she would accept the *fait accompli*. Not at all. Leicester's actions, she swore, had under-mined her royal declaration of the previous August for taking the Provinces *under her protection*. 'It is sufficient to make me infamous to all princes,' she fumed, and she wrote a reproof in the plainest language, to be personally delivered by Heneage, requiring Leicester to resign publicly from the office he had illegally assumed.

How contemptuously we conceive ourself to have been used by you, you shall by this bearer understand, whom we have expressly sent unto you to charge you withall. We could never have imagined, had we not seen it fall out in experience, that a man raised up by ourself, and extraordinarily favoured by us above any subject of this land, would have in so contemptible a sort broken a commandment, in a course that so greatly toucheth us in honour, whereof, although you have shewed yourself to make but little account, in most undutiful a sort, you may not therefore think that we have so little care of the reparation thereof as we mind to pass so great a wrong in silence undressed ...

He was to obey her on his allegiance, or face the most perilous conse-quences. She was furious that he had taken the title 'Excellency', yet – as he told Walsingham – such was his due in the rank of Earl in any case. No less serious in the Queen's eyes was his scheme to have his Countess join him, and play the great lady 'with such a train of ladies and gentlewomen and such rich coaches as Her Majesty had none such'. In a storm of temper she shouted that the very hand which had ennobled the Earl of Leicester 'can beat him to the dust'.

The campaigning season began badly for the allies. Sidney pleaded to be allowed home on his father's death to settle his affairs and comfort his mother, but Elizabeth would not let him leave Flushing, and before the end of the summer Lady Sidney, too, had died. The one success in the field was his capture of the town of Axel in the Scheldt, and then came the skirmish at Zutphen, where Sir William Russell earned from the Spaniards the tribute that he was 'a devil, not a man' for his bravery that mocked the canons of traditional warfare, while Essex once his lance was broken, wielded an axe. It was at Zutphen that Sidney was mortally wounded.

Sir Philip lingered for another twenty-six days, but before he died bequeathed to Essex his best sword, a symbolic legacy, fraught with immense significance. Sidney's remains were taken by water to Flushing for lying in state and thence were carried home in his own pinnace, rigged with sails of black bearing escutcheons of the hero's arms. The *Black Pinnace* discharged its burden near the Tower, but the funeral was postponed until Sidney's creditors had been satisfied – his father-in-law had to find some £6,000. At last, on 16 February, the hero was given the unprecedented honour of a State funeral in St Paul's Cathedral, with the almost regal cortège followed by seven hundred mourners. Walking or riding two by two in procession were officers and men from his regiment, representatives from the United Provinces, the Lord Mayor and civic dignitaries, notables from the court such as Leicester and Huntingdon, Pembroke and Warwick, and many members from the

The funeral cortège of Sir Philip Sidney, on its way to St Paul's Cathedral 1587: engraving by Theodor de Bry. Sidney's fellow poets Fulke Greville and Edward Dyer are shown accompanying the pall-bearers. Sidney was the earliest national hero to be awarded a State funeral.

dead man's wide circle of friends, Essex prominent amongst them. Also in the procession was his horse, ridden by a page trailing a broken lance, and his helmet, shield, spurs and arms borne by the heralds. Robert Sidney, his brother and heir, was chief mourner; Lady Sidney, his widow, was too weak to be present as she was also mourning a still-born child. Among the pall-bearers were his fellow poets Fulk Greville and Edward Dyer – the former a close companion from childhood, who would write as a labour of love one of the tenderest biographies in English literature.

Within the year appeared a memorial volume of thirty-four engraved plates of the funeral, prepared by Thomas Lant, a member of Sidney's household. From the time news of Sidney's death first reached London until long after the delayed funeral, there was general mourning: 'it was accounted a sin for any gentleman of quality for many months after to appear at court or city in any light or gaudy apparel'. Elizabeth cursed that he had wasted the life of a gentleman by a common soldier's fate, for she had little sympathy with his conception of the role of Shepherd Knight, the idealistic man of action who could never become a true courtier any more than he could become a successful politician. Yet she recognised the depth of others' feelings for Sir Philip and knew how badly her country needed a national hero at this hour. She might even have been at St Paul's herself, but for the execution of the Queen of Scots five days before.

The discovery of the Throckmorton Plot led to the expulsion of Mendoza, the Spanish ambassador, who was implicated in the affair; he had no successor for the rest of the reign. So long as the captive Mary remained alive she was the focus of the Catholics, inspiring others to risk their lives in her cause, and thus men swore to join a crusade to kill Elizabeth, and to enthrone Mary in her stead, restoring the old religion. Tyrannicide became almost an article of faith, with the Duke of Guise offering a reward for Elizabeth's murder, and Pope Sixtus V agreeing that such a blow for the Counter Reformation would be a most laudable act. Yet despite the danger of assassination, the Queen refused to become either the prisoner of a rigorous security system within the palace, or a recluse like Philip of Spain, for precautions framed for her safety irritated her, especially if they cut her off from her subjects.

Leicester was alarmed at the Queen's argument that 'the increase of papists in her realm can be no danger to her,' but failed to convince her that those whose Catholicism was stiffened by Jesuit missionary priests, such as Campion and Parsons, were *prima facie* traitors, no less than their mentors. She had insisted that Edmund Campion, who had once impressed her by his scholarly conversations, should be tried by the old Treasons Act and not by the draconian statute of 1581. Burghley well knew that her crown was 'not like to fall to the ground for want of heads that claim to wear it' and, fearing the poisoner, drew up fresh regulations about the preparation of her food and for denying all but a few chosen servants access to her laundry and wardrobe. He even tried to prevent her from accepting presents of perfumed gloves and sleeves, since these might contain noxious substances.

The fact that the Queen was so vulnerable greatly increased her popularity. As she returned to Whitehall in November 1583, from a stay at Hampton Court, crowds knelt by the roadside begging her to take care of her person.

The assassination of William the Silent the following summer underlined the dangers, provoking Walsingham to devise a new pledge of allegiance, the Bond of Association, which began as a round-robin at court and developed as a series of monster petitions in every city and shire, with the signatories undertaking to defend the Queen's person and to pursue her assassins, swearing that they would never accept any 'pretended successor by whom or for whom any such detestable act shall be attempted or committed'.

Sir Ralph Sadler had taken over from the Earl of Shrewsbury the onerous position of custodian to Mary Queen of Scots. Talbot had longed to be relieved of his post, and his wife Bess of Hardwick had spread libellous tales about his relations with Mary. Sadler's tour of duty lasted for a year, after which Elizabeth hoped to replace him by Lord St John, but the latter stoutly refused; he would 'suffer any extremity rather than go,' he told her, and in the end Sir Amyas Paulet, as strait-laced as Knollys in his Puritanism, was required to serve. Mary had been taken from Sheffield Castle to Wingfield in Derbyshire and then, in January 1585, was removed further south to Tutbury Castle in Staffordshire, where much stricter precautions were taken for guarding her. It was while at Tutbury and neighbouring Chartley that she put her head in the noose prepared by Walsingham by giving her assent to the plans of Anthony Babington and his associates for Elizabeth's assassination. Most of the young men who had offered themselves as Mary's champions had connexions with the court. Babington himself had been a page in Shrewsbury's service, while of his associates Edward Abington was the son of the Under-Treasurer, Chidiock Tichbourne was a servant of Hatton and Charles Tilney was the son of Philip Tilney, a distant cousin of the Queen, who had entertained her at his Suffolk home.

Several of the plots to release Mary had involved Henry Percy, eighth Earl of Northumberland, brother and successor to the Earl who had risen with Westmorland in 1569. In that rebellion Henry had remained loyal to the Crown, but soon afterwards he opened communications with the Bishop of Ross for descending on Tutbury. There was sufficient evidence to send him to the Tower for eighteen months, when he threw himself on the Queen's mercy; she fined him heavily and sent him to his mansion at Petworth in Sussex under house arrest. Northumberland had learnt nothing from experience, for ten years later he was again in the Tower on suspicion of complicity in Throckmorton's Plot. On release, he intrigued further with Mary's agent Charles Paget, who visited him at Petworth, planning Mary's release in order to extract from Elizabeth a promise of toleration for Catholics. Another plotter revealed on the rack the extent of the discussions and so Northumberland was sent to the Tower a third time. The Queen was in no hurry to bring him to trial, despite his fulsome protestations of innocence, and in June 1585 he committed suicide in his cell. The Catholics naturally interpreted it as murder, fastening the blame on Hatton.

Henry's son, another Henry, came to the earldom at twenty-one. He, too, had been suspected of favouring Mary's cause by associating with Charles Paget, but now he settled down in the family house at St Andrew's Hill, Blackfriars, rarely travelling north to Alnwick, but filling his days with collecting works of art, reading history books and studying astrology. At court he was dubbed 'the wizard Earl' and strange tales were told of his 'scientific experiments'; his reputation for being an alchemist, a heavy smoker and a compulsive gambler was far safer than the slur of doubtful allegiance. For a few months he served under Leicester in the Low Countries and then, like so many courtiers, was given a command at sea during the Armada crisis.

The Howards, like the Percies, were finding it hard to live down their earlier family disgrace. Lord Henry Howard, Norfolk's younger brother, was mistrusted by Elizabeth, who saw through his exaggerated flattery. As a penurious younger son, at one time he had hoped that his reputation as a scholar might lead to a bishopric, since a niche as a Cambridge don was a way of life 'beneath the compass of his birth', as he put it. So he had come to court before Norfolk's treason became a severe handicap. Lord Henry was himself suspected both of ardent Catholicism and of wanting to marry the Scottish Queen, but he cleared his name and Elizabeth granted him a pension. After the Duke's execution he had gone to Audley End, in Essex, to supervise the education of his nephews and nieces, yet he wrote regularly to Burghley and Hatton pressing his claims for preferment. They certainly made use of his literary abilities to pen a reply to Stubbs' tract against the Alençon match and to answer a pamphlet denouncing female government. But Howard also corresponded with the Queen of Scots.

His cousin Oxford made a great fuss of Howard's religious views in 1582, accusing him of still angling for Mary's hand, so he was arrested. In a lengthy defence addressed to the Queen, he denied having intrigued with Mary but claimed that he had advised her to 'abate the sails of her royal pride'; it was, he wrote, ridiculous for anyone to think that 'so mean a man' could win Mary, even had he wanted to risk such an enterprise. As to his religion, he admitted attending Roman Catholic worship because of personal scruples over sacramental details, and this answer satisfied Elizabeth. On release he voluntarily left court to write a *Preservative against the Poison of Supposed Prophecies*, which he dedicated to Walsingham. This attack on astrology by a man steeped in moral philosophy was not popular at court, for Dee and Richard Harvey enjoyed a strong following. Some found heresies in his text, others detected treasonable statements and in 1583 Lord Henry was put in the Fleet Prison. Through the agency of Burghley's son Robert Cecil, who was to become very close to him in the last years of the reign, Howard was released after nearly two years of captivity and chose to travel to Italy, though his sojourn in Rome did nothing to increase the Queen's confidence in him. He remained out of employment even in the hectic summer of 1588. In grave financial difficulties and spurned by the triumvirate of Burghley, Leicester and Hatton, Howard turned, like so many others, to the rising favourite Essex.

Lord Henry's fortunes had been further marred by the behaviour of his eldest nephew Philip Howard, who in 1580 succeeded to the earldom of Arundel, by right of his mother. At Cambridge Philip had disappointed his uncle by kicking over the traces of college discipline as well as by showing his distaste for book-learning, and at nineteen he came to court. His wife, Anne Dacre, was left behind at Kenninghall while Philip played the profligate peer, trying rather too hard to cut a dashing figure, running into debt and expecting Elizabeth to be impressed. He felt that he had as much to offer as the Earl of Oxford, who was in such high favour, and took it rather badly that the Queen did not treat him as an adopted son. His entertainment of her during her visit to East Anglia in 1578 made heavy inroads into his finances, whereas carefully planned festivities in the right key could have proved a sound investment.

The death of his grandfather Arundel was the turning-point in his life, for he at last put away childish things and leaving court, where he had cut such a poor figure, began to devote himself to his estates and to his wife. Anne Dacre was a strong character who had been brought up as a Catholic and Philip now came firmly under her influence. She elaborated the arguments used by Campion in his debate with the Deans of St Paul's and Windsor in the Chapel of the Tower, which had made such a great impression on her husband. Elizabeth suspected him of being involved in the Throckmorton Plot and he was ordered to confine himself to Arundel House in the Strand, while Anne, on account of her professed Romanism, was committed to the custody of a Sussex knight for a year, during which time their first child was born. Adversity turned Arundel to the consolations of religion, and in the autumn of 1584 Father William Weston received him into the Catholic Church. Next spring he decided to flee from England, leaving behind an apologia for the Queen, but he was taken off his ship in mid-Channel and brought back a prisoner to the Tower. In the court of Star Chamber he was fined £10,000 and sentenced to remain a prisoner during the Queen's pleasure.

There is no doubt that Arundel had been thick with Catholic agents, and would have aided any domestic plots or foreign invasion. Because of his potential danger to the State there was full justification for keeping him under close surveillance, though Elizabeth showed particular severity in her dealings with him, even forbidding his wife and son to see him. Unlike Philip II's other godson, Philip Sidney, Philip Howard had become a militant convert and nothing would shake his loyalty to his new faith. When the Armada was sailing up the Channel he organised other Catholics in the Tower to maintain a constant vigil of prayer for its success. Subsequently he was found guilty of high treason and sentenced to death, but the sentence was never carried out – perhaps Elizabeth still felt remorse for signing his father's death warrant. Arundel remained a prisoner in the Tower until he died of natural causes, aged thirty-eight. However, the House of Howard was rescued from complete ignominy by Howard of Effingham, the Lord Admiral.

The Act of 1585 for the Queen's safety, which an intensely loyal Commons had framed, required her to appoint a special tribunal to investigate Mary's part in the Babington Plot once Walsingham had acquired incontrovertible evidence. Yet it was some days before Elizabeth could steel herself to order Mary's removal from Chartley. The council wanted to put her in the Tower, but Elizabeth refused to have an anointed Queen treated as a common traitor and instead chose Fotheringhay Castle in Northamptonshire. She delayed interminably in deciding who were to serve as commissioners for the trial, but by 11 October scores of notables had descended on Fotheringhay Castle. Bromley, as Lord Chancellor, was chief commissioner, assisted by Oxford, Shrewsbury, six other Earls and Burghley as Lord Treasurer. These were supported by Walsingham, Hatton, Sadler and other councillors, the lords chief justice and lesser men of the law. The case for the Crown was handled by the Attorney and Solicitor General, yet Mary – like every other defendant at a State trial – was denied counsel; it was only Hatton who managed to persuade her to appear in court at all.

Leicester, still at his post in the Netherlands, was the only notable absentee. Suggested long ago as an unwilling suitor for Mary's hand, he had visited her twice in captivity, going on to stay with Shrewsbury at Chatsworth after a cure at the baths in Buxton. Yet, when he heard that Elizabeth was procrastinating about carrying out the court's sentence, he wrote at once to Walsingham urging him to pressure the council into acting decisively: 'Be you all stout and resolute for this speedy execution.' Elizabeth would never be safe while Mary breathed, and had he been at Whitehall himself he declared that he would have taken the initiative and borne the consequences.

Burghley persuaded the Queen to ease her personal burden by involving Parliament in Mary's fate and though she promised to open the sessions in person, when the day came she stayed away, not wishing, as she said, to preside over proceedings against a kinswoman. Lord Chancellor Bromley, who opened the sessions, explained that they had assembled for an extraordinary cause of 'great weight, great peril and dangerous consequence'. In the Lower House, Hatton opened the case against Mary and then Sadler prayed that God might influence the Queen 'to take away this most wicked and filthy woman'. Other speakers underlined that the Queen of Scots had been from her birth an enemy of Protestant England, for she was by nationality a Scot, by upbringing a Frenchwoman, by blood a Guise, in practice a Spaniard and in religion a papist. Both houses joined in a petition to the Queen to direct that Mary should without delay endure the penalty of the law. When in due course she made her reply to a delegation that waited on her at Richmond, she left the matter as much in the air as ever. 'As for your petition, your judgment I condemn not, neither do I mislike your reasons, but pray you to accept my thankfulness, excuse my doubtfulness and take in good part my answers answerless.' Robert Cecil prepared her speech for immediate publication and it also appeared in John Stow's new edition of *Holinshed's Chronicles* in January, but this was cold comfort for her councillors, who continued to press her to authorise proclamation of sentence against Mary under the terms of the 1585 Act.

A warrant was prepared on Burghley's instructions and left with William Davison, a protégé of Leicester's, who had been appointed a Secretary of State to take some of the burden of routine business from Walsingham. On 1 February the Queen suddenly sent for Davison and read through and signed the warrant, telling him to take it to the Lord Chancellor's for the Great Seal to be affixed. She also asked him to inform Walsingham, who was ill, saying with a twinkle that the grief of hearing the news would 'kill him outright'. Next morning she sent word to Davison that he was not to go to Chancellor Bromley until she had spoken to him again, so he immediately came to tell her that the warrant had passed the Great Seal; he was unnerved by her subsequent outburst and poured out his heart to Hatton. Together they saw Burghley, who realising the urgency of the situation summoned a secret meeting of as many councillors as were at hand the following morning, at which they took on themselves the entire responsibility for sending the death warrant to Fotheringhay. All ten present swore they would not reveal to the Queen the fact that they had acted thus and required Beal, the Puritan clerk of the council, to hasten to Fotheringhay.

Mary was executed on 8 February. When Elizabeth heard that the sentence had been carried out she was more angry than anyone had ever seen her. Hatton was the first to feel the sharpness of her tongue, Davison was put in the Tower and Burghley kept away from court, 'finding his bitter burden of Her Majesty's displeasure' intolerable. By the end of March all ten offending councillors were summoned before the Lord Chancellor, Archbishop Whitgift and the two chief justices to justify their actions, which they did on the grounds of Davison's report of the Queen's intention to have the death warrant sealed. No one revealed their oath-taking to keep the matter from Elizabeth. Secretary Davison became the scapegoat for the Queen's scruples

The execution of Mary Queen of Scots at Fotheringhay Castle, 1587: from a contemporary drawing.

of conscience, for he went for trial before special commissioners. He was fined 10,000 marks and imprisoned during the Queen's pleasure. Burghley remained in such disfavour for four months that his exile took on the character of retirement, and it was at this time that his son Robert came to the fore to help Walsingham and Hatton (Lord Chancellor since the end of April) with the mounting paperwork of diplomacy and administration. Nevertheless the threat from Spain brought the old Treasurer out of the shadows, to serve as vigorously as his gout would allow.

It was in the months following Mary's execution, with Leicester away at Bath taking the waters for his health, that the young Earl of Essex began to realise his power over the Queen. Robert Devereux, the first son of Walter, Earl of Essex, and Lettice Knollys, was born in 1567. His father died in 1576, while fighting in Ireland, leaving his nine-year-old son the heir to splendid titles and enormous debts – Robert was the poorest Earl in England. Two years later, his mother, the beautiful Lettice, married Robert Dudley, Earl of Leicester. Although this marriage so infuriated the Queen that both Leicester and his Countess were in deep disgrace, it was to be a connexion which helped the young Earl of Essex to find a favoured place at court.

At the age of ten, Robert paid a visit to the Burghleys in London, and there first met the Queen. He was a handsome child, with a tall erect figure and red curly hair – looks that he retained for the rest of his life. He then attended Trinity College, Cambridge, studying under John Whitgift, and did not appear at court again until 1584.

His good looks and fine presence quickly found favour with the Queen, and he discovered that he was stepping into the shoes of his step-father, Leicester. He alone seemed able to rescue her from acute depression: 'at night my lord is at cards, or one game or another with her, that he cometh not to his own lodgings till birds sing in the morning'. Sir Walter Raleigh could not reasonably complain at being overlooked, for he had succeeded Hatton as Captain of the Guard and netted most of the traitor Babington's estates. Some at court might sneer at Raleigh being in 'wonderful declination', but the Queen as usual held a balance between her prime favourites. At North Hall in July 1587, when Lady Warwick was entertaining the Queen, the house party unwisely included Essex's sister Dorothy Devereux, who had been banished from court for her secret marriage to Sir Thomas Perrot, an opponent of Raleigh since his early days in Ireland. As the girl's brother, Essex felt for the first time the onslaught of Elizabeth's anger and he blamed the whole affair on 'that knave Raleigh, for whose sake she [Elizabeth] would grieve me in the eye of the world'. Perhaps, as some say, he boxed Raleigh's ears, but he certainly remonstrated with the Queen, reminding her of what the favourite 'had been and what he was'. Elizabeth retaliated with devastating remarks about Essex's mother, Lettice Knollys. Looking back on the incident the Earl wrote, 'what comfort can I have to give myself over to the service of a mistress that is in awe of such a man'. On an impulse he fled to the coast, intending to find a passage to the Netherlands to fight as a soldier of fortune, but he was turned back by a messenger. Once more in the royal presence he found that all was forgiven. She refused his pleas to serve her on land or sea, for she wanted him near at hand, and to make plain that he held a special position in her favour she soon made him a Knight of the Garter and appointed him Master of the Horse on Leicester's resignation.

Such was the disgrace of the Howards at this time that only Charles Lord Howard of Effingham was able to restore the reputation of his house. Effingham was born in the year of Anne Boleyn's execution, had undertaken an embassy to France in 1559, had been general of horse in Warwick's army in the Northern Rebellion, and then was appointed to the first of many commands at sea. Howard cemented his position at court by marrying Catherine Carey, Hunsdon's daughter, a favourite lady in waiting of Elizabeth, but it was for his loyal service afloat that he was to receive, belatedly, the earldom of Nottingham. On succeeding his father, Effingham had for a decade been Lord Chamberlain of the Household, but in 1585 he had come to the post dearest to his ambitions, that of Lord High Admiral, and as such was the hero of the defeat of the Armada. Two of his daughters married sailors – Sir Robert Southwell, commander of the *Elizabeth Jonas*, and Sir Richard Leveson, later vice-admiral of England – and he also influenced his nephew, Lord Thomas Howard, to follow a naval career.

ABOVE Catherine Carey, daughter of 1st Baron Hunsdon, who married Lord Howard of Effingham: miniature by Isaac Hilliard.
RIGHT Charles, Lord Howard of Effingham, the Lord Admiral, who from his flagship *The Ark* commanded the English fleet against the Spanish Armada, 1588: an engraving by Thomas Cockson.

Two naval architects from the Tudor period.

Comparatively few of the men-of-war in Howard of Effingham's fleet were commanded by professional seamen of the calibre of Drake, Hawkins or Frobisher; indeed it is remarkable how readily so many peers and courtiers took to life afloat. For George Clifford, Earl of Cumberland, naval warfare proved a thrilling relief from gambling at court, and from this experience he was to embark on a successful career as a privateer, which happily combined both vocations. There was Lord Henry Seymour, who despite indifferent health stayed afloat for most of 1588 in the narrow seas, signing himself in dispatches 'Her Majesty's most bounden and faithful fisherman'; he was to be rewarded with the governorship of Guernsey. Both Oxford and Northumberland eagerly left for commands, Charles Blount, sick of the land campaign against Parma, found a man-of-war, while Raleigh at last felt in his element. In 1585 everyone of spirit had wanted to go to fight in the Netherlands, but in the great emergency three years later the action was likely to be at sea, and those not specifically required to be guarding the coast or serving at Tilbury Camp with Leicester were obtaining commands afloat.

Leicester, still unwell, was succeeded in the Netherlands by Peregrine Bertie, Lord Willoughby, the son of the Dowager Duchess of Suffolk. It was

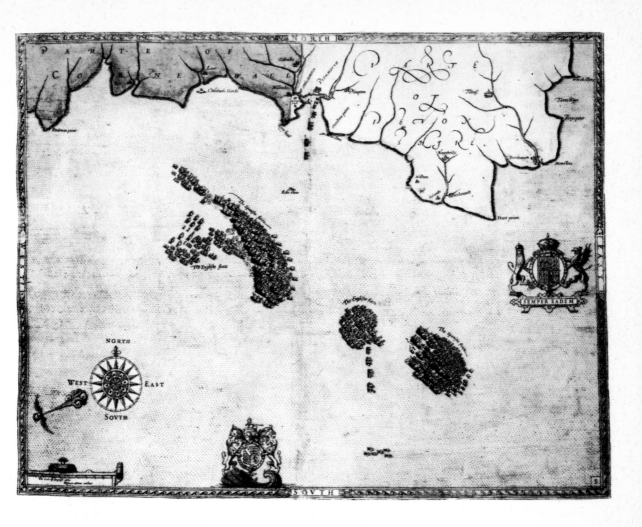

Detail of the English and Spanish fleets about to engage off Plymouth, 1588: from Christopher Saxton's *Atlas of the Counties*.

not until the Armada was off the Dorset coast on 19 July that the order was given for the main army to assemble at Tilbury and the second army, for defending the Queen's person, to report to St James's. Four days later Leicester was named as lieutenant-general for the defence of the realm. Old Sir Henry Lee, who was the Queen's Champion of the Tilt, and had organised the lavish tournaments held annually to celebrate Elizabeth's Accession Day, came to St James's with ten horses at his own charge to stay by the Queen. Walsingham knew that Elizabeth would not be content to stay hemmed in by her guards at Westminster and told Leicester that if she left he intended staying with her, to watch over her safety.

Elizabeth wanted to visit the coast for a view of the naval action, but Leicester had forbidden it, though he agreed that she could travel with her ladies by barge to Tilbury to review the troops. Here, on the day when it was feared that Parma's army might well attempt invasion, she made the most famous of all her speeches and would not leave the Camp until the danger was passed, staying the night at Rich's house of Little Leighs. Among the courtiers at Tilbury were Essex, who had equipped a private company of harquebusiers and lighthorse, wearing the Devereux livery, and his future rival Robert Cecil, who was master of Ordnance for the main army. The Earl of Hertford, who had once rashly married Lady Catherine Grey, paraded a band of his Kentish retainers.

Leicester returned from Tilbury to London with 'so many gentlemen as if he were a King' and, indeed, Elizabeth seriously considered making him her viceroy. In some ways this would have been no more than allowing him to continue to exercise his special powers as lieutenant-general of the realm

Playing cards from the 'Armada Pack', engraved in the seventeenth century as a protest against the future James II's Roman Catholicism. Significantly Leicester is represented as the King of Hearts.

Leicester's last letter to the Queen, written from Lady Norris's house at Rycote, 28 August 1588 (see p. 210). The letter bears a docket in Elizabeth's own hand: 'His last letter'.

during the emergency, but others harked back to the Queen's intentions of appointing him protector when she lay near to death in 1562. Both Burghley and Walsingham disliked the idea of Leicester being singled out now for powers more extensive than a consort would have enjoyed, and on reflection she thought it probably unwise to elevate her old favourite in this way. He watched from an upper window, by Elizabeth's side, the grand review in the Whitehall tiltyard which Essex staged to mark the defeat of the Armada.

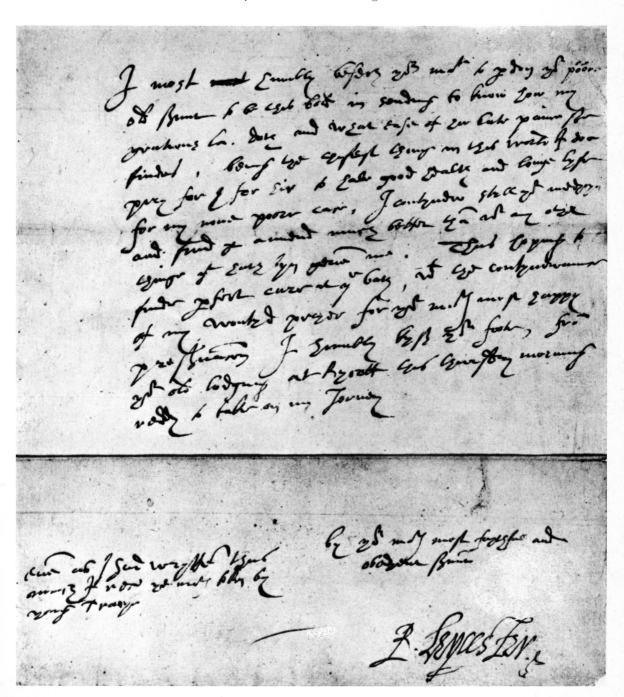

However, he was out of sorts and hoped to rid himself of his fever in time to play his role in the other official thanksgivings, so he rode off with Lettice by easy stages for the Midlands, planning to stay at Buxton. The second night they broke their journey at Rycote House, where Lady Norris gave him the room she usually kept for the Queen. Installed here he wrote to his sovereign:

I most humbly beseech Your Majesty to pardon your old servant to be thus bold in sending to know how my gracious Lady doth, and what ease of her pain she finds, being the chiefest thing in the world I do pray for, for her to have good health and long life. For my own poor case I continue still your medicine and it amends much better than any other thing that hath been given me. Thus hoping to find perfect cure at the bath, with the continuance of my wonted prayer for your Majesty's most happy preservation, I humbly kiss your foot, from your old lodging at Rycote, this Thursday morning, ready to take on my journey, by Your Majesty's most faithful, obedient servant, R. Leycester.

He added a postscript: 'Even as I had writ, thus much I received Your Majesty's token by young Tracey.' But the royal medicine could do nothing for his 'continual burning fever' and within the week he had died at Cornbury, in his own lodge as ranger of the Forest.

A great gloom descended on the court when news of the Earl's death was received, for he left a void. For almost thirty years, from the first months of the reign, he had been a dominant force, the perennial leader of a faction, the man closest to his sovereign and the one she always singled out when there was a special task to be undertaken. The Queen had remained emotionally tied to her 'sweet Robin', despite the suspicions surrounding Amy Robsart's death, despite his indiscreet marriage to Lettice Knollys. The strength of their relationship did not become apparent until much later, for after her own death there was found in a little casket she always kept by her bed the letter which Leicester had written from Rycote and on it she had written 'His last letter'. In September 1588, when she should have been rejoicing at the defeat of Philip's invasion plans, she withdrew to her apartments at Whitehall, locked the doors and refused to see even her most intimate servants, 'until the Treasurer and other councillors had the door broken open', for they feared for her health.

Perhaps because of Leicester's unique position, he had never been popular, and at court there were few tears apart from the Queen's. The Earl's political support of the Puritan cause led to no notable tract or moving sermon on his passing and his patronage of scholars and poets produced only one *in memoriam* stanza, which itself explains the dearth of further verses. Spenser, who had once served as Leicester's secretary, wrote in *The Ruines of Time*, a year later:

> He now is dead and all his glories gone
> And all his greatness vapouréd to naught
> That as a glass upon the water shone
> Which vanished quite, as soon as it was saught.
> His name is worn already out of thought
> Ne any poet seeks him to revive
> Yet many poets honoured him alive.

Some reckoned that Hatton would now come into his own, but the Lord Chancellor was content to use his influence with the Queen to support Burghley and Walsingham, and in any case his own days were numbered.

The Armada Jewel, made by Hilliard, and according to tradition given by Elizabeth to Sir Thomas Heneage on the defeat of the Armada. This illustration shows the reverse of the Jewel depicting the Ark of the True Church tossed through troubled waters. It is bordered with strapwork of opaque blue and white enamel, set with diamonds.

Leicester's mantle would fall instead on his stepson, Essex. When Walsingham became ill in March 1589 and was away from court for three months, Burghley doubled as Secretary and Elizabeth would not hear of the old man spending more than a week away from court when his wife died. With Hatton fully occupied by legal affairs, it was to Sir Thomas Heneage, newly appointed Vice-Chamberlain of the Household, that she increasingly turned.

In his will, Leicester had left Elizabeth a pendant of emeralds and diamonds, hung on a rope of six hundred pearls, in gratitude of the honours and liberality she had bestowed on him, and she relished the part of keeping a stiff upper lip that involved financial dealings with Lady Leicester. To clear Leicester's debts to the Crown and to other creditors, the Queen required the widow to auction the contents of Kenilworth, Leicester House and Wanstead, and there was still a substantial sum outstanding at Elizabeth's death. With no hope of charity or even of civility from the Queen, Lettice cut herself off still further from court by marrying within a few months of Dudley's death Sir Christopher Blount, a close friend of her son, Essex.

Soon other links with the past were being snapped and if it was a comfort for Elizabeth to have survived Catherine de'Medici and her son Henry III (the same who had years ago dubbed her 'an old woman with a sore leg'), it was a wrench to lose Walsingham's services and a bitter personal blow to see Hatton's passing. She went over to Ely Place through the rose gardens with a can of 'cordial broths', to tempt her Lord Chancellor's feeble appetite and to persuade him to stop worrying about the enormous debts he owed her. Alone of all her favourites he had remained single for her sake, a poor fish – as he put it – who had fallen for her sweet bait. Leicester's brother, Warwick, also died and of the older generation there remained only Burghley, Hunsdon and Knollys.

Such were the inevitable griefs of old age, the dubious benefits of surviving one's contemporaries. Because she felt the death of friends so acutely, no one could write a more moving letter of condolence. Still living under the shadow of Leicester's passing she wrote to Lady Paget, who had served her in bygone days in the Privy Chamber, to lament the death of her daughter, Lady Crompton: 'Call to mind, good Kate, how hardly we Princes can brook of crossing our commands; how ireful will the Highest Power be (may you be sure) when murmurings shall be made of his pleasingest will? Let nature therefore not hurt herself, but give place to the giver. Though this lesson be from a silly vicar, yet it is sent from a loving Sovereign.' And when she heard of Sir John Norris's death in Ireland she was to write to his mother, her old friend Lady Norris, addressing her by her old nickname: 'Mine own, Crow: harm not thyself for bootless help; but show a good example to comfort your dolorous Yokefellow.' For her own part the Queen had chosen Essex, not as a yokefellow but as the one man – now that Raleigh was in utter disgrace – whose presence could help her to endure her ordeals. This presaged a revolution at court.

EARLE OF ESSEX.

8 On Heroes and Heroine Worship

ABOVE Sir Charles Blount, later Earl of Devonshire and Baron Mountjoy (1563-1606): a miniature by Hilliard. The court favourite was to prove himself the match for Tyrone in Ireland.

LEFT Robert Devereux, 2nd Earl of Essex: a portrait by William Segar, c. 1590.

The mantle of Leicester fell on his stepson, Robert Earl of Essex, who moved effortlessly into the place of prime favourite. But for Essex it was not enough merely to be a Leicester; he wanted to be a Burghley as well, to share supreme power with the Queen, to wear the laurel crown of high military reputation and to sit at the head of the council. He arrived at Whitehall at eighteen to court the Queen's favour as the sole way of putting the finances of his earldom in order, and found that his sovereign, thirty-four years his senior, warmed to his flattery. Unlike so many youths at court, he had the inestimable advantages of high birth and remarkable features, as might have been expected from the son of Lettice Knollys. Though his mother remained a liability, it counted for much that Elizabeth's aunt, Mary Boleyn, had been the boy's great-grandmother. Inheriting Sir Philip Sidney's sword after Zutphen had given him a taste for military glory which he never lost, and he possessed a strange magnetism over men, assuring them by a glance that he was their natural leader under whom it would be a privilege to serve, even unto death.

Essex had in fact cast himself in a dual role which proved too contradictory for satisfactory performance, for he remained torn between the rival claims of court and military service. To achieve these ambitions required the full acquiescence of the Queen and he was slow to realise that she was serious when she told him she would not let him out of her sight; moreover she would never allow herself to be dominated and, determined to maintain a balance between factions, would never submit to what a later age would call totalitarian rule. At the final assessment, if Essex was to be 'all England's hero' Elizabeth was jealous of surrendering a particle of the heroine worship that was hers of right.

Each expected too much of the other, demanding an exclusive friendship, with no intentions of reciprocation. Elizabeth grew jealous when she saw him talking with another woman and once, when she detected two of her ladies, Mistress Brydges and Mistress Russell, gazing on the Earl as he took his exercise, she screamed at them and hustled them from court; Elizabeth Brydges had no regrets and later became his mistress. Essex similarly took offence if the Queen smiled on another courtier, especially if he had a martial bearing. In the winter after the Armada, she had been impressed by the performance of Charles Blount, Lord Mountjoy's son, in the tiltyard and in recognition she 'sent him a golden queen from her set of chessmen'. Blount tied this favour to his arm with a crimson ribbon, which provoked Essex to scoff 'Now I perceive that every fool must have a favour.' When the rival challenged him to a duel, and wounded the Earl in the thigh, Elizabeth remarked 'By God's blood, it was fit that someone or other should take him down and treat him better manners, otherwise there will be no rule in him.' Both men were forbidden the court until they had shaken hands. A month later, after a petty quarrel with Raleigh, Essex challenged him to fight, but the Queen intervened. Though in theory she was flattered that men should want to fight for her favours, in practice she was alarmed at the dangers of violence which could cost her companionship.

She had forbidden Essex to sail with Drake and Norris on the Portugal expedition in 1589, and when she heard that he had stolen from court she sent first his grandfather Knollys and then Huntingdon to secure his return. It was too late. He did not receive her summons for another two months: 'Essex, your sudden and undutiful departure from our presence and your place of attendance, you may easily conceive how offensive it is, and ought to be, unto us. Our great favours bestowed on you without deserts, hath drawn you thus to neglect and forget your duty ...' Of course, once he was back at court, she forgave him. Yet, instead of paying full homage to Gloriana and fortifying his position, he almost threw everything away by secretly marrying Frances Sidney, Sir Philip's widow and the daughter of Secretary Walsingham, who was mortally ill. To have married the widow of his brother-in-arms seemed the height of chivalry, for Frances could bring him no dowry, nor was she a great beauty. Walsingham died not long afterwards, so crippled by debts that he had to be buried at night lest creditors should seize his coffin. For a courtier of Essex's calibre to have contracted a marriage so far beneath him, and without the Queen's permission, was a gross insult to Her Majesty, and he should have known the likely consequences. Elizabeth had to be told before she found out from gossip, but, though she ranted, her fury was short-lived. After a mere fortnight – such was the Earl's hold over her – she welcomed him back to court and greeted Frances as a Countess, an acknowledgment that Leicester had never achieved for Lettice. Surprisingly, Essex's marriage made little difference to his position at court; perhaps by now Elizabeth was becoming hardened to the matrimonial adventures of the men who had vowed eternal homage to her.

Marriage and status at court were not enough for Essex, for he desperately wanted a command in the army supporting Henry of Navarre against the Catholic League. After the failure of early attempts, he pleaded with the Queen for three hours on his knees until she gave way, and even condescended to inspect his cavalry before they embarked. But in France things went badly; his younger brother was killed and Elizabeth fearing he, too, might become a casualty ordered him home in a peremptory fashion. Although he secured a temporary reprieve thanks to Robert Carey, he had to obey in the end and protested to her in person, 'I see Your Majesty is content to ruin me.' Reluctantly she agreed to let him return to France and from camp he assured her he was bent on rescuing his tarnished reputation as a soldier through gallant service. That accomplished,

No cause but a great action of your own may draw me out of your sight, for the two windows of your privy chamber shall be the poles of my sphere, where, so long

Frances Walsingham, daughter of the Secretary, who married first Sir Philip Sidney, and then Robert, Earl of Essex: miniature by Isaac Oliver.

as Your Majesty will please to have me, I am fixed and unmoveable. When Your Majesty thinks that heaven too good for me, I will not fall like a star, but be consumed, like a vapour by the same Sun that drew me up to such a height ...

Such a letter served only to convince the Queen that she must have him back at her side, for she was miserable from Hatton's death, and at Christmas she ordered him to hand over his command to Sir Roger Williams and bring home with him 'the best sort of gentlemen there'. This time Essex did not argue. At twenty-four he was not content to remain a favoured son, or a courtier who had wielded his sword in a worthy cause: he had determined to embark on a political career.

Raleigh's stock should have been at its height with Essex's marriage and Hatton's death, yet the Captain of the Guard threw away his chances by marrying Bess Throckmorton; it is doubtful whether he seduced her, for she was the oldest and least attractive of the maids of honour, but Elizabeth was prepared to believe court gossip about his 'brutish offence'. For a whole decade he had been utterly loyal to his 'Cynthia' and now he had forfeited her trust, so she sent him to the Tower. He wrote in an elaborate strain to Robert Cecil, hoping that his letter would reach the Queen:

My heart was never broken till this day that I hear the Queen goes so far off, whom I have followed so many years with so great love and desire in so many journeys, and am now left behind her in a dark prison, all alone. I that was wont to behold her riding like Alexander, hunting like Diana, walking like Venus, the gentle wind blowing her fair hair about her pure cheeks like a nymph, sometimes playing like Orpheus; behold the sorrow of this world once amiss hath bereaved me of all. Oh love that only strength in misfortune, what is become of thy assurance!

Flattery was the only weapon left to him. When the Spanish treasure-ship *Madre de Dios* was towed into Dartmouth, he was released on parole to oversee the Queen's share of the prize. After three further months in prison he and Bess were released, and settled at Sherborne Castle in Dorset; effectively his career was finished. Harington tells the tale that when Sir Walter first espied the Castle from a distance, he was so enchanted with it that he failed to control his horse, and fell. 'This fall,' wrote Harington with the benefit of hindsight, 'was ominous and no question he was apt to consider it so.' After service on the Cadiz and Islands expeditions in 1596 and 1597, he was allowed to return to his post as Captain of the Guard. Ever hopeful of extending his influence, he was to be thwarted by Robert Cecil, who kept him off the council, and Raleigh was left to carry on his own ineffective intrigues with James VI, hoping to return to power with the new regime.

In the 1590s, a group of young and discontented courtiers was forming around the Earl of Essex. Henry Wriothesley, the youthful Earl of Southampton, was rather incongruously drawn to Essex on his arrival at court. Southampton had been born in 1573, the year following his father's release from the Tower after his suspected complicity in the Ridolfi Plot, and was only eight when he succeeded to his title. The third Earl spent his minority as Burghley's ward, following in the path of Oxford, and was sent to St John's College, Cambridge. When he first came to court at seventeen everyone was struck by his delicate features, set off by long golden tresses.

Although he took part in tournaments, his principal interests were literary, he found a place in his household for the Italian John Florio and as a result of his early friendship Shakespeare dedicated to him both *Venus and Adonis* and *The Rape of Lucrece*. Yet the sensitive youth had a wild temper, and was forever becoming involved in brawls and other escapades. His mother married the widowed Sir Thomas Heneage in 1595, but the Vice-Chamberlain could not tame his stepson into the ways of a courtier. His service in the Cadiz expedition had shown him the force of Essex's leadership and once home again court seemed a bore: 'He passed away the time merely in going to plays every day.'

The one redeeming feature of court for Southampton was Elizabeth Vernon, a maid of honour. Idle gossip abounded concerning their relationship, and early in 1598 there was an awkward scene in the Presence Chamber after the Queen had retired for the night. The Earl was playing primero with Raleigh and Ambrose Willoughby (a Squire for the Body). When Willoughby indicated it was time to pack up the game, Raleigh agreed, but Southampton became obstreperous. Later that night, near the Whitehall tennis court, he struck Willoughby, who had been talking freely about Mistress Vernon, and in retaliation he 'pulled off some of his locks'. When the Queen was told, she congratulated Willoughby. Shortly afterwards Southampton was permitted to go to France, but during his absence Elizabeth found out about his liaison with the maid of honour. Hearing that the lady was pregnant, the Earl dashed home to marry her secretly, then returned alone to Paris. He might have saved himself the journey, since the Queen immediately recalled him, and had him taken into custody, while his 'new-coined countess' was hounded out of the palace into the Fleet Prison. At twenty-five, Southampton's career as a courtier was over and he turned to Essex for help.

In 1596 Robert Carey, who had spoken up for Essex four years before, was also in disgrace for contracting a marriage. Now over thirty and knighted for his service in France, Hunsdon's tenth son had become 'an assiduous attendant on the court', a way of life that ruined his pocket. With no hope of preferment, despite his parentage, he decided to marry a widow of means – Lady Widdrington. He escaped from the Queen's wrath to serve on the border at Carlisle for a year and then, on his father's advice, decided to make amends by appearing at court on Accession Day, presenting himself in the tiltyard as 'a forsaken knight who had vowed solitariness'. Incognito, he gave the Queen a rich present, but although he revealed his identity after the tilting, she took no notice of him. His brother, the Marshal of Berwick, and his father, the Lord Chamberlain, later arranged for him to carry letters from James VI to Whitehall, where, alas, his reception was 'stormy and terrible', for the Queen made uncharitable remarks about his wife and his foolishness in marrying her, though later she relented and forgave him.

With the changes consequent on his father's death, Sir Robert was required to take over the governorship of Berwick, but nothing was said about a salary and after a year of penury he risked leaving his post to plead his cause with Elizabeth. Neither Cecil nor his own brother, by now Chamberlain, would dare to introduce him to the Presence Chamber, but he was saved by a gentleman of the Chamber, who spoke up for him, announcing to Her Majesty that there stood without a man 'whose loyal service surpassed that of many whom she rewarded liberally'. Intrigued to know who this paragon of virtue might be, she was told it was young Carey, who could no longer bear to be away from her sight. The magic worked. He was allowed to kiss her hand, she gave him £500 on the spot and appointed him Warden of the East March. Lady Carey was to come into her own at the Stuart accession, when she was given charge of the future Charles I, then four, and earned fame by resisting James I's suggestions that his little son should wear iron boots to strengthen his ankles and have an operation on his tongue to ease his impediment.

On Walsingham's death in 1590 there was no obvious successor to the secretaryship of State which he had held for eighteen years. Essex unwisely, if chivalrously, sponsored William Davison for the post. Davison was still in deep disgrace with the Queen for the part he had played in the episode of Mary Queen of Scots' death warrant, and though he continued to draw his pay as an Assistant Secretary he never served Elizabeth again in any capacity. Meanwhile Burghley had been grooming his second son, Robert Cecil, for the post. Almost from birth, Robert had imbibed his father's political maxims about how to succeed at court, and never questioned their wisdom: 'Be sure to keep some great man thy friend, but trouble him not with trifles. Compliment him often with many, yet small gifts and of little charge. And if thou hast cause to bestow away some great gratuity' – a device not to be encouraged – 'let it be something which may be daily in sight. . . . Towards thy superiors be humble, yet generous. With thine equals familiar, and yet respective. Towards thine inferiors show much humanity and some familiarity.' Counsels of perfection, indeed, yet Robert saw the importance of following them and, partly by temperament, partly by training, was to become a far more astute politician than his father.

The Cecils, father and second son: a double portrait from Hatfield House of Lord Burghley and Sir Robert Cecil.

Burghley did not attempt to chart what Bacon was to call 'that deep and inscrutable centre of the court, which is Her Majesty's mind', for, despite his long association with her, he often miscalculated her reactions in these last years, when she became increasingly unpredictable and her court almost Byzantine, with rapid changes of fortune and individuals. When Burghley had been out of affairs in the spring of 1587 Robert had helped with the paper-work, but he was still under thirty and the Queen thought him inexperienced; besides, to allow another Cecil into power while Burghley remained at the helm would have courted trouble with Essex. Other potential candidates such as the poet Dyer and John Wilkes, clerk of the Council, lacked the standing to hold Essex at bay. Burghley risked putting Robert's name privately to the Queen, but without much hope of success. There was, in fact, no speedy decision; in the event he held the secretaryship himself, but delegated many routine tasks to his son until a more formal arrangement could be made.

In 1591, when Elizabeth visited the Cecils at their great mansion of Theobalds for ten days, at terrible cost as the host feared, Burghley worked hard to influence her. In a play performed for her amusement there was a dialogue between a gentleman usher and the postman in which the usher was able to pay fulsome tribute to Elizabeth's knowledge of languages, yet to make plain that her labours would be eased by appointing a Secretary of State. Though the Queen took the play in good part, she made no appoint-ment. Robert Cecil's view was that she 'was too much pressed at the first, which she liketh not'. Yet on the summer progress he was sworn a councillor and his oath of office (rather in the manner of subscription to the modern Official Secrets Acts) certainly enabled him to have sight of secret documents, which salved Burghley's conscience. Robert would write to ambassadors: 'My father's business makes him command me to answer your letter.' Soon he was seen regularly making his way down the corridors of Whitehall Palace to the Presence Chamber, with 'his hands full of papers and head full of matter', a hunchback, grave beyond his years, absorbed in the minutiae of public affairs and with no inclination to gossip with courtiers of his own age. Not for another five years did he receive the secretaryship, when Essex – by now singing the praises of Sir Thomas Bodley – was away at Cadiz.

The duel between Essex and Cecil began as early as the election to the Chancellorship of Oxford University in 1592. In the previous year Cecil had become High Steward of Cambridge, where his father was Chancellor, while Essex, though a Cambridge graduate, wanted to succeed to his stepfather Leicester's place at Oxford. Essex solicited Cecil's support, but the latter was in no mind to back a rank-outsider, for the front-runner was Thomas Sack-ville, Lord Buckhurst, the Queen's cousin and a scholar and a man of the right seniority. Moreover the University wanted a patron who could support its petitions forcefully. Essex took his inevitable failure as a personal rebuff and wrote to Cecil with bitterness: 'Sir R. I have been with the Queen and have had my answer. How it agrees with your letter you can judge after you have spoken with the Queen. Whether you have mistaken the Queen or used cunning with me, I know not. I will not condemn you, but leave you to think if it were your own case, whether you could not be jealous. Your friend, if I have cause, R. Essex.' This was a warning shot. With reason Burghley advised Robert in Old Testament terms 'Open not thy gate to flatterers, nor thine ears to backbiters.'

Essex was now twenty-four, and the darling of the court. He decided to take politics seriously, aiming at a seat on the council, which he achieved the following year, and then building up his own expertise in affairs and his own party in court, country and Parliament so that supreme power under the Queen might be in his grasp. The realm was still ruled by old men – Burghley, Hunsdon and Knollys – who were approaching the Biblical span, and the Earl sought to step into their shoes. Men noticed that he had forsaken 'all his former youthful tricks, carrying himself with honourable gravity,' busying himself in Parliament and council to gain a reputation for diligence and judgment. For advice on strategy, Essex could now count on the brothers Anthony and Francis Bacon, sons of Elizabeth's first Lord Keeper. Anthony, the elder, was born in 1558 and with Francis, he attended Trinity College, Cambridge, under John Whitgift. When his father died he took the advice of his uncle Burghley and embarked on a prolonged foreign tour, to seek out political intelligence, especially in France. On his travels he stayed with Theodore Beza and Montaigne, met Henry of Navarre and maintained close contact with many of Secretary Walsingham's agents. But his body was frail and his mother feared that residence abroad was undermining his Protestantism as well as sapping his health. At last in 1592 he returned to England, expecting his uncle to find him a post, but received nothing but promises and 'even in these no offer or hopeful assurance of real kindness'.

Forsaken by the Cecils, Anthony turned instead to Essex and undertook to supply him with foreign intelligence far more accurate than the Queen's ministers could obtain. Bacon was to sit at the centre of a web, receiving reports from Thomas Bodley in The Hague, Dr Hawkins in Venice and from a host of agents and spies throughout Europe, which made his study in Essex House an independent foreign office. Essex hoped as a result to trump ministers' cards at every deal and promised to let the Queen know that it was Anthony who was the master-mind behind a system far superior to that run by old Walsingham. He was to stay beside Essex to the end.

Francis Bacon, three years younger than Anthony, had intended to follow his father in the law. However, when Burghley thought him far too young for promotion, he turned to politics, sitting in Parliament and penning cogent letters of advice to the Queen, since advancement necessitated becoming a courtier. He had the most brilliant mind of his generation; when only seventeen Hilliard had painted him, adding to his portrait the motto 'if one could but paint his mind'. As he contemplated the political scene he shrewdly analysed the structure of power and developed many original ideas, drawing up a programme of reform. Essex, amazed at the range of his abilities, drew him into his service, to direct his thoughts on men and measures, and in this way Francis Bacon may be said to have headed the earliest party political research office. But he was not to be an *éminence grise*, to write speeches for a leader, for he himself took part in the in-fighting. In the Parliament of 1593, when the Devereux interest achieved an independent identity in the Commons, with men like the Earl's new step-father, Christopher Blount, Bacon sat for Middlesex and won a tactical victory over Cecil by obstructing the subsidy bill. Essex gloated over the discomfiture of the Cecils, rather overlooking the essential fact that it was unbelievably tactless for a councillor's supporters to embarrass the government. The Queen did not quickly forget the incident and it badly set back Francis's career.

In 1594 Essex exploited the intelligence provided by Anthony Bacon over the affair of Dr Roderigo Lopez. Lopez, the Queen's physician, was accused of plotting her murder for Philip of Spain. It is impossible to establish the truth in this murky episode. Essex at first kept what he knew to himself – rather as Walsingham had done in the Babington Plot – but the Earl wanted to appear as a national hero who had saved the Queen's life, and to play on anti-Spanish feelings at a time when Burghley and others were pondering the merits of putting out peace-feelers. When Essex arrested Lopez, Robert Cecil was convinced that the alleged treachery could not be proven and hastened to Hampton Court to unburden his suspicions to the Queen. Later that day, when the favourite came to Hampton Elizabeth was short with him – he was 'a rash and temerarious youth' for daring to arrest her doctor. He rode back to Essex House, locked himself in his chamber for two days, and then wrote to Anthony Bacon: 'I have discovered a most dangerous and desperate treason. The point of conspiracy was Her Majesty's death. The executioner should have been Dr Lopez; the manner poison. This I have so followed as I will make it appear as clear as the noon day.' Together with Cecil, he examined the Portuguese Jew and others in the Tower. Under torture enough circumstantial evidence was acquired to send the doctor for trial and on to certain death, while loyal Londoners flocked to performances of Marlowe's *The Jew of Malta*, applauding Essex as much as the players.

At this time Essex was throwing all his weight behind Francis Bacon's candidature for the vacant office of Attorney-General, while the Cecils were no less determined to see Edward Coke appointed. The two Roberts had shared a coach on returning from the Tower, where they had been examining Lopez, and Cecil pressed home his advantage. 'Good Lord, I wonder your Lordship should go about to spend your strength in so unlikely and impossible a man. Give me only one precedent for the appointment of so raw a youth to that place of such moment.' Essex, referring to Cecil's own suit for the Secretaryship, retorted 'I could name a younger than Francis Bacon, of less learning and of no greater experience, who is suing and shoving with all force for an office.' Cecil was not to be drawn; if the Earl had been putting forward Bacon for the solicitorship, rather than the attorneyship 'that might be of easier digestion to Her Majesty'. Essex had had enough. 'Digest me no digestions. The attorneyship for Francis is that I must have.' Any who stood in his way was an enemy, 'for now do I fully declare myself'.

The battle won, Cecil sent the Earl a terse note: 'I am glad that the Queen is cleared by some of her friends from some suspicions that might have troubled you. Your friends will not alter without expostulating the cause. I doubt not but you will observe the same course'; this was more than agreeing to differ. There was still to be some give and take: Cecil assured Essex that while the latter was away on the Islands Voyage he would do all he could to keep Parliament from meeting until after the expedition returned. Again, when Cecil was on an embassy to France early in 1598, the Earl undertook to do nothing 'disagreeable' while he was abroad.

When the attorneyship went to Coke and the junior post to Sergeant Fleming, Essex impetuously offered Bacon some land in Twickenham Park, which the latter eventually accepted. In later years, when Francis had left his service it was said by another dissatisfied retainer that Essex could get anything for himself, but nothing for his friends. This was, in fact, an unfair

Francis Bacon (1561-1626), once the political adviser and friend of Essex, he became one of the Queen's counsel at the Earl's trial after his rebellion. Like his father, he eventually achieved the Woolsack. Portrait attributed to Paul van Somer.

comment on Elizabeth's distribution of patronage, for over the years the Earl's supporters received a fair share of such pickings as were going, if they were suitably qualified for the post in question. The Queen was not going to be dictated to and was convinced she must balance the Cecil and the Devereux factions at court.

When Essex offered himself to scrutinise all claims to Elizabeth's patronage to relieve her, he said, of a great burden, she saw through the suggestion. Essex already had a secretariat in Essex House, directed by Henry Cuffe, once Professor of Greek at Oxford, and staffed to deal with applications for appointments, but Elizabeth was well aware that whoever disposed of patronage would become ruler of the court. Controlling the issue of titles of honour, rewarding past and future service by grants and pensions, and making appointments throughout the public service were an essential aspect of government, and Elizabeth would never surrender her exercise of patronage to anyone else. To compete for the prizes involved the growth of factions, and the fewer and smaller the prizes offered in the 1590s (because of the Crown's strained financial position), the more intensive the faction fighting, yet the Queen insisted on remaining as umpire. She needed freedom to manœuvre so that she could override the dictates of party leaders, prevent the emergence of a 'single-party' rule at court, and gratify her own whims in exercising her prerogative rights of dispensing grace and favour.

In the year of the Lopez affair Essex became embarrassed by the appearance of a tract on the succession which had been printed abroad, probably by expatriate Catholics, and smuggled into England. R. Doleman's *A Conference on the Next Succession to the Crown of England* was on the face of it an impartial survey of potential claimants to the throne, including James VI of Scotland, the Infanta of Spain, the Earls of Derby and Huntingdon, and Lords Beauchamp and Seymour. To circulate a book on the forbidden topic was anathema to the Queen, but to make it worse the author, reckoning there *would* be a disputed succession on Elizabeth's death, called on Essex, to whom he had dedicated the work, to intervene on the demise of the Crown, since no other figure could 'have a greater part or sway in deciding of this great affair'. It was indeed dangerous to suggest that England would be ripe for a Kingmaker. Although the Queen was sure that the Earl had been the victim

ABOVE Sir Henry Lee (1530-1610). A nephew of Sir Thomas Wyatt, he became Queen's Champion of the Tilt and Master of the Ordnance: a portrait painted in the Low Countries by Antonio Moro, 1568.
LEFT Tilting at the barriers in the sixteenth century.

RIGHT Design by Joseph Halder for a suit of tilting armour for Sir Christopher Hatton: from the design book for the courtiers of Elizabeth I.
FAR RIGHT George Clifford, 3rd Earl of Cumberland, dressed for the tilt: portrait by Hilliard.

of propaganda, probably devised by Robert Parsons, others were to ensure that the mud stuck.

Essex sought to rehabilitate himself at the Accession Day Tilt of 1595. This annual contest of arms in an allegorical setting to honour the courtiers' sovereign lady had been devised by Sir Henry Lee, the Queen's Champion of the Tilt, in 1580. Seeded champions issued their challenges some days before and on the great day would process with their splendidly attired retainers into the Whitehall tiltyard. Each champion had a well-coached spokesman to mount the steps beneath the Queen's window either to recite a polished verse, perhaps commissioned from Edward Dyer or Thomas Churchyard, or sometimes to make a comic speech. The spokesman 'in the name of his lord offered to the Queen a costly present which was accepted and permission given to take part in the tournament'.

This tilt on 17 November, the date of Elizabeth's accession, was the principal event of organised sport in the Elizabethan calendar. Seats in specially-erected stands cost 12d. each. 'On this day not only very fine lords were seen, but also beautiful ladies, not only in the royal suite, but likewise in the company of the gentlemen of the nobility and the citizens.' The victors were expected to present their shields for hanging in the Shield Gallery, by the river. When Lee succeeded Warwick as master of the Ordnance in 1590, he decided to retire from the honorific office he had invented as Champion. Two years later he entertained Her Majesty at Ditchley, his Oxfordshire home, and to commemorate the visit, he commissioned a portrait of the Queen to be painted standing upon the map of England, her feet on Oxfordshire – a loyal touch that delighted her.

He was succeeded as her personal champion by George Clifford, Earl of Cumberland, the prince of privateers who always wore in his hat, as a symbol of chivalry, a glove which Elizabeth had dropped. Hilliard characteristically portrayed him wearing fancy dress over his full armour, standing beside an allegorical tree on which he had hung his shield. In 1595 Cumberland entered the tiltyard riding 'a dragon laden with fair spoils', while Essex dressed himself in 'innocent white and fair carnation', Drury in 'flames of gold' and Sussex in 'raven's feathers'. The poet George Peele put out a broadsheet describing the secular devotion of the lists on this occasion, when an ageless Queen was fêted by her true knights:

> What troop of loyal English knights at arms
> Right richly mounted and appointed all
> In shining arms accoutred for the wars,
> Small number of a number numberless
> Held jousts in honour of Her holiday . . .

The same evening Essex secured the performance at court of a play written by Francis Bacon to flatter the Queen and make plain the Earl's absolute devotion to her. A character representing Essex, held Her Majesty's glove, while he talked with an old hermit (easily identifiable as Burghley), a Secretary of State (Robert Cecil, even more hunch-backed than the original) and a soldier. In turn this triumvirate tried to persuade the Earl to turn his back on Love and follow singlemindedly the way of life of a hermit, or of a secretary or a soldier. Then 'comes into the tiltyard, unthought upon, the ordinary postboy of London, a ragged villain, all bemired . . . and delivered the secretary a packet of letters, which he presently offered my Lord of Essex'. This was an audacious send-up of the play devised for Elizabeth's visit to Theobalds in 1591, though some of Bacon's jokes misfired since Burghley was away from court suffering from gout. It ended on a more serious note for 'the Earl' in a flowery speech refused to abandon 'that mistress who made divine his meditations and whose beauty inspired him to command armies'. Behind the allegory and the allusions to chivalric romance, the statement was unequivocal. Essex had announced himself to the court as the hero not only of England, but also of the Queen. Elizabeth was not unimpressed by this display, remarking 'if she had thought there had been so much said of her, she would not have been there that night'. It seems she had rather enjoyed herself.

Soon there was employment of the kind Essex enjoyed, for it was decided to send an expedition against Cadiz, to make impossible the launching of another armada. At the last moment Elizabeth hesitated, for the Spaniards were at the gates of Calais and she could hear their artillery from Greenwich. She postponed plans for an assault on the Peninsula and instead appointed Essex to cross the Channel with an army to aid the French, though in a secret note to him she implored him not 'to peril so fair an army for another prince's town'. But the expedition came too late; before it could embark, Calais was in Spanish hands – a safe harbour for a potential armada.

The Queen kept changing her mind about Cadiz – whether or not to send the expedition and who was to command it; in the end Lord Howard of Effingham and Essex went as joint commanders and she wished the fleet of

RIGHT 'Queen Elizabeth leading the Dutch Cow', an allegorical picture of Philip II riding the cow of the Netherlands, his spur drawing blood. The Duke of Alva is seen milking the cow, while the Duke of Alençon (whose proposal Elizabeth had at length rejected), is attempting to pull the beast backwards. William the Silent is steadying the cow's horns, while the Queen feeds it with hay. By the Treaty of Nonsuch, April 1585, Elizabeth sent an army to the Netherlands.

OVERLEAF Nonsuch Palace in the early seventeenth century.

Clemens et Regni moderatrix iusta Británi
Hac forma insigni conspicienda nitet.

Tristia dum gentes circùm omnes bella fatigant,
Cæciíq errores toto grassantur in orbe.
pace beas longa, Vera et pietate Britannos:
Iusticia moderans miti sapienter hactenas.
Chara domi, celebrisq foris, longænaq regniu
Hic teneas, regno tandem fruitura perenni.

Añ·Dñi 1579

one hundred sail Godspeed, for a great victory 'with the least loss of English blood'. When news of the sack of Cadiz reached her she at once wrote to her commanders, 'Let the army know I care not so much being Queen as that I am sovereign of such subjects.' But undignified squabbles broke out between Howard and Essex about the spoils and these soured the flavour of victory for the Queen. Essex received a withering welcome from Elizabeth and wrote to Anthony Bacon: 'I am as much distasted with the glorious greatness of a favourite as I was before with the supposed happiness of a courtier,' all was vanity.

Yet if he was out of favour with the Queen, the Cadiz expedition had made Essex the darling of the adventurers, many of them younger sons, who looked on soldiering as a glorious profession. In reciprocating their warm affection for him, Essex was playing with fire. 'I love them for mine own sake, for I find sweetness in their conversation, strong assistance in their employment and happiness in their friendship. I love them for their virtue's sake and for their greatness of mind.' They were the real heroes of England – 'if we may have peace, they have purchased it; if we must have war, they have managed it'. Essex was compared in sermons with the great soldiers of the Ancient World and in taverns and alehouses his name was widely toasted.

Unlike the earlier favourites – Leicester, Hatton and Raleigh – Essex was popular and he now courted further popularity in a most dangerous way, expecting as a matter of course to reward friends with the Sovereign's patronage. Where Elizabeth was concerned, however, the only idolatry allowed was heroine worship. After Cadiz, instead of stealing the limelight, Essex should have been content to bask in the light reflected from the Queen. Bacon had once written, 'Her Majesty loveth peace. Next she loveth not change,' but in playing the military hero to the extent of embodying a war party Essex was flouting the first, and to get his own way he would have to flout the second. With his usual perception, Bacon analysed the situation and with remarkable frankness told the Earl that his Queen must conclude he was 'a man of a nature not to be ruled, that hath the advantage of my affections and knoweth it; of an estate not grounded to his greatness; of a popular reputation; of a military dependence'. These four traits in his character spelt ruin, since there could not be 'a more dangerous image than this represented to any monarch living, much more to a lady and of Her Majesty's apprehension'.

Francis Bacon was sure now that he had hitched his waggon to the wrong star. When Essex demanded and was given the command of the Islands Voyage to Ferrol in 1597, seeking to capture the Spanish plate fleet, he showed how Bacon's advice had gone unheeded. Raleigh, restored to some measure of his old favour, was chosen as rear admiral for the attack on the Azores, but as at Cadiz, Essex quarrelled with him. Raleigh deemed it prudent to be first back home to present the Queen with his own version of an expedition that had been dogged by wrong decisions, putting the blame firmly on Essex. On the favourite's return Elizabeth questioned him searchingly about his treatment of Sir Walter. Essex was even more put out to discover that during his absence Cecil had netted the lucrative post of Chancellor of the Duchy of Lancaster, while Archbishop Whitgift, a Cecilian, had been brought on to the council and, much worse, Admiral Howard had been promoted to an earldom. Essex fell ill, but made no effort when he was better to attend council, instead sulking at Wanstead. Bacon again proffered advice: 'The greatest subject that is or ever was greatest in the prince's favour, in his absence is not missed, and a small discontinuance makes things that were, as if were not, and breeds forgetfulness which gives way to wrath; and the wrath of a prince is as the roaring of a lion.' Yet Essex still thought he could tame the Queen!

The Lord Admiral's earldom of Nottingham dismayed Essex on two scores: in the first place the wording of the patent, besides lauding his actions in 1588, praised his service at Cadiz – a victory Essex insisted was his own; secondly, a Lord Admiral who was also an Earl took precedence over an Earl who did not hold one of the great offices of State. Nottingham had at last turned the tables on the favourite, for whom he had little love; when Essex at Cadiz had followed his invariable practice of placing his signature so high on a document that there was no room for the Lord Admiral to sign above it, the latter had cut out Essex's signature. He now challenged the Admiral or any other member of the Howard family to single combat. When Lord Hunsdon, the Chamberlain, pointedly suggested that the Queen 'rather imagined you should look into the state of the realm as a councillor than respect your private state, when you might take a more quiet time hereafter to look into it,' these were prophetic words. He failed to honour the Queen by attending the Accession Day Tilt, yet by the end of the year, to attract him back to court, she created him Earl Marshal, an office which again gave him precedence over Nottingham and had overtones of martial greatness dear to his heart. He should have been prepared to take another disappointment in his stride.

In 1597 Lord Cobham's death made the wardenship of the Cinque Ports vacant. Although Cobham had been under suspicion at the time of the Ridolfi Plot, he easily regained royal favour and in due course his daughter married Robert Cecil. Their marriage was tragically short, for she predeceased her father by a matter of weeks, and though Robert hid his feelings

Charles Lord Howard of Effingham, in his robes as Earl of Nottingham, the title given to him by the Queen in 1596 for his part in the victory of Cadiz and the defeat of the Spanish Armada: portrait by Daniel Mytens.

in public he was overwrought with grief. At a time like this, Cecil was not likely to allow the claims of his brother-in-law, the new Lord Cobham, to the lord wardenship to be set aside. Essex put forward Sir Robert Sidney, but upon being told that he had insufficient weight beside Cobham, he had the temerity to ask for the post for himself. Elizabeth called him in to tell him that she was appointing Cobham, but did not tell him then about his consolation prize. As he was shaking the dust of London from his feet next morning he was stopped by a messenger who summoned him again to the presence, where the Queen announced that he was to become master of the Ordnance, in succession to old Sir Henry Lee.

However, unhappy Ireland, the graveyard of so many English politicians' and commanders' reputations, was to prove the undoing of Essex. From the early days of the reign, when Sussex had attempted to outwit O'Neil, down to the surrender of Tyrone in the year of Elizabeth's death, English expeditions to end the succession of rebellions cost the enormous sum of £2,410,000. 'Pacification' seemed a will-o'-the-wisp. There is a contemporary ring about the tragedy of Elizabethan Ireland; for 'there is no land in the world of so continual war within himself, nor of so great shedding of Christian blood, nor of so great robbing, spoiling, preying and burning, nor of so great wrongful extortions continually as Ireland'. Tyrone now had promise of Spanish aid to win a crown of a united Ireland as Philip's satellite, and since Henry IV of France had signed peace with Spain the threat to Elizabeth was indeed great.

Essex attended the meeting with the Queen to discuss the appointment of a new Lord Deputy. Elizabeth suggested Sir William Knollys, Essex's uncle, but the Earl argued that Sir George Carew, a friend of Cecil's, should be sent, as he wanted him away from court. The Queen refused to countenance this, and Essex lost his temper daring to turn his back on Elizabeth, 'as it were in contempt, with a scornful look. She waxing impatient gave him a cuff on the ear and bade him be gone with a vengeance.' Foolishly he laid his hand on his sword, but Nottingham stepped between him and the Queen. Before he left he swore in a passion he 'neither could nor would swallow so great an indignity' and would not even have taken it from Henry VIII.

Soon after this incident, Burghley died. He had mellowed with the years from his early self-conscious Protestantism and on his deathbed prayed in Latin. His experience of government was incomparable, his output of papers impressive, and of all Elizabeth's councillors he had come nearest to achieving detached judgments. He always regarded himself as her principal representative and had been reluctant to appear as leader of a faction, though he had gladly opposed Leicester and was enjoying seeing his son stand up to Essex. A few charged him with erecting 'a Regnum Cecilianum', keeping a stranglehold on appointments, but the evidence points the other way; had nepotism been his way his Bacon nephews would have found early promotion. To keep the peace at court he had risked investing £500 in Raleigh's 1595 voyage. Of his integrity, by the standards of the age, there is no question. Burghley had risen by devoted work and if his perquisites as Master of the Wards helped him to build Theobalds, Burghley House, Northamptonshire, and his house in the Strand, he still reckoned that the fees of the Treasurership would not meet the expenses of his stable. He obviously enjoyed the exercise of power and had been delighted at his barony, yet the pomp and the frills in which many courtiers revelled were for him irrelevancies. Now in August 1598, after almost forty years of office, he was dead – a monolith removed from the scene. As a statesman he was irreplaceable. To some courtiers he had become 'Old Saturnus', a father figure for Elizabeth, just as Saturn had been the father of Jupiter, but the Queen referred to him as '*pater pacis patriae*', and there could be no finer commendation.

Essex, meanwhile, could not bring himself to apologise to the Queen for his outburst.

> Madam, when I think how I have preferred your beauty above all things and received no pleasure in life but by the increase of your favour towards me, I wonder at myself what cause there could be to make me absent myself one day from you. But when I remembered that Your Majesty hath by the intolerable wrong you have done both me and yourself, not only broken all laws of affection, but done against the honour of your sex, I think all places better than where I am, and all dangers well undertaken, so I might retire myself from the memory of my false, inconstant and beguiling pleasures. ... I was never proud, till you sought to make me too base. And now, since my destiny is no better, my despair shall be like my love was, without repentance. ... I must commend my faith to be judged by Him Who judgeth all hearts, since on earth I find no right. Wishing you all comforts and joys in the world and no greater punishment for your wrongs to me, than to know the faith of him you have lost, and the baseness of those you shall keep.
>
> Your Majesty's most humble servant
>
> R. Essex

Much as she wanted him back, Elizabeth would not give way to his petulance. If he came in person and repented, she would reconsider the affair. 'He hath played long enough upon me,' she said, 'and now I mean to play a while with him and stand as much upon my greatness as he hath upon his stomach.' A courtier neatly summed up the problem: 'I know but one friend and one enemy my Lord hath; and that one friend is the Queen and that one enemy is himself.' He attended the Accession Day Tilt on 17 November, but less to please the Queen than to snub Raleigh, at long last allowed to return to his place as Captain of the Guard. Essex had discovered that Sir Walter was to dress his men for the tilt in orange tawny plumes, so to deflate him he equipped his own army of retainers in identical plumage. Elizabeth was so annoyed at such behaviour at a public event that she closed the proceedings early.

After Christmas there appeared the first book of John Hayward's *Life and Reign of Henry IV*. It was much concerned with the deposition of Richard II and because of its extravagant dedication to Essex Elizabeth suspected that this was a tract for the times put out by the Earl's faction. Hayward was tried in the Star Chamber for daring to treat of so dangerous a topic as a sovereign's deposition, and was sent to the Fleet Prison.

In council Essex opposed every name suggested as commander-in-chief in Ireland, to replace Sir Henry Bagnal, who had been slain. It was clear that he wanted the command himself and in the end the Queen took him at his word. If by his military skill he could subdue Tyrone and pacify Ireland, all well and good; if not then the campaign would cure him of his ambition. He was delighted to accept the challenge and escape from court; 'methinks it is

Captain Thomas Lee (1500-1601) the nephew of Sir Henry Lee. He served in the Irish campaigns, 1581-99, and became an adherent of Essex: he was

the fairer choice to command armies than humours,' he said, 'I am tied in my own reputation.' He left for Ireland at the end of March 1599 with an enormous army. Among the courtiers to accompany him was Sir John Harington, serving as Master of the Horse for the army in place of Southampton, whose appointment Elizabeth had vetoed, although he still travelled to Ireland, together with Sir Christopher Blount and a host of veterans from the Cadiz expedition.

Essex disobeyed his instructions from the outset. Against the Queen's precise orders not to confer knighthoods except for great valour, he dubbed captains freely. Instead of marching into Ulster to meet Tyrone he stayed put. Elizabeth chided him for inactivity and feared 'your purpose is not to end the war'. She asked Francis Bacon for his views on the situation and received a most frank assessment:

Madam, if you had my Lord of Essex here with a white staff in his hand, as my Lord of Leicester had, and continued him still about you for society to yourself, and for an honour and ornament to your attendance and Court in the eyes of your people, and in the eyes of foreign ambassadors, then were he in his right element. For to discontent him as you do, and yet to put arms and power into his hands, may be a kind of temptation to make him prove cumbersome and unruly. And therefore if you would send for him, and satisfy him with honour here near you, if your affairs – which I am not acquainted with – will permit it, I think were the best way.

Away from court, Essex suspected that Cecil and others were planning his overthrow, for all the intelligence reaching him pointed that way. There was vague talk about marching on London, but Blount restrained him, though he was still bent on seeing the Queen. On an impulse he signed a truce with Tyrone and despite Elizabeth's letters left for England on 24 September, with a few chosen friends. In the morning of the 28th, after strenuous riding, he reached Nonsuch Palace, immediately pushing his way into the Queen's bedchamber. She had only just risen and was scarcely dressed, so that Essex saw her as no man had ever seen her before: without her wig and her rouge, bare of the jewels and the great ruff, with none of the trappings of regality, so that she appeared a rather ugly woman of sixty-six. He knelt self-consciously to kiss her hand and left to change from his riding clothes, having no doubt that he could charm his way out of his predicament.

Later in the morning Elizabeth gave him a long private audience. While she dined alone, he fed in the hall with courtiers keen to learn the latest news from Ireland, though both Cecil and Raleigh kept their distance. After dinner the Queen interrogated him with great thoroughness on his reasons for disobeying her instructions, and on the morrow the Earl faced a lengthy examination from the council, while Harington, who had accompanied him, felt her biting tongue. Essex's appeal to the Queen as a woman had failed, and he expected to be sent to the Tower. Instead the Queen sent him to York House in the custody of Lord Keeper Egerton, where his health deteriorated through acute depression, and he feared he was dying.

At the end of Michaelmas term Egerton's customary speech in the Star Chamber dwelt on Essex's disobedience and the dangers of sedition, while plans were made for his trial. This was cancelled when he wrote a full submission acknowledging his faults, and he was allowed home to Essex House,

executed on Tower Hill for his part in the rebellion of 1601. This portrait, by Marcus Gheeraerts the Younger, 1594, shows Lee attired as 'Hybernus Miles'.

233

though as a prisoner. He made a further appeal to Elizabeth in May, reminding her that she had always said she wanted to correct him, not ruin him, 'for I said to myself, "Between my ruin and my Sovereign's favour there is no mean, and if she bestow favour again, she gives it with all things that in this world I either need or desire." But now that the length of my troubles and the increase of your indignation have made all men so afraid of me as my own poor state is ruined and my friends and servants like to die in prison,' he was subject to malicious gossip and felt 'thrown into a corner as a dead carcass'. He prayed that she might conclude his punishment and his life, so that he could pass from an unkind world 'in which I have lived too long, and once thought myself too happy'. The Queen was deeply moved by this letter, but could not bring herself to reply. She spared him a State trial, but he had to appear before the judges at York House – Francis Bacon, who had once been so close to him, Egerton and Coke. They censured him for his conduct of the Irish campaign, but all underlined the Queen's mercy. Essex was to remain confined in Essex House until further orders and to be forbidden from exercising his offices of Earl Marshal, Master of the Horse and Master of the Ordnance. Twelve weeks later he was set free, and announced that he would spend the rest of his days in retirement.

Essex was now troubled not by his life but by his debts, amounting to some £16,000. The principal source of his income, the lease of the duties on sweet wines, expired at Michaelmas and if Elizabeth were not to renew it he would be undone. He wrote with a new urgency: 'Haste paper to that unhappy presence, whence only unhappy I am banished. Kiss that fair correcting hand. ... Say thou comest from shaming, languishing, despairing SX.' She sighed when Lady Scrope spoke up for him, and said 'Indeed, it is so.' He wrote again bluntly pointing out that his creditors were hungry and spelling out how desperately he needed the renewal of the wine lease. It was no good his signing himself 'Your Majesty's humblest, faithfullest and more than most devoted vassal'; she knew at last he had been beaten, and as he grovelled she decided to teach him a lesson he would never forget. She would not renew the lease, but if he mended his ways there was a chance of receiving a fresh grant in time.

The Queen's conditions for curbing him, he said, were 'as crooked as her carcass'. He could not accept the fact that his star had fallen. Illness, confinement, imminent bankruptcy and fears for his life increased the streak of megalomania that had been apparent from his début at court. Any chance he had of making a rational decision to retire from the scene and wait for a change of fortune was nullified by the evil genius of Henry Cuffe, his secretary, who persuaded him that to save his own reputation he must resort to arms and not behave like a coward, for his supporters were relying on him. Thus Essex was driven to make a final gamble, in which young adventurers joined with companions of past campaigns to overturn the government.

The leading figures in the revolt were disappointed aristocrats who had come to court, like Essex himself, for the tangible rewards that could be obtained only from the Queen's hands. To achieve their ambitions they had attached themselves to the Earl as the prince of patrons. Among them were the Earls of Southampton, Rutland, Sussex and Bedford, who had lived so extravagantly that they were dubbed 'fantasticals'. In four years Rutland had thrown away £12,400 of his inheritance. All were living on borrowed money, with their estates mortgaged to the hilt. In the lottery for profit and place at court they had lost, partly through Essex's own tactics, partly because the dividends were much smaller.

Essex's ranks also included Catholics, Devereux tenants from the Welsh border summoned by the Earl's fiery steward Sir Gelli Meyrick, and other malcontents. Some survivors of the revolt were to become involved in the

Main and Bye Plots of 1603, after James I's accession, and to conspire with Guy Fawkes in 1605. Essex sent messengers to Ireland and Scotland and was convinced that Mountjoy would come to his aid by bringing over an army, while James VI committed himself in writing to the general design. The conspirators planned to take the Tower, to hold the city of London and to surround the court to wring from Elizabeth Essex's appointment as Lord Protector. In theory they were rescuing the Queen from evil advisors, the traditional formula for English rebels, yet if need be they would risk shedding her blood. As a manifesto they paid the actors at The Globe to play Shakespeare's *Richard II* for the night of Saturday 7 February.

Next morning, after Essex disobeyed a summons to attend the Queen on his allegiance, she sent Egerton, Sir William Knollys, the Earl's uncle, and others to Essex House to try to reason with him, but they were taken prisoner. Earlier, from a boat on the river, Raleigh had tried to extricate his kinsman, Sir Ferdinando Gorges, from certain trouble and win him over to the Queen, but the latter had told Sir Walter 'You are like to have a bloody day of it.' Many in the Essex camp, which had been roused before dawn, urged an immediate attack on Whitehall Palace, but instead he rode off through Temple Bar to the City to force the Lord Mayor and Sheriffs to surrender, shouting as he went, 'For the Queen! For the Queen! A plot is laid for my life.' He was followed by a herald, sent by Cecil, to proclaim him a traitor.

From Whitehall, where barricades were erected, Nottingham mustered a small army against the rebels. London, Elizabeth's city from the first moment of her reign, remained loyal, and any brief tactical advantage Essex might have had was squandered; by dusk he was back at Essex House, knowing that all had failed and that it was a matter of time before the house was surrounded and his person seized. For the present he was locked in Whitgift's Palace at Lambeth and, until after the State trial, London and Westminster were regularly patrolled by companies of militia.

Cecil and the law officers worked hard at the preliminaries for a State trial at Westminster Hall, in which Essex was accused of attempting to usurp the Crown and, together with Southampton, Rutland and Sandys, of conspiring to depose and slay Her Majesty and subvert the government of the realm. On 19 February Essex and Southampton went for trial before their peers, with the verdict a foregone conclusion. Lord Treasurer Buckhurst presided over the proceedings in which Essex was at the mercy of Coke, the Attorney General, Fleming, the Solicitor General and, ironically, his former friend Francis Bacon. The evidence of treason was overwhelming; there were the confessions of Rutland, Sandys, Danvers, Blount and others, as well as the testimony of Raleigh. When Sir Walter was called to take his oath before relating his conversation with Gorges on the river in the first light of that fatal Sunday morning, Essex commented 'What booteth it to swear the fox?' The tension rose when Francis Bacon began his speech, comparing Essex to the Athenian conspirator Pisistratus, and exploiting the weakest areas of the Earl's defences. Essex believed that he was motivated by personal malice and told the court Bacon had forged letters between himself and his brother Anthony to deceive the Queen. Coolly Bacon answered: 'This is no crimination. I loved my Lord of Essex as long as he continued a dutiful subject and I have spent more hours to make him a good subject to Her Majesty than even I did about my own business.'

The 'Rainbow portrait' of the Queen, attributed to Marcus Gheeraerts the Younger, *c.* 1600. The rainbow is synonymous with peace and has allusions to the sun. The artist has produced an idealised portrait of the aging Elizabeth, making use of Nicholas Hilliard's 'Mask of Youth' miniature portraits.

Floundering like a cornered creature, Essex charged Cecil with favouring the claim to the throne of the Infanta of Spain, but the Secretary, who had been listening to the proceedings from behind a curtain, emerged to defend himself. 'My Lord of Essex, the difference between you and me is great,' he began, and although it was an extempore speech, it showed his oratorical brilliance:

For wit I give you the pre-eminence – you have it abundantly. For nobility also I give you place – I am not noble, yet a gentleman; I am no swordsman – there also you have the odds; but I have innocence, conscience, truth and honesty to defend me against the scandal and sting of slanderous tongues, and in this Court I stand as an upright man, and your lordship as a delinquent. I protest, before God, I have loved your person and justified your virtues: and I appeal to God and the Queen, that I told her Majesty your afflictions would make you a fit servant for her, attending but a fit time to move her Majesty to call you to the Court again. And had I not seen your ambitious affections inclined to usurpation, I would have gone on my knees to her Majesty to have done you good; but you have a wolf's head in a sheep's garment. . . . Ah, my Lord, were it but your own case, the loss had been less; but you have drawn a number of noble persons and gentlemen of birth and quality into your net of rebellion, and their bloods will cry vengeance against you. For my part, I vow to God, I wish my soul had been in heaven and my body at rest that this had not been.

He demanded that the prisoner should name the councillor who claimed that Cecil had supported the Infanta's claim. Essex called to his fellow prisoner Southampton to reveal that the councillor was the Comptroller of the Household, Sir William Knollys. This was a dramatic moment. The proceedings were stayed while a messenger was sent to the court to fetch Knollys, who was to remain ignorant of the vital question that would be put to him. When Essex's uncle appeared, Lord Buckhurst repeated the accusation about Cecil. Knollys made it plain that the Secretary had been referring at the time to Doleman's tract on the succession, and recalled Cecil as saying: 'Is it not strange impudence in Doleman to give an equal right in the succession of the crown to the Infanta of Spain as to any other . . .' He concluded: 'Hereupon was grounded the slanders upon the Secretary, whereon he is as clear as any man present.' Essex's diversionary tactics had failed. A few further bitter exchanges and the peers considered their verdict: both Essex and Southampton were guilty of high treason.

Elizabeth believed Essex's admission that she could never be safe so long as he lived; it was the same inexorable logic of statecraft that had necessitated the death of Mary Queen of Scots. Southampton could be safely left a condemned man in the Tower, but not her former favourite. She signed his death warrant on Shrove Tuesday, 24 February, half expecting a last desperate appeal for mercy, but he realised the hopelessness of his case and so spared her the anguish of having to reconsider his position. On Ash Wednesday 1601 Essex's life was ended at the age of thirty-four in an enclosed courtyard at the Tower. As a result of his own crass self-destruction Elizabeth had lost the only man she had really cared for since Hatton's death. At court the most troublesome faction of the whole reign had been annihilated and Robert Cecil remained at last in undisputed command.

9 Sunset

With the failure of Essex's *coup*, Sir Robert Cecil had no serious competitor left at court. Though he had come to the secretaryship relatively late in life, he had in a sense always been in office, for under his father's rule he had acquired a vast experience of government, incredible knowledge of the state of England and a flair for discerning what was in the minds of other courtiers and of the Queen they professed to serve. Try as he might to pass on to Raleigh the obloquy for the unpopular proceedings against Essex, public opinion came firmly down against Cecil himself, and the quips of the ballad-mongers that

> Little Cecil trips up and down
> He rules both Court and Crown

came very near the truth. They were not completely true however, since the authority of the Principal Secretary, the Queen's chief minister, was undoubtedly limited by Elizabeth herself, who even in her last years was no passive ruler. Moreover, as Cecil so readily appreciated, his tenure of office was not necessarily bound to outlast the Queen's life.

Those noblemen who had risen in February 1601 were dealt with by the law, and other secret sympathisers with his cause were too disillusioned by his fate to look for another leader to challenge the Tudor system of government at its height. Southampton remained in the Tower for the rest of the reign; the Earls of Bedford and Rutland and Lords Cromwell, Mounteagle and Sandys bought their release by heavy fines on instalments, remaining under a terrible cloud. With the sole exception of Cecil, the new generation of ministers was a pale reflection of their predecessors, and sons stepping into their fathers' shoes were usually of indifferent calibre. The new Lord Hunsdon, who succeeded his father as Lord Chamberlain, was insignificant at court, old Knollys's son was a nonentity, while the second Lord Burghley, Robert Cecil's half-brother Thomas, would never have gained the post of Lord President of the Council of the North in his father's day. Soon men were saying 'there are none of noble blood left of the Privy Council'. Yet the fact that there was a dearth of talent did not make Cecil's main problem of settling the succession for James I any easier.

Thomas Sackville, Lord Buckhurst, the Treasurer, was now sixty-six but seemed much older, for he was sickly and much occupied about the state of

James VI and I in 1604: portrait in the style of John de Critz.

241

Thomas Sackville, Lord Buckhurst, as Lord Treasurer in 1601. Elizabeth, who was his cousin, gave him Knole Park in Kent. Portrait by an unknown artist.

his health. On the eve of Essex's rebellion the council had met at his house because he had a chill, and two days later he missed the meeting; 'having put off my double caps and coifs and put on a very warm night-cap' he felt still in 'such a chillness as though I were towards an ague'. He secretly supported the Infanta's claim to the throne. In the remaining months of the reign he almost traded on being distantly related to the Queen to excuse his attendance from public business, and his name frequently featured among the 'apologies for absence' at court and council. 'I have by the space of this month or more foreborne to take physic by reason of Her Majesty's business,' he wrote, 'and now having this only week left for physic I am resolved to prevent sickness, feeling myself altogether distempered and filled with humours, so as if Her Majesty should miss me I beseech you in respect thereof to excuse me.' He still could not gain possession of Knole, which the Queen had given him in 1566, because of sitting tenants and pondered the 'fleeting course of fast-declining life' about which he had written so movingly years before in his 'Induction' to the *Mirror for Magistrates*.

Sir John Fortescue had spent the entire reign at court. He was the stepson of Sir Thomas Parry, who secured him the post of Keeper of the Wardrobe at Elizabeth's accession. Fortescue had clung to this minor office down the years despite other preferments, for he had succeeded Mildmay as Chancellor of the Exchequer and for a time also held the Chancellorship of the Duchy of Lancaster. His fees helped him to build a fine mansion at Salden in Buckinghamshire and to embellish his house at Hendon, but in political terms he was a nonentity. The Queen had a high regard for both his integrity and his scholarly tastes, for he had kept up his Greek and become a close friend of Sir Thomas Bodley, the founder of the Bodleian at Oxford. Sir John Stanhope, Treasurer of the Chamber for the last decade, had earned his office by marrying into the Knollys family and his appointment as councillor in 1601 is an indication of the paucity of really able men at the centre of affairs.

To his acute dismay Raleigh was again passed over in favour of the safe, insignificant men, for Cecil made it plain that he would never have him appointed a councillor unless he surrendered his post of Captain of the Guard, which afforded a regular, private access to Her Majesty. The Secretary could not risk favour and power being allied in the person of a man he could not trust, a potential breeder of faction.

Another new member of the council was Gilbert Talbot, the seventh Earl of Shrewsbury, who had once written his father such amusing letters about events at court, but subsequently quarrelled with him. After his father's death he directed his anger at Bess of Hardwick, who was both his step-mother and his mother-in-law. Indeed he was prickly with all his relatives and such a tyrant to his tenants that the Queen had once caused his arrest. His passion for blood sports at Worksop and his skill as a falconer were the only qualities which Elizabeth found redeeming; she used him for honorific duties in embassies and Garter ceremonies. Shrewsbury and his wife were reputed 'great favourers of recusants', but it was to secure a better regional balance rather than for religious reasons that he was sworn a councillor, and his presence was a guarantee that there would not be potential trouble from the supporters of his wife's niece Arabella Stuart.

Worcester's recusancy was more straightforward; it was said that the Queen's favour reconciled 'a stiff papist to a good subject'. He had at last fallen on his feet by succeeding to Essex's post of Master of the Horse. As the reign drew to its close, though Cecil certainly never took him into his confidence, Worcester took comfort in the fact that he had been Elizabeth's special envoy to Edinburgh to congratulate James on his marriage. He could make capital out of that contact, and no one was surprised when James I confirmed him in his office.

One councillor of a much older vintage was Sir John Popham, who had first sat in the council room thirty years before he had been imprisoned by the rebels in Essex House. Like Lord Egerton he had risen through the law, serving in turn as Speaker, Master of the Rolls and (from 1592) Chief Justice of Queen's Bench. He had kept afloat financially by marrying a Glamorganshire heiress, but was of no consequence outside Westminster Hall.

Anthony Bacon died soon after Essex's execution, but Francis, no nearer high legal office than in the Earl's heyday, stored up his brother's support of Essex as capital for the future. He was too shrewd, while the Queen lived, to open communications with Edinburgh, but once James had come south he sought his favour of 'the infinite devotion and incessant endeavours (beyond the strength of his body and the nature of the times) which appeared in my good brother towards your Majesty's service' – and his success was dramatic.

Elizabeth had left the key question of the succession unanswered, but Cecil was by now in no doubt that the Crown must pass to James VI of Scotland: 'I am resolved in my mind ... whom no device nor humour shall make a changeling.' He was to stage-manage the transition with such adroit circumspection that when the time came there would not be a split second's hesitation in the customary, 'The Queen is dead. Long live the King.'

Having come to his decision Cecil knew that he must begin to plan without delay, and from that moment there came into being in Whitehall a rival court to Elizabeth's, the court of her most obvious successor. As Cecil put it once to Francis Bacon 'The Queen indeed is my sovereign and I am her creature. I may not least deceive her,' yet making plans for the good of the State, in an area of policy in which Elizabeth had steadily refused to give guidance, counted not as high conspiracy or even as constitutional intrigue, but as statesmanship. He had to win James's absolute confidence and warn him of others who were volunteering themselves in his service. For Cecil's plans to succeed, the secret must be confided to as few as possible and correspondence therefore had to be in cypher; George Nicholson, the English ambassador in Scotland was on no account to be privy to the negotiations and James's idea of appointing a resident agent in London had to be discreetly quashed.

In overthrowing Essex Cecil had, perforce, to form an uneasy alliance with Cobham and Raleigh, but now he had no need of them, and was determined to outmanoeuvre them. So long as Essex lived the council had been weakened by faction, and Cecil could not risk faction returning. Enough had come out at Essex's trial to make plain James's involvement at a distance in the rebellion. He intended to send the Earl of Mar to Essex House by 1 February, and could not believe, even when he heard of the failure of the revolt, that Essex was finished. Mar and Bruce still travelled to London under hastily revised instructions, to see whether a general rising was still possible

Tudor to Stuart: a series of early seventeenth-century ivory knife handles, representing Henry VII, Henry VIII, Edward VI, Elizabeth I and James I.

Letter in cypher from secret correspondence on the succession, written by James, 30, to Sir Robert Cecil, 10.

and to make it their business to 'dally with the present guiders of the court', walking warily 'betwixt these two precipices of the Queen and the people, who now appear to be in so contrary terms'. James had also required them to extract from Elizabeth a statement that he had no share in Essex's revolt and they were to be firm with Cecil, who was to be told he could expect no future favours unless he acted favourably towards the King at once. The

Queen received the envoys somewhat frostily on 22 March and in her letter to James, which was baroque and allusive in style, she hinted broadly that she knew rather more about his past intrigues. 'Let not shades deceive you, which may take away best substance from you, when they can turn but to dust or smoke.' Here indeed was a warning, and she asked him to scan her words as 'becometh best a King' – which could be interpreted in more than one way. Unknown to him his envoys were already enjoying remarkable success with the Secretary.

Cecil had examined likely candidates, for the task of approaching the King, with more than his customary care. The Master of Gray, a potential go-between, had been employed by James on several diplomatic missions, but while Cecil rated his ability high, he reckoned that he was not a man to be trusted; he had in turn betrayed Mary Queen of Scots, then Arran, and in 1600 had revealed to the English James's negotiations with the Papacy. To use Gray in such a delicate affair was putting it at risk, and the Secretary made sure to discredit him at Holyroodhouse. Lord Huntley, another possibility, he wrote off as too weak a character. He needed men of utter dependability who were of sufficient weight at the Scottish court, and in the end satisfied himself that the Earl of Mar and Edward Bruce were the most suitable intermediaries. John Erskine, Earl of Mar, once a playmate of James, had now become governor of the royal children; in London he was reckoned 'a courtly and well-advised gentleman'. As a lad he had engineered the Ruthven Raid to capture the King, but he had lived down that escapade and was easily the most formidable character around James and probably the man closest to him. Edward Bruce was by title secular abbot of Kinross, but by profession a judge, a Lord of Sessions. He had come to London on missions in 1594 and 1598 and made a good impression, for he liked the south and envied the English judiciary their fees and perquisites. Bruce was to become Master of the Rolls in 1604 and on his deathbed insisted on being buried in the Chapel of the Rolls.

At the end of April 1601 Cecil summoned the two envoys to a secret interview at the duchy of Lancaster office in the Savoy; effectively this was the first meeting of King James's English court. Unlike Raleigh's cabals at Durham House, the duchy office could keep its secrets, for it was away from the main thoroughfare of politics and gossip. From a lifetime of experience Cecil was able to advise James how to behave towards Elizabeth; he must never again mention the succession, but by clean and temperate courses he should be able to 'secure the heart of the highest, to whose sex and quality nothing is so improper as either needless expostulations or over-much curiosity in her own actions'; he must not court popularity in England while she lived and, above all, he must trust the men now in power for they alone could pilot his ship into the safe harbour. Subsequently a code was devised, with Northumberland 0, Raleigh 3, Cecil himself 10, the Queen 24 and James 30 – this numerical progression was itself a neat piece of psychology. The only other Scot in the secret was David Foulis, James's secretary; the only Englishman besides Cecil was Lord Henry Howard.

Lord Henry could in no sense be regarded as a competitor of Cecil, yet there was a part in this for him to play, for he was a peer and a Howard, and could win over the Lord Admiral at the appropriate time. He was a crypto-Catholic who could assure James that there would be no opposition to his accession from his co-religionists, and he could also be used to solve some of the Secretary's principal problems, notably blackening the characters of Raleigh, Cobham (with whom Howard had a personal feud) and Northumberland. He was to write that Raleigh had 'a pride above the greatest Lucifer that hath lived in our age' and, with the others, made up a trio of wicked plotters, 'hatching treasons from the cockatrice eggs that are daily and nightly sitten on'. To his pen, too, fell the awkward task of warning James against his consort, Anne of Denmark. Howard could also corroborate all that Cecil promised to undertake for James and bring home to him the Secretary's key position at court. He did all that Cecil expected of him; his letters were as the King termed them, 'Asiatic and endless volumes', interleaved with heavy flattery, adulation even.

Cecil, by contrast, graced his letters with classical and Biblical quotations that he knew would appeal to James. Initially he had to win the King's confidence, living down past suspicions – 'those hard obstructions which other men's practice had bred within your heart' – and show him it was reciprocated:

Although it has pleased you to let me read in royal characters, what the constitution of your mind is towards me, what you esteem my disposition towards you and upon what arguments both your favour and opinion are and shall be grounded, yet can I not deny my mind that justice which it exacteth from me, to be heard speak as much (with his proper organ) as hath already been reported by other means.

He rejoiced at what the King had written to him, 'because you promise hereafter in all accusations to deal with me as God did with Adam, *Ubi est?*' He had been forced by events to oppose Essex, 'for who knows not that have lived in Israel, that such were the mutual affections in our tender years, and so very reciprocal benefits interchanged in our growing fortunes'.

From such beginnings confidence was established. There was the constant fear that this correspondence might be discovered and brought to the Queen's notice, and because Cecil feared that his secretary, Simon Willis, might have an inkling of the affair he dismissed him on the grounds of 'insolence and harsh behaviour'. He succeeded in covering up his tracks from contemporary spies and subsequent historians far better than did Lord Henry Howard and their rival Northumberland. Elizabeth was too shrewd to be unaware that sundry communications with Edinburgh were taking place; after all, her motto remained *Video et Taceo*, and she must secretly have admired the discretion being shown. As she told the antiquary William Lambarde, 'now the wit of the fox is everywhere on foot, so as hardly one faithful or virtuous man may be found,' but the exception to the rule was Cecil. If she said that she was a Richard II, surrounded by flatterers, then she knew that James was her Bolingbroke.

The second Duke of Lennox, a favourite at Holyroodhouse, came south in the autumn, ostensibly for an audience with the Queen at which he was expected to press his master's claim to the throne. By then, however, James had changed his tactics on Cecil's advice and so the awkward topic was avoided in the interview. While in London, however, Lennox saw something of Raleigh and Cobham. Raleigh told Cecil that the Duke had asked for private discussions, but that he had excused himself, being 'too deeply engaged ... to his own mistress to seek favour elsewhere'. He was hoping

that the Secretary would let the Queen know of his unshaken loyalty to her,
but Cecil trumped this by suggesting that Elizabeth might deduce that
Lennox would never have approached him if he thought that loyalty could
not be shaken. This answer persuaded Raleigh to hear what Lennox had to
say, but their various discussions proved barren.

Another correspondent was Henry Percy, 'the Wizard Earl' of Northumberland, who was eighth on the list of heirs presumptive to the Crown. Fellow
Catholics had suggested ten years earlier that he should strengthen this weak
claim by marrying Lady Arabella Stuart, but he had disappointed them by
marrying Essex's sister, the widowed Dorothy Perrot. They made an ill-
assorted pair and lived chiefly apart. In 1600 his countess resided at court
and was said to be 'often with the Queen', but her favour did not outlast

Essex's treason. With his curious intellectual interests, Northumberland enjoyed Raleigh's company and they would smoke their pipes into the night at Durham House, discussing the supernatural. In 1601, however, when they were joined by Cobham they turned to the burning topic of the succession.

Cecil was with reason suspicious of 'the Durham House trio' and, anticipating that Northumberland would approach King James, stole a march on him, to vilify his character. Early in 1602 Percy decided to open communications with Edinburgh off his own bat, without reference to Raleigh or Cobham, for now his main concern was the future of English Catholicism. Moreover, unaware of James's fundamental timidity, he wanted to dissuade him from attempting to seize the Crown by force – as in Essex's plan – for he knew that the country as a whole was apathetic to James's cause and, because he was the greatest Border lord, Northumberland might be forced to declare himself, which did not at all suit his plans. In his first letter, entrusted to his cousin Thomas Percy, he wrote 'it were a pity to lose so good a Kingdom for not tolerating mass in a corner'. James thanked him for his 'most wise advice' and answered 'I will neither persecute any that will be quiet and give but an outward obedience to the law, neither will I spare to advance any of them that will by good service worthily deserve it.' Northumberland made known James's promise to the chief members of the Catholic community and as a result many were weaned from the phantom of the Infanta's claim. Bruce had, however, copied both Northumberland's letter and the royal reply for Cecil, and it was all the more incongruous that the Earl should himself approach Cecil with the original letter from James. In the event only two other letters were sent.

Francis Knollys had died in July 1596, when his grandson Essex was on the crest of the wave, ironically buoyed up by that same strong Protestantism that had long ago almost swamped the old man's career. Six of his seven sons sat frequently in the Commons, chiefly for Oxfordshire or Berkshire constituencies; the eldest, Henry, predeceased his father, but the second, William, succeeded to his father's seat on the Council and, like him, became successively Comptroller and, from 1602, Treasurer of the Household. William married the widow of Lord Chandos, but she was much older than he and they had no children; her health was indifferent and he prayed she might not last long, for he had fallen in love with Mary Fitton, the youngest and most beautiful of the maids of honour.

Sir Edward Fitton, a Cheshire knight, had written to William Knollys after Mary's appointment to the Queen's household, asking him to keep an eye on her – in truth he could not keep his eyes *off* the nubile creature – and he agreed to play 'the good shepherd and will, to my power, defend the innocent lamb from the wolfish cruelty and, fox-like subtlety of the tame beasts of this place'. The man in whom the girl's father placed such trust proved an utter snake-in-the-grass. Clearly, Mary Fitton did not altogether discourage the Comptroller's advances, for he was in a most influential position, yet she looked for a husband nearer her own age, rather than a man in his forties waiting for his wife to die. In 1599 she was ill with a nervous complaint known as 'the mothers', enduring long bouts of melancholy, with hysterical fits, crying and insomnia, and had to be sent away from court. Her absence nearly caused Knollys to have a break-down. When she returned

Monument in the church of Rothersfield Greys, near Henley, to Sir Francis Knollys (d. 1596) and his wife, Catherine Carey. Above the recumbent effigies of Sir Francis and Lady Catherine are the kneeling figures of his eldest surviving son, Sir William Knollys, Comptroller of the Household, and the wife from whom he longed to be free. At the foot of the tomb are shown the daughters of the family, headed by the fascinating Lettice.

to her duties he wrote to her married sister that Mary had 'not been troubled with the mother for a long time. I would God I might as lawfully make her a mother, as you are.' (Alas, the disconsolate lover's wife survived for another six years.) Soon after this letter was written, Mary put Knollys out of her thoughts, for she had become the lover of William Herbert, heir to the earldom of Pembroke.

Herbert, whose mother was Philip Sidney's sister, inherited her literary interests and looked forward, after two years at New College, to coming to London to mix with the poets and dramatists who were writing a glorious chapter in English letters, to which he could make his own contribution. His father had hoped that he might marry Burghley's grand-daughter, Bridget Vere, then only thirteen; later there was talk of a match with Hertford's daughter. With Essex in disgrace, some courtiers backed Herbert's chances of becoming a royal favourite – he 'very discreetly follows the course of making love to the Queen,' it was observed, but he lacked the essential charm

Within the portrait, top right: Mary 2nd Daughter of Sir Edward Fitton. Maid of Honour to Queen Elizabeth.

Mary Fitton, maid of honour from 1595 until 1601, when she was disgraced as a result of her liaison with the Earl of Pembroke. Mary, who was an outstanding beauty, was possibly the 'dark lady' of Shakespeare's sonnets: portrait by the circle of George Gower.

and single-mindedness to succeed and was soon 'blamed for his weak pursuing of Her Majesty's favour. Want of spirit is laid to his charge, and that he is a melancholy companion.' Herbert practised rather hard in the tiltyard, but his heart was in books, not the tournament. He suffered from migraine, which responded to no other treatment but taking strong tobacco. Then, in June 1600, at the wedding of his cousin, Worcester's son, to Lady Anne Russell, he discovered Mary Fitton. The festivities were held in Cobham's house at Blackfriars and included 'a strange dance, newly invented' by the maids of honour. Elizabeth was present, and asked Mary the character she represented in the dance. Her answer was 'Affection', whereupon the Queen replied in a vinegarish phrase, 'Affection! Affection's false!' But Mary Fitton soon reckoned that she had found true love. It is not entirely fanciful to think that, as a result of Herbert's friendship with Shakespeare, she was the original of the 'Dark Lady of the Sonnets' or of black-eyed Rosaline in *Love's Labour Lost*.

251

In order to escape from the matronly rule of the mistress of the maids and the ogling Comptroller so as to keep her assignations with Herbert, Mary would 'put off her head-tire and tuck up her clothes, and take a large white cloak and march as though she had been a man' well clear of the palace. By the New Year, just before the Essex rebellion, she could no longer conceal that she was pregnant and Herbert, who had just succeeded to his earldom, admitted responsibility. Knollys was amazed at what had been happening under his nose and, envious of Pembroke's success, was in great distress that the girl he had singled out to be his future comfort should have acted thus. Elizabeth, in a furious temper, swore she would send both culprits to the Tower, but in the event the Earl was sent to the Fleet Prison and Mary was put into the care of Lady Hawkins. While in her house she was delivered of a stillborn son. Pembroke absolutely refused to marry the girl, excusing himself in his poem *To a Lady residing at Court*:

> Then this advice, fair creature, take from me
> Let none pluck fruit, unless he pluck the tree.
> For if with one, with thousands thoul't turn whore.
> Break ice in one place and it cracks the more.

This attitude did not speed his release from prison, where he complained to Cecil that being cut off from the Queen's presence was 'hell' and he asked for a change of climate to 'purge me of melancholy, for else I shall never be fit for any civil society'. Eventually he returned to Wilton, then married Lady Mary Talbot and settled down to become the 'Maecenas' of Jacobean England, patronising Ben Jonson, Massinger, Chapman, Inigo Jones and many others. Mary was sent back to Cheshire in disgrace, her career at court in ruins, a reminder to other maids of honour and their admirers to behave more circumspectly. As Sir John Stanhope, Treasurer of the Chamber, commented, 'Fitton's afflictions' were 'a discouragement of the rest'.

When Parliament assembled in October 1601 to vote supplies for the war with Spain and for continuing operations against the rebels in Ireland, the government was requesting an unprecedented sum. As Elizabeth came to open Parliament, the cries of 'God save your Majesty' were muted and on leaving the House of Lords some members treated her with scant courtesy. A gentleman usher shouted for them to make room for the Queen to pass but no one obeyed and one made a disagreeable rejoinder, so that 'she heaved up her head and looked that way towards him that spoke'. This augured ill for the mood of the Commons, so Cecil opened the subsidy debate himself, in place of the less experienced Fortescue who, as Chancellor of the Exchequer, should have made the principal speech. His peroration was persuasive: 'What we freely give unto her [the Queen], she living, bestows it to our good, and dying doubtless will leave it for our profit.' In the debate he had several brushes with Raleigh and throughout the session they were to cross swords, their exchanges spiced by personal animosity, for on a very different political level, as we have seen, they were battling for the Stuart succession. Yet the chief threat to the government which Cecil had to face in the House was the attack on monopolies.

An integral part of the royal prerogative, grants of monopoly rights in commercial and industrial ventures – once a sensible way of rewarding inventiveness and encouraging men to risk capital for backing new processes – had degenerated into wholesale political patronage. With totally insufficient resources at her disposal the Queen had to provide from her court a growing bureaucracy to run the State. Inflation had reduced fees in most cases to a pittance and, with the increasing drain of war finance, as the Queen's supply of chested treasure ran out and the availability of Crown lands for granting or leasing to courtiers ceased, she had been forced to turn to monopolies, or rather courtiers turned to her for patents. Over the last five years everyone had been complaining about the Queen's 'nearness', how no one received his deserts, how 'all advancements at court stand of a long stay', and in 1600 she was obliged to apologise to a deserving servant that the costs of the war had made it imperative for her to 'restrain her bountiful hand'.

Even the supply of monopolies seemed to be drying up. Critics of the system talked openly of 'the late grasping days', making an unanswerable case that monopolies affecting so many everyday commodities, like salt, and soap, had made the cost of living leap. These potentially rich pickings had gone to courtiers in place of realistic salaries and more traditional rewards, and to exploit their rights patentees had erected a top-heavy system of agents, middlemen, promoters and informers, all taking their cut. Pamphlets underlined the public scandal, suggesting widespread robbery and corruption:

> The courtiers craved all,
> The Queen granted all.

Again:

> Courtier leather, courtier pin and soap
> And courtier vinegar and starch and card
> And such as shall not count it long we hope . . .

Wilkes, clerk of the council, was Mr Salt, Raleigh the knave of Playing Cards and Cecil and Buckhurst the kings of Starch – a most profitable acquisition with fashion's demands for stiffened ruffs.

In the last Parliament in 1597 there had been an outcry, and the Queen had promised speedy redress. She undertook to scrutinise existing patents and to issue no new ones, but did not keep her word. Four years later, Lawrence Hyde mounted a full-scale onslaught, and courtiers realised that it was not just an attack on the royal prerogative but an attempt to undermine the entire system by which the court was maintained.

When a bill was introduced to curb monopolies, Francis Bacon defended them in a legalistic speech, since the right to issue such patents was 'the head pearl in the Queen's crown'; but Cecil made more impact, reproving the Speaker for accepting the bill and members for their disorderly behaviour that was 'more fit for a grammar school than a court of Parliament'. Elizabeth then sent a message giving way; she would completely reform the system and, after referring each patent to the law officers, would decide which should be suspended. Already she had a proclamation drafted. She received a deputation from a most thankful Commons, in the Council Room at Whitehall, and ended the affair by making a remarkable speech that won their hearts. She counted it 'the glory of my crown that I have reigned with your loves', and if her 'kingly bounty' had been abused and her grants turned 'to the hurt of my people', she hoped that God would not lay the offence to

her charge. She had told the Speaker that she would receive a deputation of one hundred, but *all* members wanted to attend, and in fact one hundred and fifty were fortunate enough to witness this great event; the others were soon able to read the text of what came to be called her 'golden speech'. Her words dwelt upon the idealistic relationship between subjects and sovereign in the golden age of monarchy, an age which the monopolies debate had shown was all but ended. Monopolies were not dead and buried, but court finance would never be the same.

Three weeks later, Elizabeth came to Parliament before members dispersed to their homes, to survey the domestic and foreign scene in a splendid sweep, showing the development of policy from her accession. As always, however, she remained silent on the question of the succession; although Parliament had first dared to discuss it in 1559, by 1601 it had never been more topical.

The English Catholics were divided on the problems of the succession, as on so much else. The claims of Isabel, the Infanta of Spain, which Essex had foolishly accused Cecil of upholding, were certainly being supported at this time by such crypto-Catholics as Buckhurst and Nottingham, who were in

ABOVE The family of Edward, 3rd Lord Windsor, playing cards and chess, 1568: attributed to the Master of the Countess of Warwick.

ABOVE RIGHT Henry Wriothesley, 3rd Earl of Southampton, by John de Critz. He had this portrait painted to commemorate his period in custody in the Tower after the Essex Rebellion. BELOW RIGHT Robert Devereux, 2nd Earl of Essex, attributed to Marcus Gheeraerts the Younger. This was painted after the Earl's return from the Cadiz expedition.

254

touch with Father Parsons in Rome. Northumberland, as we have seen, was attempting to assure James VI of his co-religionists' support. Cecil was eager to steal a march on Northumberland so that he could be the one to convince the King that the recusants would not oppose him. He first succeeded, through Lord Henry Howard, in detaching the Lord Admiral from Buckhurst and his fellow travellers, who still favoured the Infanta, and then he intervened in a masterly way in the endemic struggle within the Catholic community between the secular priests and the Jesuits.

Following Cardinal Allen's death, it had been decided in Rome that the English secular priests should be ruled by an arch-priest, George Blackwell. Though not a Jesuit himself, he was given wide powers and required to consult the Jesuits on significant matters. Blackwell's arbitrary rule embittered the seculars, who resented interference from Rome and the new-style discipline and intolerance of members of the Society of Jesus towards the ways of others. One of the secular priests railed hard against the Jesuits whose 'insolent challenge to the whole realm was the cause of all the hard laws and edicts made to the utter undoing of so many Catholics in England'. Here was a feud that could be exploited. Cecil, in league with Richard Bancroft, Bishop of London, received news in March 1601 of a certain Father Bluett, imprisoned at Wisbech for the last twenty-four years, who would be happy to betray the Jesuits to the government. The man was released from Wisbech and told to go to a prison in London, where he would doubtless find friends who would know him. The plot worked splendidly, for a captive priest recognised him and the jailer had the visitor taken away for examination by the authorities. In this way Bancroft and Cecil were brought into touch with him without raising suspicion and he informed them of the state of affairs at Wisbech. Bishop Bancroft allowed Bluett to travel to Rome, with colleagues, to appeal to the Pope against the Jesuits. At the same time they petitioned Elizabeth, promising allegiance of Catholic clergy and laity in all temporal affairs, and asking for their worship to be tolerated, as well as for Jesuitical books to be suppressed. The feud between seculars and the Society was now extended to Rome, where Parsons fought tooth and nail to defend his activities. There were recriminations throughout the Catholic world and in the end Bluett and his companions were censured by the Inquisition. English Catholicism was hopelessly discredited by the affair, and to add fuel to the fire Bancroft relaxed censorship on certain books written by secular priests. On 5 November 1602 a proclamation accused the Jesuits of plots against the State and the seculars of civil disobedience; toleration was out of the question. The Jesuits were required to leave the realm forthwith, though subsequently those who submitted to the Queen's mercy and signed a declaration of loyalty to her were allowed to remain. Cecil had succeeded in showing the dissensions among the English Catholics and their political impotence, so that he could truthfully write to King James that most of them 'do declare their affections absolutely to your title'. The toleration Elizabeth had refused they now expected as of right from her successor.

In these final years, Elizabeth was still restless and anxious to get away from London in the summer, though councillors tried hard to dissuade her from journeys that would tax her health. Having slipped off to Nonsuch in 1600, she decided to move further afield: 'the Lords are very sorry for it, but Her

The Booke of Faulconrie or Hau-
KING, FOR THE ONELY DE-
light and pleasure of all Noblemen and Gentlemen:
Collected out of the best aucthors, asvvell Italians as Frenchmen,
and some English practifes withall concernyng Faulconrie, the contentes
whereof are to be seene in the next page folowyng.
By George Turbervile Gentleman.
NOCET EMPTA DOLORE VOLVPTAS.

Imprinted at Londen for Christopher Barker, at the signe of
the Grashopper in Pavles Churchyarde. Anno. 1575.

The booke of Hunting.
Of the place where and howe an assembly should be made,
in the presence of a Prince, or some honorable person.

Majesty bids the old stay behind and the young and able to go with her'.
She hunted vigorously throughout August and September when 'her daily
music is the sweet cry of the excellent hounds', and when Sir William Howard,
the Lord Admiral's brother, died, she rode off to Hampton to cheer Nottingham and 'call him from his solitariness' to the chase. To keep her from roam-
ing too far from Whitehall, ministers would entice her to May Day festivities
at Highgate or Lewisham, or persuade her to make a day visit, as when she
was entertained by Sir Robert Sidney at Penshurst. The host wrote:

She seemed most pleased at what we did to please her. My son made her a fair
speech, to which she did give most gracious reply. The women did dance before her,
whilst the cornets did salute from the gallery, and she did vouchsafe to eat two morsels
of rich comfit cake, and drank a small cordial from a gold cup. She had a marvellous
suit of velvet borne by four of her first women attendants in rich apparel; two ushers
did go before, and at going upstairs she called for a staff, and was much wearied in
walking about the house, and said she wished to come another day. Six drums and
trumpets waited in the court and sounded at her approach and departure. My
wife ... did wear a goodly stuff of the bravest cut and fashion, with an under body
of silver and loops. The Queen was much in commendation of our appearances, and
smiled at the ladies, who in their dances came up to the step on which the seat was
fixed, to make their obeisance, and so fell back into their order again.
  The day well nigh spent, the Queen went and tasted a small beverage that was
set out in divers rooms where she might pass, and then in much order was attended
to her palace ...

  The last grand reception of the reign was held in August 1602 at Harefield
Place, Middlesex, when the Queen was the guest of Lord Keeper Egerton.
Although the natural son of a nonentity, Egerton had gone far through his
great legal ability. In 1600, following the death of his first wife, he married
Lady Alice Stanley, the dowager Countess of Derby. Egerton's remarriage

Elizabeth enjoyed hunting
and falconry throughout
her life. As late as
1600, a courtier declared:
'Her Majesty is well and
excellently disposed to
hunting, for every day
she is on horseback and
continues sport long'.
ABOVE LEFT Title-page to
George Turberville's
Booke of Faulconrie,
published in 1575.
ABOVE RIGHT Woodcut
from Turberville's *Booke
of Hunting* published
in 1575, showing
the Queen and courtiers
at a picnic during
the chase.

258

The lake in the gardens of Elvetham House, Hampshire, with three islands capped in turn by buildings representing a fort, a ship, and a snail, prepared for the Queen's visit to the Earl of Hertford in 1591.

put the seal on his position at court, for Lady Derby's younger sister was wife of Hunsdon, the Lord Chamberlain.

It must have been Lady Alice, rather than the Lord Keeper, who planned the elaborate festivities at Harefield, where two 'rustics', the Bailiff and Joan the Dairymaid, spoke a welcoming dialogue in the gardens and presented the Queen with a jewelled rake and fork, for she was 'the best housewife in all this company'. On the steps of the house two further characters, Time and Place, acted out their scene. 'The great that we are to entertain doth fill all places with her divine virtues, as the Sun fills the world with the light of his beams,' announced Time, with an hour-glass in his hand. 'But say, poor Place, in what manner didst thou entertain the sun?' 'I received his glory and was filled with it,' came the reply. There were banquets, masques and concerts, and then a 'seaman' organised a lottery, although the draw had been arranged so that Elizabeth and all her ladies won prizes. As she departed, Time and Place made a reappearance, now in mourning, to present the Queen with a jewelled anchor, as 'this little harbour is too little for you, and you will hoist sail and be gone'. Courtiers who had not been present at Harefield were able to read an account that was in print within a few days of the glory of the Sun Queen, still apparently far from setting.

The House of Howard had returned to prominence, and Cecil could write to Nottingham: 'Never treble strings were higher stretched than all the race of your kinsmen are.' In mid-December the Admiral entertained the Queen at Arundel House in the Strand, where the gossips said she had expected him to give her his splendid series of tapestry hangings depicting the defeat of the Armada. Just before removing for the last time from Whitehall to Richmond, that 'warm winter-box to shelter her old age', as she put it, Elizabeth visited the Charterhouse as she had done on her entry to London in 1558, to be entertained by Norfolk's second son. She had developed an affection for this Thomas Howard, who had served her well at sea, and referred to him as her 'good Thomas', thinking back to his father's treason. Reluctant as she was to create new titles, she made him Lord Howard de Walden. His first wife was Mary Dacre, from the northern Catholic family. Mary might have tried to convert him to Catholicism – as her sister had so notably succeeded with Arundel – but she died young and his second marriage was to the widow of Lord Rich's son.

In mid-January 1603, the Queen and the Lord Admiral were on their way to Richmond, when Elizabeth declared: 'I told you my seat has been the seat of Kings and I will have no rascal to succeed me; and who should succeed me but a King?' Within the month his wife, Lady Nottingham, the most long serving of the Queen's ladies, died at Richmond. This death of old Hunsdon's daughter affected Elizabeth as much as the Admiral, and she became very melancholy. In her final illness, when so few came to the Queen's presence, it was to Nottingham that she remarked that she was 'tied with a chain of iron about her neck'. He spoke to her in a kindly way about her courage, but she denied she had any left: 'I am tied, I am tied, and the case is altered with me.' He remained at Richmond until the demise of the Crown.

Yet it was a third Howard, Lord Henry – so long in disgrace with Elizabeth – who, as the 'dear and trusty No. 3' of King James's letter, stood close to Cecil and near the centre of affairs at this period. Once the transition to Stuart rule was safely made he became a councillor, ousting his enemy Cobham from the wardenship of the Cinque Ports, officiating at the trial of his other adversary Raleigh, finally becoming Earl of Northampton. Lord Henry had come a long way since the days when he threatened 'to retire to a grove and a prayer book'.

From Christmastide, careful observers began to wonder how long the Queen could survive, despite the brave face she put on. Sir John Harington was much struck by her frailty and wrote to his wife at Exton to report on her 'most pitiable state', for her appetite for food and even for life itself had gone. At her request he read her some of his verses, but she found little to hold her attention and told him 'when thou dost feel creeping Time at thy gate, these fooleries will please thee less'. Her nephew Sir Robert Carey, whose marriage had so irritated Elizabeth, came in to cheer her at the end of February, but found his task impossible. 'No, Robin, *I am not well*,' she told him, her insomnia by now a byword. It was at this time that Cecil took Carey into his confidence, commissioning him in advance to take tidings of the demise of the Crown to James VI. He awaited his cue, but by 21 March had come to the conclusion that the Queen was *in extremis* and wrote to the Scottish King that she could last for no more than three days, and that he was remaining at court to be the first with the news. He had ready the best horses at stages all along the road to the north.

Cecil saw to it that the pretender Arabella Stuart was being closely watched at Hardwick Hall, for she still remained a threat. During these last days, news about Her Majesty's health was forbidden to be reported, in order to maintain public order and deny potential enemies crumbs of comfort. Tradition has it that when the councillors stood round her bed on 23 March she indicated James as her successor (she could not have named him, for she had

by then lost powers of speech), though Cecil apparently asked, if 'you remain
in your former resolutions and that you would have the King of Scots to
succeed you in your Kingdom show some sign unto us', and with a tremendous effort she affirmed that this was so. Only Whitgift stayed by her side to
pray with her until she fell asleep for the first time for several days.

The Queen died in her sleep about 3 a.m. on Thursday, 24 March. Before
dawn Carey began his ride north. Although he fell badly on the way he
continued at a breathless pace, so that by the Saturday night he reached the
palace of Holyroodhouse, and was the first to kneel before James to salute
him as King.

Cecil insisted that no one else leave Richmond Palace without written
authority, and by 7 a.m. the councillors present rode to Whitehall for a formal
meeting to draft the Accession Proclamation. Northumberland maintained
that councillors had no status in acting during an interregnum, and that
senior peers should take their places of right. Lord Keeper Egerton saw the
force of his argument, but treated it as merely a question of precedence, ruling
that privy councillors who were not peers should sit at the lower end of the
table. Significantly it was Robert Cecil who performed the first reading of
the Proclamation at Whitehall Palace, opposite the tiltyard, for he had
almost single-handed made sure of James's peaceful accession. For this he
deserved the gratitude not only of the new Sovereign, but also of the nation
at large. James's shadow court in England, over which Cecil had presided
for the last two years, now acquired constitutional status. All the courtiers of
the old Queen – who had passed away 'as the most resplendent sun setteth
at last in a Western cloud' – now looked inevitably to their new monarch,
some with hope, others with fear and many uncertain whether, despite their
passive acquiescence in the accession, they would be ousted by favourites
from Scotland. Of a truth a new age had begun.

Genealogical Tables

Elizabeth I and the House of Stuart

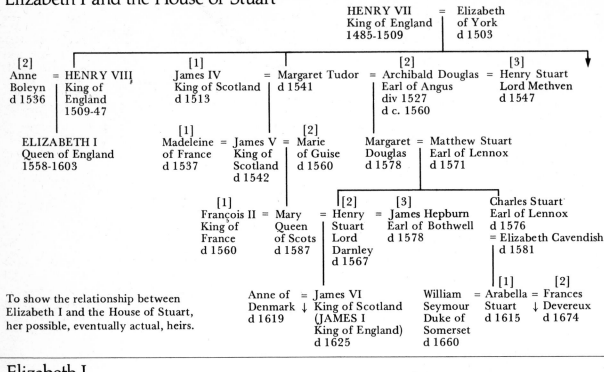

HENRY VII = Elizabeth
King of England | of York
1485-1509 | d 1503

[2] Anne Boleyn d 1536 = HENRY VIII King of England 1509-47

[1] James IV King of Scotland d 1513 = Margaret Tudor d 1541

= [2] Archibald Douglas Earl of Angus div 1527 d c. 1560

[3] = Henry Stuart Lord Methven d 1547

ELIZABETH I Queen of England 1558-1603

[1] Madeleine of France d 1537 = James V King of Scotland d 1542 = [2] Marie of Guise d 1560

Margaret Douglas d 1578 = Matthew Stuart Earl of Lennox d 1571

[1] François II King of France d 1560 = Mary Queen of Scots d 1587 = [2] Henry Stuart Lord Darnley d 1567 = [3] James Hepburn Earl of Bothwell d 1578

Charles Stuart Earl of Lennox d 1576 = Elizabeth Cavendish d 1581

Anne of Denmark d 1619 ↓ = James VI King of Scotland (JAMES I King of England) d 1625

William Seymour Duke of Somerset d 1660 = [1] Arabella Stuart d 1615 = [2] Frances ↓ Devereux d 1674

To show the relationship between Elizabeth I and the House of Stuart, her possible, eventually actual, heirs.

Elizabeth I and the House of Howard

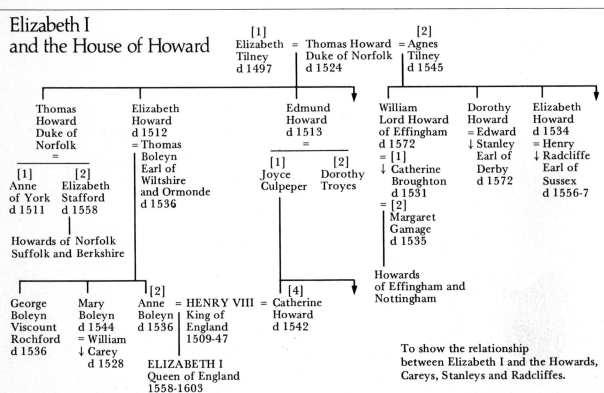

[1] Elizabeth Tilney d 1497 = Thomas Howard Duke of Norfolk d 1524 = [2] Agnes Tilney d 1545

Thomas Howard Duke of Norfolk =

[1] Anne of York d 1511

[2] Elizabeth Stafford d 1558

Howards of Norfolk Suffolk and Berkshire

Elizabeth Howard d 1512 = Thomas Boleyn Earl of Wiltshire and Ormonde d 1536

Edmund Howard d 1513 =

[1] Joyce Culpeper

[2] Dorothy Troyes

William Lord Howard of Effingham d 1572 = [1] ↓ Catherine Broughton d 1531 = [2] Margaret Gamage d 1535

Howards of Effingham and Nottingham

Dorothy Howard = Edward ↓ Stanley Earl of Derby d 1572

Elizabeth Howard d 1534 = Henry ↓ Radcliffe Earl of Sussex d 1556-7

George Boleyn Viscount Rochford d 1536

Mary Boleyn d 1544 = William ↓ Carey d 1528

[2] Anne Boleyn d 1536 = HENRY VIII King of England 1509-47

[4] = Catherine Howard d 1542

ELIZABETH I Queen of England 1558-1603

To show the relationship between Elizabeth I and the Howards, Careys, Stanleys and Radcliffes.

Elizabeth I and the Suffolk Line

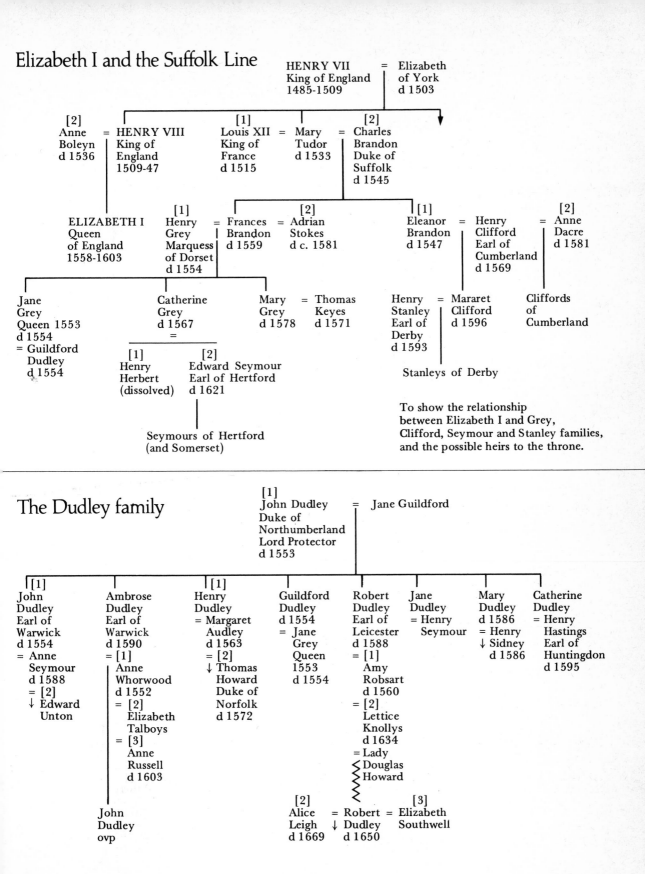

HENRY VII = Elizabeth
King of England | of York
1485-1509 | d 1503

[2] Anne Boleyn d 1536 = **HENRY VIII** King of England 1509-47 | [1] Louis XII King of France d 1515 = Mary Tudor d 1533 = [2] Charles Brandon Duke of Suffolk d 1545

ELIZABETH I Queen of England 1558-1603

[1] Henry Grey Marquess of Dorset d 1554 = Frances Brandon d 1559 = [2] Adrian Stokes d c. 1581

[1] Eleanor Brandon d 1547 = Henry Clifford Earl of Cumberland d 1569 = [2] Anne Dacre d 1581

Jane Grey Queen 1553 d 1554 = Guildford Dudley d 1554

Catherine Grey d 1567 =

Mary Grey d 1578 = Thomas Keyes d 1571

Henry Stanley Earl of Derby d 1593 = Mararet Clifford d 1596

Cliffords of Cumberland

[1] Henry Herbert (dissolved)

[2] Edward Seymour Earl of Hertford d 1621

Stanleys of Derby

Seymours of Hertford (and Somerset)

To show the relationship between Elizabeth I and Grey, Clifford, Seymour and Stanley families, and the possible heirs to the throne.

The Dudley family

[1] John Dudley Duke of Northumberland Lord Protector d 1553 = Jane Guildford

[1] John Dudley Earl of Warwick d 1554 = Anne Seymour d 1588 = [2] ↓ Edward Unton

Ambrose Dudley Earl of Warwick d 1590 = [1] Anne Whorwood d 1552 = [2] Elizabeth Talboys = [3] Anne Russell d 1603

[1] Henry Dudley = Margaret Audley d 1563 = [2] ↓ Thomas Howard Duke of Norfolk d 1572

Guildford Dudley d 1554 = Jane Grey Queen 1553 d 1554

Robert Dudley Earl of Leicester d 1588 = [1] Amy Robsart d 1560 = [2] Lettice Knollys d 1634 = Lady ⟨ Douglas ⟩ Howard ⟨

Jane Dudley = Henry Seymour

Mary Dudley = Henry ↓ Sidney d 1586

Catherine Dudley = Henry Hastings Earl of Huntingdon d 1595

John Dudley ovp

[2] Alice Leigh d 1669 = Robert ↓ Dudley d 1650 = [3] Elizabeth Southwell

The House of Howard

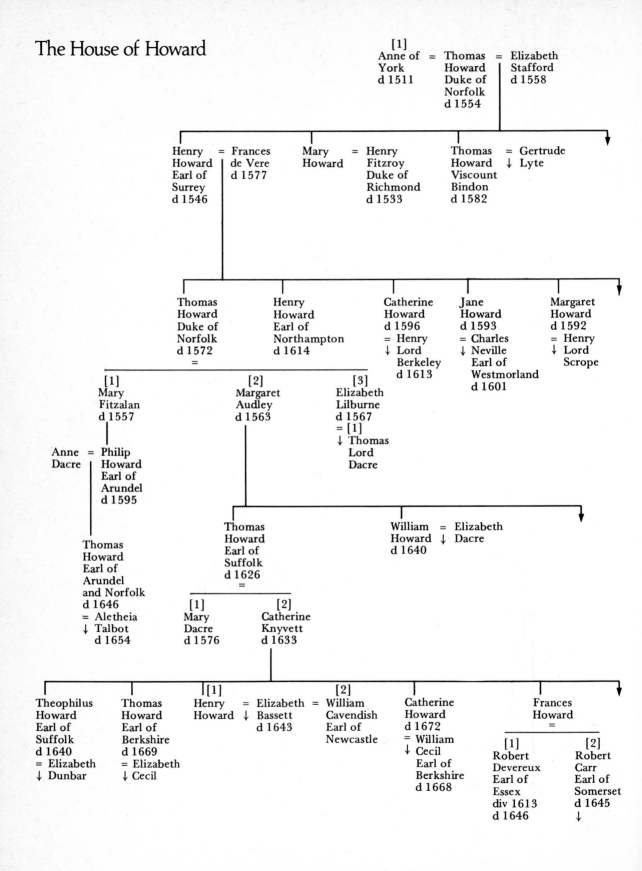

The Seymour family

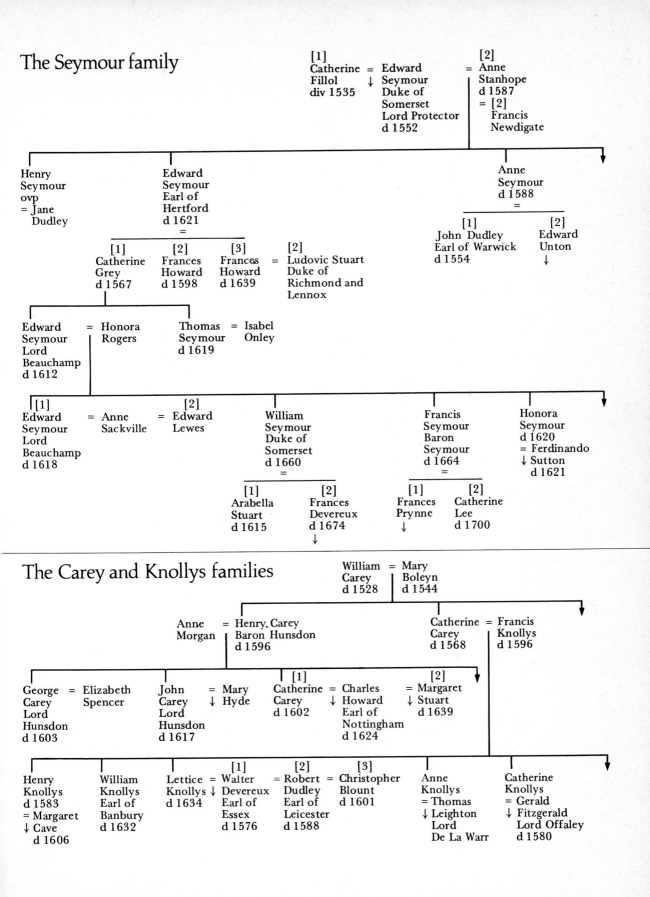

[1]
Catherine = Edward = [2] Anne
Fillol ↓ Seymour Stanhope
div 1535 Duke of d 1587
Somerset = [2]
Lord Protector Francis
d 1552 Newdigate

Henry Seymour ovp = Jane Dudley

Edward Seymour Earl of Hertford d 1621 =

Anne Seymour d 1588 =

[1] John Dudley Earl of Warwick d 1554

[2] Edward Unton ↓

[1] Catherine Grey d 1567

[2] Frances Howard d 1598

[3] Frances Howard d 1639 = Ludovic Stuart Duke of Richmond and Lennox [2]

Edward Seymour Lord Beauchamp d 1612 = Honora Rogers

Thomas Seymour d 1619 = Isabel Onley

[1] Edward Seymour Lord Beauchamp d 1618 = Anne Sackville = Edward Lewes [2]

William Seymour Duke of Somerset d 1660 =

Francis Seymour Baron Seymour d 1664 =

Honora Seymour d 1620 = Ferdinando ↓ Sutton d 1621

[1] Arabella Stuart d 1615

[2] Frances Devereux d 1674 ↓

[1] Frances Prynne ↓

[2] Catherine Lee d 1700

The Carey and Knollys families

William Carey d 1528 = Mary Boleyn d 1544

Anne Morgan = Henry Carey Baron Hunsdon d 1596

Catherine Carey d 1568 = Francis Knollys d 1596

George Carey Lord Hunsdon d 1603 = Elizabeth Spencer

John Carey Lord Hunsdon d 1617 = Mary ↓ Hyde

[1] Catherine Carey d 1602 = Charles Howard ↓ Earl of Nottingham d 1624

[2] = Margaret ↓ Stuart d 1639

Henry Knollys d 1583 = Margaret ↓ Cave d 1606

William Knollys Earl of Banbury d 1632

Lettice Knollys d 1634 = [1] Walter Devereux ↓ Earl of Essex d 1576 = [2] Robert Dudley Earl of Leicester d 1588 = [3] Christopher Blount d 1601

Anne Knollys = Thomas ↓ Leighton Lord De La Warr

Catherine Knollys = Gerald ↓ Fitzgerald Lord Offaley d 1580

Index

Sr Anthony
Broward

Sr Wm Cordell knight   Suffolk

Essex

Sr Robert Catly knight Lord chief Justice

Sr John Gorne knight

Dorothy